From Tobacco Road to Amen Corner

On Sports and Life

Ron Green

Down Home Press • Asheboro, N.C.

First Printing, October, 1990

ISBN 0-9624255-9-1

Library of Congress Catalog Card Number 90-062197

Printed in the United States of America

Cover design by Al Phillips
Book design by Elizabeth House

Most of the material in this book originally appeared, some in slightly different form, in the *Charlotte News* and and *Charlotte Observer*. Some first appeared in *Sports Illustrated, On The Green, Golf* , *Golf Illustrated* and *Golf Yearbook* magazines.

Down Home Press
P.O. Box 4126
Asheboro, N.C. 27204

With love and gratitude,
this book is dedicated to Beth Green.
Beth, it's been an honor knowing you.

Foreword

By Arnold Palmer

One of the pleasures of a long career is the opportunity to look back over the years and remember the many persons, places and incidents that have been part of it. In my case, the happenings have been many, the friends legion and I am grateful for this.

So much has occurred along so many avenues, but it all sprang from my golf and the wonders that it has wrought. Golf has been a big part of my life from the time that my father put a cut-down set of clubs in my hands when I was three years old, showed me how to put my fingers on them and instructed me that I should "hit it hard."

By the time I was moving through my high school years, my love for golf and the pure joy I found in practicing the game had manifested itself in a fair measure of success in my home area of Western Pennsylvania and my first exposure to "the press" – in my hometown of Latrobe and the nearest "big city" of Pittsburgh.

Before long, the media attention was national, then international, and it has remained so to this day. For many athletes and celebrities, such attention has been an unwanted burden; for me, it has been a pleasure. I count many journalists – golf writers, columnists, magazine and book authors – as friends, as men and women I enjoy seeing and visiting with when I am on the road. I guess it's natural that the writers for whom I have a particular affection are those who have been around and writing through much of my career. That's why I was happy to offer these words as a preface to this selection from among the many fine columns that have been authored through the years by Ron Green, one of the Carolinas' (and nation's) finest sportswriters.

Ron was just getting started as a sportswriter when I was still an amateur – we're the same age – and we first met at the old Azalea Open in Wilmington, N.C. In 1955, I went to the Masters for the first time and so did Ron Green. Neither of us has missed Augusta since. Three years later, I won the tournament that has always meant so much to me and I recall well that my wife, Winnie, and I spent some time on the Saturday eve of that very important win for me with Ron and another long-time writer friend from the Carolinas, Irwin Smallwood of Greensboro, in the Bull Bat Lounge of the Richmond, a hostelry long gone from downtown Augusta, and went to the course that Sunday after having breakfast with the two of them. Obviously, the right send-off.

Ron was an observer at another of my treasured victories, my second British Open win in Troon in 1962. I'm sure he remembers – I do – the luncheon after my first-round 71. It was quite a group. Winnie and I sat down with Ron, Bob Drum, the Pittsburgh golf writer who had covered me since high school days; Dan Jenkins, the long-time *Sports Illustrated* golf author and raconteur, and John Bibb, the fine Nashville sports columnist. Naturally, the conversation quickly turned to my round that day, a verbal give-and-take that may well have led to what I have always considered to be one of my strongest overall performances in a major championship. Drum, a boisterous Irishman never shy about expressing an opinion, as viewers of golf telecasts saw and heard for a couple of years not long ago, said that I seemed to be moving my head on my putts. We turned to Winnie, as always an excellent observer, though not a golfer herself, and she agreed with Bob. I have never putted better than I did during the next three rounds and that played a major part in my six-stroke victory.

Perhaps the main reason why Ron Green has always written so well about golf and golfers for so long is that he plays the game himself. Not badly either, although I must say that his fingers are more effective beating on a typewriter or computer keyboard than clinging to the grip of a golf club. I think that you will find this to be true on the pages that follow.

June, 1990

Introduction

I read this somewhere. I think it was *Time* or *Newsweek*. Anyway, I clipped and saved it because it was about what I do: write columns.

"The individual column does not count, because a column is not supposed to exist alone. A columnist looks to erect a whole assembly of columns, each single effort standing patiently at attention after it is created, until eventually a civilization emerges.

"The civilization is both an accumulation of the columnist's ideas and of his being; he is his collected works. More: he has shown that collecting the works is the way a life ought to be built, column by column, displaying both continuity and changes in the structure and in the architect. He has shown the way to make and use a mind."

Here, within these covers, is some of my "civilization."

Most of what you read here, collected from the last three decades of my four in the business, is intended to be either warm or humorous or simply interesting. There's little or none of the harsh criticism that is necessarily a part of the job, and not a lot of sadness, although there is some of that. This is not by design, but I'm glad it turned out that way. Sports should be fun for the participants and for those who watch.

You'll find an abundance of golf here. That's because it's my favorite and is filled with a wide range of emotions that keep running into each other, and because the game lends itself to writing. Golf is filled with interesting people who do wonderful or crazy things.

Only baseball has as many good stories.

My favorite among all the people about whom I've written over the years is an amateur golfer, Billy Joe Patton, from Morganton, N.C. If you'll read the column about him included here, I think you'll see why.

It's people like Billy Joe and a lot of the others in this book who have made writing sports a pleasure for me for more than four decades now. I don't like what has happened to our games, which is essentially a forsaking of the spirit in favor of the dollar. But I've managed to keep my love burning because I've continued to encounter the Billy Joe Pattons and Michael Jordans and Richard Pettys and Max Patkins and Mickey Mantles and the intriguing pool shooters and pier fishermen and old fighters and their like, people who are interesting and do interesting things.

I'm indebted to them, to everyone I've encountered along the way, actually, even the bad guys. It's the best way I can imagine to make a living, possibly outside of playing the pro golf tour or being Tom Cruise.

I owe a special debt to some of my current and former associates, most especially Sandy Grady, now a Washington bureau chief for the Philadelphia Daily News. By hanging around him during some of my early years of newspapering, I learned to love the written word. He wrote sports the way I wanted to write sports, so I paid attention to everything he said or did.

He read Hemingway, so I read Hemingway. We went through a period when every jock writer on the staff, smitten by Hemingway, began stories with lines like, "In the autumn of that year..." or, "Eddie Jones sipped a Coke in the dust beside the dugout, and it was good."

When we were serving together on the late lamented *Charlotte News,* my paper for most of my career, Sandy taught me to appreciate books, jazz, fishing, foreign cars and sports writing with blood in its body and a smile on its face.

I also owe Perry Morgan, one of my former managing editors, and Bob Quincy, one of my former sports editors, who counseled me well in the art of newspapering. I've also tried to draw quality and style and caring from conversation or simply reading stars like Dave Kindred, Furman Bisher, Blackie Sherrod, Jim Murray and Red Smith.

And along the way, I've kept company with a lot of good ones like my buddies Bruce Phillips, Irwin Smallwood, Lenox Rawlings, Wilt Browning, Dan Foster, Ken Alyta, Leonard Laye, Larry Keith and

Ron Green Jr., who have helped me by setting a pace with companionship and conversation and exchange of ideas and kind words when the work has gone well.

I've also been blessed with a family who thought what I was doing was important and treated it that way. All of them – Beth and our young 'uns, Ron Jr., David and Edie – love sports. That has made it easier and more fun. They've also been nice to come home to. And while I'm about it, let me acknowledge my late dad, who made sports a big part of my life, and my mom, whose arm has been around my shoulder along the way. And Dr. Daniel Gianturco, for his counseling.

And the people at the *Charlotte Observer* (and formerly the *Charlotte News*) for giving me a job that has taken me places I would never otherwise have gone, given me thrills I would never have known, gotten me the best seat in the house and given me an opportunity to write about sports, and then put it in the paper. And paid me for doing it. I don't understand it.

Contents

Baseball

Basketball

Football

Golf

Boxing

Racing and Running

From Pool to Politics

These Are Personal

From Tobacco Road
to
Amen Corner

Baseball

March 22, 1973

Sounds of Spring

The words fairly waft out of Florida on warm, orange-scented zephyrs. They are the language of baseball, cliches describing spring training, an event that is itself a cliche, conjuring up fascinating visions...

"...The Grapefruit League campaign.. the longest stint by a Tiger hurler this spring..the slender southpaw...the long blast was the rookie's second homer in as many contests...the skipper said he intends to use the big righthanded slugger mostly against lefthanded pitchers this season...'The kid's playing his way into a job. I think we'll take him north with us. He's got a good set of wheels and he can go to his left'...It was the fastballer's first outing of the spring..."

They are the sounds of this season and last season and the season 10 years ago and the season a thousand years ago, as unchanging as the immutable game itself.

They are interspersed with imagined noises like the crack of bat, the pop of a well-thrown ball smacking into a glove, the hen-clucking of the catcher squatting there in his armor, the ancient litany of the players afield, the clatter of spikes on dugout steps, the soft thud of tobacco juice in the dust, all of the ritualistic noises of the summer game.

It is spellbinding, this news from the training camps, for buried somewhere in all of it is the secret of the future, embryonic pennant winners, the rookies who will not wilt under the spotlight, the veterans who will falter or find new glory.

We listen, trying to sort through the multitude of sounds for some sign that the Yankees will reign again, that the Phillies have found some help for Carlton, that the madman Durocher can still manage a champion, that the Braves finally have some pitching...

But that's all we get, really, signs, like a catcher's signal to a pitcher. There is no assurance that the curve won't hang. (Every home run ever hit was off a hanging curve, if the pitchers are telling the truth.)

These distant events are reassuring, though. They are rustles of springtime, warm breezes blowing through the gray chill as winter exits snapping and snarling. Even as the cold rain drums on the windows, we can feel the sun raising beads of sweat to be wiped away with the back of a glove when we read, "Lee May singled, doubled, then slammed a 450 foot two-run homer off Lew Krausse..."

We should have learned by now that developments in spring training are not as significant as we make them out to be but we choose not to accept that.

We read this titillating dispatch today:

"Larry Hisle hit three homers to account for five runs as the Minnesota Twins bombed the Los Angeles B team 10-7. Hisle now has six home runs this spring..."

We know that Hisle is a derelict fished out of the sea of mediocrity by the Twins but we recall that he hit 20 homers for the Phillies one year and this is the season he regains that old form. And his mighty bat will take over when Killebrew can no longer drive them beyond the fences.

That is what we choose to believe because this is spring training and reality has not yet set in for the year. The homers are being struck off winter-softened arms. The hitless innings are being hurled against eyes not yet focused on the snake-slide curveball. The standings are myths.

But spring training is not a time for reality. It is a time for speculation, anticipation, hope, a soft time when things don't really count, when we only imagine they do.

June 20, 1967

The Last Baseball Clown

Max Patkin ate too much dirt last night and got sick but he gulped an Alka-Seltzer and went on being funny.

He's the last of the baseball clowns.

It's not ever easy but he had an extra tough game to work at Griffith Park last night. There was a crowd of only 872, better than normal for Charlotte but not so hot for Patkin, who measures his success by the gate. ("Small crowds get me down.")

You've probably seen him do his act. He's been here about 30 times in the last 15 years. You know the part where he throws the handful of dirt in his face. He got too much of it in his mouth and nose ("I weigh 190 pounds, mostly nose") and between bits on the diamond he went in and treated himself.

In the fifth inning, the ballplayers crabbed the act when they threatened a brawl. Both teams spilled onto the field and glared at each other while the umpires and managers went around trying to make peace. Patkin has been through this before. He simply laid down with his head on first base and pretended to be asleep. He was suffering inside. When the crowd gets stirred up, his act isn't so funny.

"The same thing happened to me in Winston-Salem the other night," he said. He talks in machine gun style, in deep-throated bursts.

"It's a doubleheader. First, the umpires show up an hour late. Then Winston-Salem makes eight errors in the first game and I'm going on in the second. The home manager gets run by the umpire before the second game ever starts.

"And I'm supposed to make the fans laugh. Gee!"

He's funny. Even when a fight's brewing or the home team is kicking every ground ball or the enemy pitcher has the bats under lock and key, he's funny.

When he comes flapping out, all loose and wiggly, the first thing you see is his nose, followed by a putty (that's putty, not pretty) face that was made for his line of work. There's a cap on it, sideways. Then comes the neck. It must be a foot long when he stretches it. An then there's the body, rear end stuck way out, and the works covered by a pair of baggy baseball pants and a shirt with a question mark on the back.

By the time he's been on five minutes, he's an awful mess, all wet and dusty and disheveled.

"I've been a clown for 22 years," he said. "I've made half a million dollars. I'd hate to tell you where it went. Wine, women and song–and I didn't do much singing."

Patkin, 47 now, has had his schedule curtailed a bit by the shrinkage of minor league baseball and he now gets home to Philadelphia for a lot of weekends during the season. ("My wife has never seen my act in a ballpark. She wonders why I'm gone so much. She thinks I'm a corporation lawyer.")

He still makes 60 parks and 30,000 miles by plane and bus.

Quit? He talks of it but admits he doesn't want to give it up as long as he has an audience. Besides, it's good advertisement for his janitorial supply business back home in Philly.

Max started in baseball as a pitcher with an arm that one writer said "gave up in disgust." He pitched in places likeWisconsin Rapids and Oshkosh and Wilkes Barre.

He began by being sold from Waterloo to Wisconsin Rapids for $100 ("And the guy who bought me thought he got cheated.")

"In 1941," he machine-gunned, "I struck out over 200 batters for Wisconsin Rapids and set a new league record–42 wild pitches. Boy, was I wild.

"One day, I almost knocked a sports writer out of the press box with my curve ball. No kidding, I threw it so wild, it flew into the press box and nearly killed a writer. No, on second thought, it wouldn't have killed him. My curve wasn't that good."

Max loaded up his baggy pants and the rest of it and headed off into the night. He's going on to Asheville, Knoxville, Evansville, Chicago, Davenport, Cedar Rapids, Denver, San Diego, Vancouver, Dallas, El Paso, Oklahoma City...laughing all the way.

Al Schacht, Jackie Price, Johnny Jones and the tank town guys are all through now but Max keeps flapping along.

September 19, 1972

The Abandoned King

The symbolism, though unconscious, would have been acclaimed by the critics if it had been an Ingmar Bergman movie.

A two-bit circus, in Charlotte yesterday, in Reading, Pa., tomorrow, was running through its matinee at Griffith Park, one withering aspect of American life playing on the freshly dug grave of another.

Just last Friday afternoon, the Minnesota Twins had announced that minor league baseball was dead in Charlotte after decades of residence in what was widely regarded as a bastion of the bushes, the keystone of its league.

Even as the announcement was being made, the Miller-Johnson Circus was setting up on the infield grass for a performance as sparsely attended as last season's baseball games.

There were lions and there were clowns, as there had been on the diamond through the years. The smell of popcorn was heavy in the concrete-floored, greenwood lobby with its ugly ribs exposed and things stacked around.

Turnstiles, little used this summer despite the presence of two teams – the Charlotte Hornets of the Class AA Southern League and the Charlotte Twins of the Class A Western Carolinas League – stood around to one side, like men out of work in desultory conversation.

Trucks and trailers of the brassy, painted intruders lined the outfield walls beneath the insurance and cola and beer signs. The clock sat still, the scoreboard mute.

A ring for the unicyclists encircled home plate. The steel cage where the lion tamer performed was on third base and the trapeze was set up behind the mound.

A man and a woman cursed each other loudly in the lobby before he grabbed her arms and forced her out of earshot of the kids drifting in for the show.

The pictures peering down on this ugly scene from the walls seemed ludicrous. Tony Oliva. Harmon Killebrew. Rick Renick. Early Wyatt. Chuck Manuel. Tom Hall. Dick Woodson. Joe Haynes. Sherry Robertson. Rich Reese. Paul Ratliff. Frank Quilici. Bob Allison. Ray Corbin. George Mitterwald. All of them made it to the majors.

And Minnie Mendoza, the eternal Hornet. He left sometimes but always returned to play the best third base anybody ever played here.

Red Dwyer, the general manager of the teams that no longer exist here, looked around the lobby yesterday and said, "I don't know what I'll do with all these pictures."

Red and Buster Sloan, the groundskeeper for more than 20 years, are on the payroll for the rest of the year. They are uncertain what they'll do after that. Both stood around and speculated hopefully about the arrival of a new team, clinging to their fading way of life.

Signs on the walls down the hall from the lobby spoke of happy nights – "Ballplayers Only" and "Popcorn, peanuts, cotton candy, snow cones, hot dogs, soft drinks."

If you wandered to the end of the hallway, you could find a place for silent contemplation, interrupted only occasionally by a scampering youngster.

The sound of a bat meeting ball solidly, the thunderclap of cheers when a racing centerfielder hauled in a deep drive, the raspy condemnation of the umpire who could do no right.

The ghosts were there with their lovely sounds, drowning for a moment the discordant four-piece circus band.

"On the bleak shore now lies th' abandoned king, a headless carcass, and a nameless thing."

May 31, 1974

The Game's Over

Griffith Park is a fading, weedy hulk now, in its second season without the old Charlotte Hornets. The franchise died after the 1972 season, a disastrous one at the gate, but minor league baseball didn't die in Charlotte until yesterday, when Phil Howser drew his last breath.

Howser, general manager of the Hornets for 32 years, suffered a stroke in January, 1973, and a heart attack a few months later. A series of minor strokes since finally ended his life at age 63.

Griffith Park was a museum of baseball in Howser's time there, groaning with memorabilia of the game. But the most interesting item through it all was the roundish, cigar-smoking man, Howser himself.

The photographs yellowed and the souvenir ashtrays cracked and the structure itself began to creak with the years but Howser remained as much a part of their age as he did a part of the present.

The atmosphere at Griffith Park was that of a country store. People hung around. The conversation was invariably about baseball, spiced with salty lines out of the past, trimmed with hopeful speculation about tomorrow.

Howser was a man for each of the 32 seasons he served as general manager, as comfortable as a well-worn mitt but as usable this year as last.

Thirty-two years on the job taught Howser not to attack it but to calmly fend off each problem as it arose, chomping contentedly on his cigar and chatting in his high-pitched drawl with anyone who happened to be visiting at the time, and there was always somebody.

Oh, he would get riled. He expected perfection from his employees and when he didn't get it, he would sputter and fume awhile, but the eruption would end as suddenly as it had begun.

He knew baseball and had a keen eye for talent, but that was almost secondary to the image that emerged over the years.

He could never conquer the National Anthem, for example, a problem some of our most famous singers have also encountered. There was a standard procedure for the playing of the Anthem. When the pitcher reached the mound to begin his warm-up tosses, the public address man would announce the Star Spangled Banner. Howser was supposed to be standing by the public address console, ready to flip the switch that would play the record.

Sometimes, it went smoothly. At other times, he got caught in conversation and forgot to stand by and there would be this embarrassing silence after the introduction, then a crash of furniture as he dashed across his office to switch on the song. Sometimes, it came out on the wrong speed and Kate Smith sang basso profunda.

During his years as general manager, Howser maintained two offices at Griffith Park. One, downstairs, was his official office. The one upstairs was originally intended to be the press box but it proved to be a perfect place for Phil and his cronies to watch the game and the press moved on up to the top of the stadium.

Phil had a desk in both offices, both of which sagged under the weight of papers, books, souvenirs, food and gifts heaped upon him by friends. The walls groaned with dozens of photographs of baseball people like Clark Griffith and Judge Landis and a Cuban kid named Tony Oliva whom Howser had discovered.

In the corners and under the tables were cardboard boxes full of goodies. Howser was forever poking around in them and passing out caps and baseballs and pennants and such to youngsters. He loved kids. He could be pitching a fit at one of his employees and if a youngster walked in, he would cool off, smile, say something like, "Hi, Mickey Mantle," and hunt around until he found the kid a baseball or some free passes.

One young man went to work for Howser as a scoreboard operator and after he got to know him well, he said, "Mr. Howser, I used to sneak over the fence every night to see the games here."

Howser's brow furrowed and he snapped, "Why didn't you come and ask me for a ticket? You know I'd have given you one."

Howser never lost his faith in Charlotte or minor league baseball. He loved both and thought they belonged together. His love is what kept them together all those years.

Now the game is over.

July 17, 1974

Diz

In this day of gray flannel athletes with agents, stock portfolios, unions, carpeted clubhouses and a maddening lack of showmanship, it is difficult to accept Dizzy Dean as a reality.

You get the feeling the old St. Louis Cardinal pitcher was the creation of someone like Ring Lardner, a fictional character too outrageous to be believable – wildly independent, remarkably talented, a lovable clod from Arkansas who was a migratory cottonpicker with a second grade education.

He was a braggart of championship caliber. A few years ago, he said, "They'll never be another one like me." And there won't.

Ol' Diz died this morning, the victim of a heart attack at age 63. At death, he was still the last National League pitcher to win 30 games, a record that has stood for the big righthander since 1934.

Dean will be remembered for his records. In the 1934 pennant race and World Series, for example, Diz pitched nine times in 19 days. In that series, he won two games off Detroit and his brother Paul won the other two to clinch the championship.

But far more than his records, Dean's antics will be remembered, the stories told and retold by a sporting world longing for the likes of him.

A man named Bruce Ogrodowski nudged Diz toward one of his most remarkable feats. Ogrodowski was his catcher. They got into an argument about their relative importance, whether the pitcher was more valuable than the catcher.

"All you have to do is catch 'em," Diz argued. "I'll throw 'em."

Ogrodowski replied that Dean's effectiveness would be lost without the signs and strategy of the backstop.

"That's a lot of bull," Dean said. "I don't need no signs. I'll run my own game. You just hang onto the ball."

He went out against the Boston Braves and beat them 13-0, never once taking a sign from Ogrodowski. What's more, he announced to each batter as he came to the plate, "You ain't gonna get nothin' but fast balls, so don't look for nothin' else, and be ready."

Perhaps his greatest moment came in the final game of the 1934 World Series.

He had the Tigers beaten 11-0 with one out in the ninth. Hank Greenberg, one of the great sluggers, came to bat. He had struck out twice in earlier appearances.

Dean called time out, walked toward the Detroit dugout and said, "Hey, ain't you got no pinch-hitter?"

The Cardinal manager, Frankie Frisch, blanched. He raced to the mound and said, "Diz, what are you trying to do? We've got a lot at stake here." Dean said, "Frank, you're a great guy but you worry too much."

When Frisch was back in the dugout, Dean fired his high, hard one and struck out Greenberg on four pitches.

Diz had caused Frisch many a fretful moment, one of them in 1933 when he started slowly against the Cubs, trailing 1-0 after the first inning.

"If you don't get better," Frisch told him, "you're going to the bullpen next inning." Dean replied that he simply hadn't warmed up enough.

He went back out and fanned 17 batters, breaking the National League record.

Dean will be remembered by many as a color man on radio and TV baseball broadcasts. An unfettered soul in any situation, Diz walked all over the English language with spikes on as he gave his cursory descriptions of the games and delighted himself and his audience with tall tales of days gone by.

When things got a little dull, Diz would burst forth with a few bars of "Wabash Cannonball."

Like ol' Diz said, "They'll never be another like me."

June 29, 1976

The Feistiest Skipper

He came bustling into Griffith Park late in the afternoon wearing yellow trousers, a yellow and white shirt, a yellow hat and a large pair of sunglasses. He went to the Orioles' office window and said, "Hi, I'm Ellis Clary, scout for the Minnesota Twins. Could I have one of your rosters, please?"

It is necessary for Ellis Clary to introduce himself at Griffith Park now. It has been 15 years since he managed the Charlotte Hornets in the Sally League. But those who knew him then are not likely to have forgotten him. He was perhaps the feistiest manager Charlotte ever had.

They will remember the night catcher Wendell Antoine hit a game-winning inside-the-park home run ("I waved him home but I said to myself, 'You ain't gonna make it'") and a fan leaped out of the stands to congratulate the big catcher. Clary, thinking it was a drunk who had been heckling Antoine all night, knocked the fan unconscious. When the knockout victim was finally revived, Clary ushered him into the clubhouse, dusted him off and gave him an autographed baseball.

"The next day, I picked up the *Charlotte News* and there was my name in the box score" said Clary. "It said, 'Clary hit for Antoine in the 12th.'"

Clary was a fighter. On another occasion he went into the stands after a man who had ridden him hard, but that time he didn't catch his tormentor.

Whenever some leather-lung got on his hitters, Clary, coaching at third, did not hesitate to reply with language that would make your socks roll up and down, loud enough to be heard out on Magnolia Avenue and salty enough to make the late Phil Howser, then general manager, flinch as he visualized another dozen or two sensitive customers being driven away.

Clary parked in the stands on this afternoon and chuckled about those days.

"Let's see," he said. "I had Minnie Mendoza at third, Nestor Velazquez at second, Babe Daskalaskis was one of my pitchers – hell, I had about three Greeks and seven Cubans on that team and I had to come out to the park at 2 o'clock everyday to have enough time to fill out my lineup card 'cause I couldn't remember how to spell the names.

"We had plenty of money back then but not much talent in the system. Now it's just the opposite."

Clary did not enjoy managing. He had been a coach with the parent club for several years and had been reluctant to give that up but did so at the request of the Twins' front office. After a year in Charlotte, he became a scout and has remained one.

"I never wanted to manage," he said. "If I had gone out after it, I might have been a major league manager but I didn't. I was tickled to death as a coach. We had a lot of fun, laughed a lot, didn't have much pressure on us and got to travel big league style. Once you've been up there, you don't ever want to come back down."

Clary played for 19 seasons and was good at it, once being named most valuable player in the Southern League and spending several years in the majors as an infielder, but he likes to joke about his career.

"I played on three teams with Early Wynn," he said, "and Wynn always said he would've won 600 games instead of just 300 if I hadn't been playing behind him. I screwed up third base so bad in St. Louis, they had to move the team out of town.

"When we left St. Louis the Lipton Tea Company asked for my glove. I'd used it for eight seasons but it was like new because I hadn't caught anything in it. Lipton used it as a model for the first flow-through tea bag."

Clary even wisecracked when he was staring death in the face some six years ago. A heart attack felled him in Mobile. When he was placed in an ambulance, he told the attendants, "Be sure and mark down how far it is to the hospital. I get paid mileage."

Now, he tells people he is only six years old "because I actually died in the hospital and I got last rites. Dropped dead as hell at a ballgame. My heart stopped. You can only make it four minutes like that, you know, and when I got to the hospital, the clock was already in the red. They said I was a goner. They gave me shock treatment and it didn't revive me. So they stepped up the voltage so high, I hit the ceiling and it worked. I came down talking like an auctioneer."

And he still is.

May 10, 1978

The Only Race

Jackie Robinson had battled across the racial line in the major leagues five years earlier and opened the way for other blacks to follow.

But in 1952, in the hot, dusty minor league ball yards of the South, racism still flamed. Blacks were allowed to watch the games from their designated sections of the bleachers, but were not welcome to play on the same field with whites.

It was into this cauldron of fear and hatred that David Mobley, who sprouted from the farmland outside Lancaster, S.C., and learned to play baseball on the flinty upstate sandlots, was thrust. He was the first black man to play in the Tri-State League, a class B league that embraced towns like Charlotte, Rock Hill, Knoxville, Spartanburg, Anderson and Greenville.

It was a brief, terrifying experience but Mobley, 50 now and supervisor of a brick mason crew here, looks back on it with some pride and with no apparent bitterness. He is a man of unmistakable dignity, but there are traces of the old back-of-the-bus submission lingering in his soft, almost shy manner.

Everybody knew him then and knows him now as "Pepsi Cola" or "Pepsi" or "Pep" for short. It's a name a couple of friends – "Headquarters" and "Cold Air" – gave him when he drank five Pepsis after a high school boxing match a long time ago.

The baseball exploits of "Pepsi" were widely known by the time Rock Hill summoned him to play in the Tri-State. He had been playing sandlot games with adults since he was 12 and had played a couple of months with the Birmingham Black Barons in a Negro league in 1949 before he got homesick and quit, but he was best known for his heroics with the Lancaster Tigers, a semi-pro club.

"We used to play at a park near the Springs Mill," Mobley recalls. "I hit a lot of home runs. I used to knock balls up agin' the mill and break the windows but they said I could break all I wanted to, as long as I kept hittin' home runs.

"Sometimes there would be 500 or 600 mill hands come out to watch me play. They'd give me shirts and money and food and all kinds of things when I'd hit a homer. They liked to see me cut up, too. They called me a hot dog but I wasn't. That was just my natural way."

The Rock Hill team owner had seen Mobley play and envisioned him as the answer to sagging attendance problems. He sent the general manager to find Mobley and bring him to Rock Hill.

Mobley, sitting in an easy chair in his apartment one evening this week, speaking softly, his eyes to the floor most of the time, said, "I went and tried out but I had to stay on the sidelines because when I went to the field, I got so many catcalls. I got scared and went home.

"A couple of days later, they told me to come on back. They sent for a photographer and a newspaperman and signed me up at $90 a week.

"They had been drawing about 600 or 700 people to their games but when word got out that I was gonna play, 16,000 people showed up. No, not 1,600. It was 16,000. There was a lot of my white friends there and the whole Indian nation from down there came to see me. They were my friends, too.

"I guess they had this big crowd because people had heard there was some controversy about me playing."

Before he ever took the field, the management received phone calls threatening Mobley's life if he played.

He was left in the cement block clubhouse, under guard of four or five men, while the first few innings were played. "I couldn't see the game from there," he recalls, "but I could hear that crowd. I was brave, all right, but I was raised in the country and there was 16,000 people out there and that's a heap of difference and some of them had said they were gonna shoot me if I played. I sat there hoping they wouldn't send for me to play."

But they did, in the fifth inning. "I felt light as loaf bread walking out there into that park," said Mobley, who has a mustache and thick hair that is starting to show some gray in the sideburns. "I could hear the people yelling at me, calling me bad things.

"They put me in left field. I'd never played there before. I think they put me over there because that's where the colored folks were sitting.

"The first ball hit to me was hard to catch, you know, but the next one was easier. I had started to think maybe they wouldn't bother me and I had faith in the Lord. I almost beat out a bunt my first time at bat and I got a single the next time."

But Mobley didn't last long enough to be a true pioneer. He didn't get to play for Rock Hill again. Knoxville (against whom he played that night) and Charlotte, whose general manager, the late Phil Howser, knew and liked Mobley, made it known that he was welcome to play against them. But he said Greenville, Spartanburg and Anderson had threatened to break up the league because of him and there had been more threats on his life if he showed up in those towns to play.

"So they told me I couldn't play anymore," he said.

The next year, Mobley played with Knoxville in the Mountain States League and, as he recalls, was hitting about .375 at midseason, then tailed off some. As the season wore down, "a man offered me more money than I was making in baseball to build a church so I just took it."

He went back to his beloved labor – carpentry and masonry, which he had learned by the time he was 14 years old – and playing some sandlot ball. He broke away to make two cross-country tours with the Indianapolis Clowns playing the Willie Mays All-Stars. And even today, he plays a bit but mostly he coaches a semi-pro team.

"After that debacle in Rock Hill," he says, his eyes reflecting thoughts of bygone times, "it was like it had added some bad luck to me. I didn't have nobody to talk to me, you know. If I'd had somebody to talk to me...

"I never did seem to play as good after that.

"If I'd come along maybe seven or eight years later, I think I might have made it all the way. I'd never been sick, didn't drink or smoke, was hard as a rock and people told me I was good. But I don't have no cutback on nobody about not making it. I never was one to hold no grudge agin' anybody. I love everybody. I couldn't hate white folks. I lived with some white folks for awhile when I was working for 'em. They told me I should've been white.

"Thanks to Jackie Robinson, sports have brought people closer together. There ain't no race now. The only race is from home plate to first base."

April 26, 1982

The Boss Lady

Frances Crockett grew up in a big house that was a favorite haunt of ghosties, ghoulies and things that go bump and do stepover toeholds in the night. Actually, these weird creatures were professional wrestlers, men with cauliflower ears who plied their trade disguised as Indian chiefs, English lords, masked marvels and storm troopers. They came to her home in a leafy, affluent section of Charlotte to conduct business with her late father, a successful promoter of wrestling in several Southern states. Everybody knew him as Big Jim Crockett and Frances was his little girl.

Her favorite wrestler was Gorgeous George, the legendary bobby-pin thrower himself. But she also has fond memories of dining with her family on Oriental cuisine prepared by Mr. Moto, the wickedest of all the postwar Japanese villains, and on seafood caught and cooked by the Dirty Duseks, Emil and Ernie, members of wrestling's most infamous family.

Young Frances was unaffected by the circus atmosphere that swirled around her. Well, not totally unaffected. When she walked into the living room one day and discovered Maurice Tillet, the French Angel, there, she almost jumped out of her bobby sox. Tillet had a face that would have frightened John Wayne.

While wrestling fans wondered if gentlemanly George Becker would ever unmask the Great Bolo, Frances lived an everyday life and dreamed everyday dreams. She was going to marry, have three sons and confine her work to high-minded civic projects. "I guess I was going to be just like Doris Day," she says. "I believed all those movies I saw."

She never suspected that she would become something of a curiosity herself. In 1976, at age 35, she was named general manager of the Charlotte O's baseball team, in the Class AA Southern League. A handful of other women had held similar positions. There are currently two other female G.M.s – in Walla Walla, Wash., and Rohnert Park, Calif. – but it's still an unusual job for a divorced mother of five children.

Crockett's baseball career – business career, really – began in 1975 when with her mother, Elizabeth, and her brothers, Jim Jr., David and Jack, she bought the team. Charlotte had been a bastion of the bushes since 1911, having been a way station for such hot prospects as Early Wynn, Harmon Killebrew and Tony Oliva. But minor league baseball had died in Charlotte in 1972 because of poor teams and poor management and was replaced for a while by pro softball. Clearly, the Crocketts had their work cut out for them when they paid off the Asheville team's $20,000 indebtedness and moved the club to Charlotte.

The first year Frances kept the franchise's books. The second season the family agreed she should run the club herself, while her brothers concentrated on the wrestling and real estate portions of the family enterprise. Most observers considered that decision to be nothing more than hype. After all, the clan that had foisted the Fabulous Moolah and the Purple Flash on the world would also recognize the promotional value of having a woman general manager. As far as baseball executives go, Crockett remains the object of uncommon interest, but she's no longer viewed as just another Crockett promotional gimmick. The last vestiges of that notion disappeared in a sea of black ink in 1980 when she put 198,528 customers in the stands of 5,500-seat Crockett Park. Baseball had never drawn more than 146,000 in Charlotte before. This success, which coincided with the city's first league championship in eight years, helped make her the Sporting News Class AA Baseball Executive of the Year. Last year the O's drew even better – 211,161 – though they finished only second in their division. Last week they had 12,897 for their four-game season-opening stand.

Crockett was the first woman to win the Sporting News award at any level. Faint praise, one might say, considering how few women had been in baseball ownership and management. But Crockett says, "That plaque is a statement that I have finally been accepted."

To fully appreciate what it meant for her to pack in record crowds, sell out the fence advertising and double the size of game programs to 48 ad-rich pages, one needs to know that the only surefire winners on the Charlotte sports scene have been automobile racing and, of course, professional wrestling. Indeed, after an early surge in fan interest when baseball returned to Charlotte, attendance fell so precipitously that the franchise almost expired again. The soft voice of Frances Crockett saved it.

Jim Jr., president of Jim Crockett Promotions, Inc., which includes all the family's business interests, was inclined to fold the O's after they drew only 64,163 in 1978. Frances urged him to keep the club going.

"O.K.," he told her, "you've got one more year."

"O.K.," she said, "but I do it alone."

During her first two years as general manager, Jim Jr. and David had hovered over her. After all, her previous business experience was limited to some office chores in 1974 and that bookkeeping stint in '75 when David was the O's general manager.

"We tended to fight a lot, like brothers and sisters do," Frances says. "I told them we were going to destroy each other the way we were going. They said, 'Fine, it's yours. Sink or swim.' Now when they show up at the park, it's just to enjoy a game."

Before he washed his hands of the baseball operation, Jim Jr. teamed with Frances to put a hammerlock on the parent Baltimore Orioles, threatening to find a working agreement with another organization if Baltimore didn't give Charlotte the talent to field a contender. When the Orioles obliged, Frances began to promote in a style that would've made Big Jim – not to mention Gorgeous George – proud. She almost doubled attendance in one season, raising it to 122,889 in 1979.

Big Jim never tried to teach his daughter the ropes of promotion, didn't think it was women's work, but Frances hasn't forgotten something she heard him say many times about dealing with the public: "Never lose touch with the people. Be on the same foot with them. Never drive a Cadillac because those people paid for it."

That's not the only reason Frances drives a Chevy station wagon. It's also handy for hauling her young ones around. The Doris Day thing didn't quite work out the way she expected. She married when she was 18, and after having five children in nine years, she wound up with a divorce and custody of what could have been a major babysitting problem.

She ultimately solved that by hiring the whole bunch to work at the ballpark. Debbie, 22, pops the popcorn and supervises vendors in the stands. Lisa, 19, is a Pepper Girl, sort of a uniformed hostess. Jimmy, 17, works on the grounds crew. Betsy, 15, runs the souvenir stand. Ron, 13, is a ball boy.

"It saves on allowances," says Crockett, "and it allows us time together to do something we enjoy. They seem to like the arrangement. During the off-season, I play mama for about a month, cooking them big meals and all that, but after a while, they want me to quit being such a good mother."

When it comes to business, Crockett says, "I think being a woman is an advantage in dealing with people around the league and in the Baltimore organization. When I go to a meeting, who do you think they're going to listen to or remember? They may not pay a lot of attention to what I have to say but I'll catch their attention first."

When she introduced halter-top and jogging-shorts uniforms for the Pepper Girls, she said, "They won't offend women and men will like them." As for women who might disagree with Crockett, she says, "That's just being unrealistic."

Once the season starts, she sits behind her cluttered desk, kicks off her shoes – the keeps three to five pairs under the desk so she can be prepared for everything from an emergency dress-up situation to tired feet – smokes three packs of cigarettes a day and works 12-to-15-hour shifts running her ball club.

When the Crocketts bought the ball park in Charlotte from the Minnesota Twins, they poured money into improvements. They tore out the splintery old seats and put in new ones, dressed up the concession stands and rest rooms, painted everything, added a club room, built a new press box and reworked some old office space into a room that groups could rent to party in during a game. Frances now has a staff of nine full-time employees and a horde of part-timers, but when she started out she did whatever was needed herself, including cleaning the ladies' room.

But mainly, she promoted. Crockett has staged 200 promotions, most of which she learned about at off-season seminars she attended with other general managers from around the country. Along with the usual giveaways she has imported the San Diego Chicken and Baltimore's Wild Bill Hagy, held ostrich and go-cart races, given out kazoos for "the world's biggest kazoo band," passed "the world's largest ice cream sundae" around the stands for fans to help themselves, given a full admission to anyone bringing to the park a banana or a picture of a banana – one man made it with a picture of Richard Nixon's nose – and rewarded the pure of heart by discounting Sunday ticket prices for those who brought church bulletins.

Looking back, Crockett says it scares her to think how little she knew when she became general manager. Now she's not only running the O's but has also bought into teams in Greensboro and Salem, Va., and is looking to invest in more. She has put together a radio network that broadcasts all O's games in four towns and expects to increase that number. Her attendance goal this year is 235,000.

Her groundskeeper at Crockett Park, by the way, is a beefy fellow who looks like some of those guys who used to parade through her home. Bill Soloweyko is his real name, but most folks call him Klondike Bill. He's a former wrestler.

April 15, 1983

Settle in for Summer

It is the national pastime. It is youth, springtime, a trip to the country, part of our past. It is the roaring excitement of huge urban crowds and the sleepy green afternoon silences of midsummer. Without effort, it engenders and thrives on heroes, legends, self-identification, and home-town pride.

– From "The Summer Game," by Roger Angell.

The first heroic deed I can remember seeing in sports occurred a million miles away from Yankee Stadium or Fenway Park on a dusty baseball diamond cut out of flinty ground in Greenville, S.C.

Two mill teams were playing.

I was probably shirtless and barefoot and wearing a baseball cap because that's how I remember being attired in summer for much of my youth.

With two outs in the ninth inning, the batter for the opposing team drove a shot straightaway and deep. The centerfielder turned and fled toward the vast openness behind him. There was no fence. He made a leaping catch and, clutching the ball in his glove, tumbled to the ground and did a backward somersault, finishing on his feet with the ball held high.

Nothing I've seen on any playing field since has been more wonderful than that play seen through the eyes of a boy.

He had saved the game. People whooped and hollered and slapped him on the back and someone bought him an ice cream cone from a pushcart vendor.

That was the stuff of which dreams were made. What a glorious thing it must be, I thought, to be a baseball hero, to save the game and, of course, tumble over backward to underscore the difficulty of the feat.

I repeated that play many times in my fantasies.

On reflection, it may not have been all that difficult a catch, nothing Willie Mays couldn't handle routinely, but that moment has stuck with me and holds a prominent place among my memories.

I'm no longer the baseball fanatic I was as a kid. Then, I played every day it didn't rain between April and October. I wore my baseball cap to bed sometimes. I played with borrowed gloves until I finally got my own. I loved that glove as if it were human. I oiled the pocket and spent hours popping a ball into it to shape it just the way I wanted it. It became a part of me.

I gave up playing the game as I rounded the corner into my teens without ever becoming a baseball hero, except in the fantasies. It didn't have anything to do with disillusionment. I was working afternoons and had no time for the game.

My passion for the game took a turn away from the path most follow out of their youth. I didn't bring a favorite major league club along with me. I had an off-and-on romance with some minor league teams as my family moved from town to town before finally settling in Charlotte.

I attached myself to the Charlotte Hornets for several years and even read their box scores.

Box scores are ingenious creations, stacks of categorized numbers through which much of a game can be traced, but none occupies much of my time anymore. Standings get cursory examination and are not committed to memory. On the other hand, I hold Roger Kahn's *The Boys of Summer*, a baseball book, to be the best sports book I've ever read.

My fondness for baseball lies in its aesthetics, not its statistics.

I don't go regularly to the park to watch the locals play. I could never be a season ticket buyer. That's hard core, a commitment that one who doesn't read box scores isn't likely to make, certainly to relish. I'm not one who loves the game for its pace, its long ebbs between its sudden waves of action, although I understand and appreciate why many do prefer this game that permits time for little dramas and big ones to build.

What lures me to the park from time to time is not so much a concern for victory for our nine as a fondness for the place, the smells, the tastes, the sounds, the clean geometry of the field, the timeworn rituals, the possibility that a centerfielder might haul down a deep drive to save the game, then do a backward somersault.

June 4, 1982

Where Have You Gone, Mickey Mantle?

The man said it was kind of sad, seeing Mickey Mantle, the way it turned out.

Mantle slipped quietly into Charlotte to play what athletes call corporate golf, which means playing with business folk for a fee.

"He came in from the course and you could tell he'd had a couple of beers," the man said. "And he was hittin' on some of the female help at the club."

This is no great revelation, that the one-time New York Yankees star will sip the amber and admire a well-turned ankle.

What the man said brought to mind a story written for *Esquire* by

Pete Gent, the marvelously gifted author of *North Dallas Forty*.

Gent sat with Mantle at Preston Trails Country Club in Dallas, headquarters for Mantle's leisure hours, and wrote about what life is like for the living legend now that the cheers are nothing but an echo.

They talked of how their wives had told them they had alcohol problems. And Mantle related how he earns large fees for playing golf with corporation executives and their hirelings and how occasionally he rents himself out for $3,500 to some woman who wants to have him present for her husband's birthday party.

The story of their afternoon together, Gent and Mantle, was a narrative that needed no commentary to generate a feeling of sadness, like that of the man at the club here.

This is not an indictment of Mantle. Quite the contrary.

What the hell is a legend supposed to do when he has pulled off his uniform for the last time, anyway?

I mention all this now because the man's comments called up memories of the athlete who, as much as anyone I've ever seen or heard of, was the Great American Hero.

Even his name was right. Mickey Mantle. What a wonderful name for a hero. He came from Oklahoma and brought a sort of cowboy way of speaking with him. He had a magnificent body and a face that could have been created by an artist in search of the perfect features for a baseball star.

He could hit from either side, with power, and run like a deer.

And he played for the mighty Yankees, one of sport's greatest dynasties.

He was, simply, perfect for America.

The fans adored him. Once, in the autumn of his career, he pinch-hit in the All-Star game and struck out (as he had so humanly done in his prime) but the fans gave him a huge ovation, simply because he was Mickey Mantle.

After the man had told me about seeing Mantle in Charlotte, I began to think about all that and to wonder if we had anyone like him today in this country, in any sport.

Sorting through the stars of the present, the closest thing I could find to Mantle was Sugar Ray Leonard, the fighter.

A case could be made for Pete Rose. He is a great baseball player, beloved by most, but his image is that of a sweaty, dusty, contentious scrapper. He lacks the elegance of a Mantle, whose feats had a clear, clean definition. He slew the enemy with a single swipe of his terrible swift sword. Rose worries them to death.

Ten or 15 years ago it would have been Arnold Palmer but the years have eroded The King's golf game.

Reggie Jackson's manner and performance lack the flavor and consistent qualities Mantle gave us.

America does not embrace a Mike Schmidt or a George Foster. It can embrace a Carl Yazstremski but he is not Mickey Mantle. It can embrace Tom Seaver but pitchers cannot produce the sudden drama of hitters.

Roger Staubach came close to filling the bill when he was with the Dallas Cowboys. He was a genuine Great American Hero but he's gone now. The same is true of O.J. Simpson. Terry Bradshaw had the qualities too, but, in stride with his Pittsburgh Steelers, he's fading.

Julius (Dr. J) Erving is basketball's most elegant figure but the sport doesn't capture the fancy of the people the way baseball does.

We admire, in various ways, the heroes of all sports but, in various ways, they fall short.

Sugar Ray Leonard has all of the qualities we seek in our athletes – skill, style, grace. Even he comes up short of Mantle, though.

This leaves us to sing softly, substituting for the name of another of our Great American Heroes, "Where have you gone, Mickey Mantle, a nation turns its lonely eyes to you."

We know, of course, where he has gone and because he is Mickey Mantle, we can forgive his transgressions in his leftover time to kill.

And long for another like him.

July 8, 1986

Of Horner and Homers

When Bob Horner, the Atlanta Braves' beefy, blond bomber, smashed four home runs out of Fulton County Stadium Sunday afternoon like a man playing Ping-Pong, the lights came on in the halls of baseball history, illuminating memories.

A place had to be made for Horner, there in that special room where the home run hitters go, and while we were about it, we slipped a glance at some of the other residents.

We reserve a special place for them, away from the wily pitchers, the deft glovemen and the consistent hitters, because home runs are special. As someone said, had Babe Ruth pointed to a spot in the infield where he was going to bunt the ball and then laid it down there, we would never have had the rich tale about that home run he supposedly earmarked in advance for centerfield. Not for a bunt.

In all of U.S. sports, there is nothing more dramatic, more emphatic, more electrifying than a home run.

Horner said something about the fact that the Braves had not won the game. Long after the 18,000 who were there have forgotten who won, they'll remember that Bob Horner hit four home runs. They saw something wonderful, something only 10 men before him had done and something no one had done since 1976. Something even Babe Ruth never did. It doesn't matter who won.

Horner's feat opened the door to that special room, and we gazed again at some of the most memorable of home runs.

The one in 1951, the Miracle of Coogan's Bluff, is the one generally acknowledged as the most dramatic.

The Brooklyn Dodgers had the National League by the throat, leading by 13 1/2 games on August 12, but the New York Giants won 16 in a row and 37 of their last 44 games to catch the Dodgers and force a three-game playoff.

They split the first two games of the playoff. In the third game, the Dodgers led 4-1 going into the bottom of the ninth but the Giants got a run across and two men on and then Bobby Thomson drove a home run over the left field fence to win it. All factors considered, no man ever hit one to equal it.

Bill Mazeroski won the 1960 World Series in similar fashion for the Pittsburgh Pirates, hitting a home run in the bottom of the ninth inning of the seventh game to break a 9-9 tie and beat the New York Yankees.

I have a special fondness for two home runs.

One was Roger Maris' 61st in 1961, breaking Babe Ruth's single-season record.

Maris was nothing like the home-run hitter Ruth had been, but in 1961 he was stalking the record. This troubled much of the public. It also troubled Commissioner Ford Frick. Maris was playing a 162-

game schedule. Ruth had played a 154-game slate. Frick ruled that any record set after the 154-game mark would carry an asterisk.

Maris was under such intense pressure his hair began to fall out, but he kept hitting homers, and when he came to the 154th game, he needed two homers to tie Ruth's mark. He hit one.

He hit his 60th a few days later and then, in the Yankees' last game of the season, he hit another.

To my mind, the record belongs to Roger Maris. The record is for most home runs in a season. He hit the most. I was happy for him. He was doing something extraordinary, and yet there seemed to be a widely-held feeling that he was violating something. He never claimed to be Babe Ruth. He just hit more home runs.

My other favorite home run was the one Ted Williams hit in his last time at bat with the Boston Red Sox in 1960. John Updike's account of that event, published in the *New Yorker* and adorned cleverly with the cliche-style headline popular at the time – "Hub Fans Bid Kid Adieu" – stands as perhaps the best sports story I have ever read.

Space won't permit me to quote enough of it to do it justice here, but I will give you the few climactic sentences:

"Jack Fisher, who was now pitching, was wide with the first pitch. He put the second one over, and Williams swung mightily and missed. The crowd grunted, seeing that classic swing, so long and smooth and quick, exposed, naked in its failure. Fisher threw the third time. Williams swung, and there it was."

And there it was. What a perfect line, not only for Williams' career-ending home run but for every homer ever hit.

Basketball

February 12, 1987

The Dean's 600th

When time ran out on Dean Smith's 600th victory as coach of the North Carolina Tar Heels Wednesday night, he didn't wait around to take any bows.

He never has, and the reaching of a milestone that he considers insignificant is not going to change his habits after 26 years. When the horn sounded and scrappy Wake Forest had finally been dispatched 94-85, Smith waved his team off the floor, hurried to shake hands with Deacon coach Bob Staak and then ran for the dressing room. If he heard the surge of cheers and applause as the public address announcer proclaimed the 600th win, he didn't acknowledge it.

Those who wanted to make something special of the moment managed to get in a few licks. With 35 seconds left and time out, some students paraded alongside the court carrying a huge banner reading, "Congratulations Coach on No. 600."

The message board flashed the number.

And the fans chanted, "Six-oh-oh!"

Responding to a question about his 600th, Smith said the expected. "This is not a day to reflect any more to me than last week when our staff won 599. What's the difference?

"I do remember my first game. We beat Virginia and I was pretty nervous. I could probably recall a lot more games, both wins and losses, but I haven't reflected on that."

Asked about milestones that might be ahead, Smith, in his 26th season as a head coach, gave a hint about his future.

"I don't have a blueprint for my future," he said, "but I won't be a 35 or 40-year coach, and you can quote me on that." That simply means that he won't be around over eight more years, but that's probably enough to start opposing coaches counting the days. He's beaten them 600 times. They've beaten him 173.

Smith said he appreciated all the attention being given his 600th win but said, "It just means I've coached a long time. You can bet I'm one person who's not counting. Every year I get a new team and that's the only year I'm interested in."

One of Smith's most admirable qualities is that, unlike most of us, he measures little by numbers. In basketball, the only number important to him is the final score. Give him a statistic and he can negate it with another. The pick-ax parts of the game such as steals, assists, rebounding, blocking out, setting picks and his beloved defense are more pleasing to his eye than a soft jumper.

He sees the game, the whole game, as both high-tech mechanical function and art form. He couldn't care less who leads the scoring.

By the same token, his place in the sport can't accurately be measured by the number of his victories. They reflect the successful application of a unique coaching philosophy but they don't fully define the classical style of his program that has set standards for the college game. They don't show the extra effort opponents give to playing North Carolina, game in and game out. They don't testify to the pristine conduct of his recruiting, the graduation rate of his players or his fatherly caring for them after they leave school.

They don't tell us what a good man he is, only what a good coach.

Watching Dean Smith's North Carolina Tar Heels play is a privilege we may not fully appreciate right now, but we should mark each time well because what we are seeing will someday be legend.

We're seeing greatness at work.

In time, Smith will take his place in the misty pantheon beside the likes of Adolph Rupp, Henry Iba, Phog Allen and John Wooden. What you do comes into clearer focus after you've finished.

Six hundred wins. That's a remarkable number for a career spanning 26 years. Coming into this season, his teams had averaged 23 wins a year. Wooden matched that but nobody else has.

Other teams in the powerful ACC rise to glory and fall. N.C. State and David Thompson, Virginia and Ralph Sampson, Maryland and Duke and all those splendid performers have come up to challenge him. And still, every year, Smith's Tar Heels remain the standard by which all teams in the ACC are measured.

May 5, 1967

The Signing of Bill Bradley

Word that Bill Bradley, the untouchable of basketball, had been touched by the offer of half a million dollars to play four years for the New York Knickerbockers caused some deeply imbedded emotions to rip loose.

A man has to go to work sometime, and $125,000 a year is not a bad starting salary, even for a bright young man who is a graduate of Princeton as well as a Rhodes Scholar. One of the things that you could like best about the incredible story of Bill Bradley, though, was that he had turned his back on professional basketball like Hank Luisetti out of the misty past and would let his feats at Old Nassau stand on their own.

Perhaps the strongest emotion stirred by Bradley's signing is the fear that he will spoil the image, that he will verify that uneasy feeling we always had that he was too good to be true.

Not that there is any doubt that he will make it as a professional and do well. The Knicks, who have been shopping around for a super star for the past 20 years, probably got themselves one in Bradley.

In fact, Joe Lapchick, a former Knicks coach, thinks the signing of Bradley will change the entire league.

"Bradley has so many assets and competes so beautifully," he said. "Nobody takes his territory, and he doesn't act like a rich kid but like one of those battle-hardened guys who came out of Brooklyn.

"He is capable of the incredible.

"Take his play in the Holiday Tournament at the Garden a few years ago. Princeton wasn't supposed to have a chance against Michigan, the best college team in the land. But Bradley dominated the game so completely that he made those Michigan stars look like apple pickers."

It's stuff like that, like the Michigan game, that you are afraid will melt into pure fiction.

It was Dec. 30, 1964. Having been accorded almost every honor that could be bestowed on a collegiate basketball player, including selection to the Olympic team, Bradley felt compelled to prove himself in this game against America's best. Michigan, he felt, would provide an exact measurement of him as an athlete.

Adding to the challenge was a face-to-face duel with All-American Cazzie Russell, who until that night was regarded by many as the hottest thing on an American college court. Too, it was Bradley's first appearance in the Garden.

The six foot, five inch, dark-haired son of a Missouri bank president slept 12 hours, arose at noon and deliberately read the New York newspapers, absorbing the excitement of the headlines that boomed: "Festival Duel: Bill Bradley vs. Cazzie Russell" and "Bradley Or Cazzie? Showdown at Hand."

He felt chills and he knew he was ready. He spent the afternoon alone, thinking about the game, not just about matching or beating Russell but about beating Michigan. He decided it could be done, even though few, if any, gave Princeton the faintest chance.

Bradley scored 41 points and held his man to one point in a performance that one critic described as having "all the depth and variation of theoretical basketball."

With four and a half minutes to play, he fouled out and 20,000 people stood and cheered for three minutes. Garden veterans said it was the most clamorous ovation ever accorded an athlete in that building.

When Bradley went to the sidelines to join two other starters who had fouled out, his play and that of his inspired teammates had threatened to rout Michigan. He left the Tigers holding a 12 point lead.

Without Bradley, though, Princeton collapsed and Cazzie, who scored 27 points, and his tall, husky mates overran the Tigers and won by a basket.

As the season thundered down the home stretch, Bradley carried his team past one favored opponent after another in the playoffs. The Tigers finally lost again to Michigan in the semifinals but in the consolation game of the finals, Bradley gave his greatest performance. He scored 58 points in smashing powerful Wichita, 118-82. Twenty-six of the points came in a nine minute stretch in which he missed only once. Sixteen of them came in the final five minutes, in which he did not miss a shot.

What can he do for an encore?

The Knicks got themselves quite a basketball player and quite a young man when they got the Olympic captain and clutch star that the Russians called "Shootnik."

At Princeton, Bradley was voted by his classmates to be "Most

Popular," "Most Likely To Succeed," the student they most respected and one of Princeton's two greatest assets, the other being a deceased woman who had just left the university $27 million.

He was also chosen the best athlete.

His is a rare and wonderful story. Fix it in your mind. It is the truth.

March 16, 1973

A Mere Mortal

Out on the coliseum court, Tom McMillen, wearing the No. 54 jersey of the Maryland Terrapins, loped through pre-game warmups. His pleasant, Lincolnesque features showed none of the emotion associated with the NCAA Eastern Regionals in which he would soon be pitching in short baseline jumpers and tapping in missed shots and fetching down rebounds to help plunder Syracuse 91-75.

George Raveling, who left an assistantship at Maryland to become head coach at Washington State this season, watched the 6-11 junior move about and said, "He would have had to be a saint to live up to the reputation he brought to Maryland.

"The pressure on him was as great as it was on Wilt Chamberlain and Lew Alcindor when they entered school. Nobody knows the pressure Tom has endured, not only on the court but in the academic world and trying to live up to his image. He's lived up to all of it well."

The normal pressure put on a gifted 6-11 basketball player was greatly compounded by a cover story in *Sports Illustrated* which proclaimed him "the best high school player in America," noted that "recruiters often simultaneously compare Tom to Lew Alcindor and Bill Bradley" and added that "he may help the school he chooses to the same dominance of college basketball that UCLA enjoyed during Alcindor's varsity years."

The pressure reached the explosive stage when McMillen chose North Carolina over the protests of his parents and the family disagreement became public.

The sensitive young man eventually yielded and went to Maryland and since has rarely escaped banners in enemy arenas that say things like, "How's Mommy, Tommy?" He saw them at football games before he ever shot a basket for the Terrapins but he shrugged and told Maryland's sports information man Jack Zane, "It's something I'll have to live with."

And the final heaping of pressure has been brought forth by McMillen himself. He is incredibly intense.

When the game began on this night, you could see it in the firm, almost angry set of his jaw, in the way he clawed for everything – an open shot, a rebound, victory. He got a couple of quick baskets, then hardly touched the ball again until early in the second half as his talented mates did their own number. For a player with his moves and touch, he doesn't get many shots. He got six in the second half and hit all of them.

For the night, he was eight for 10 from the floor, two for two from the line and had six rebounds. He averages 21 points, 10 rebounds.

"He does everything intensely," said Coach Lefty Driesell. "Sometimes he's too intense. He's a lot like I am, he gets too emotional, he plays too hard because he wants to win so much.

"But if he isn't an All-American, I don't know what one is. He's done a super-duper job."

The Carolina Cougars' coach, Larry Brown, watched McMillen play for the sixth time this season and said, "He's an amazing shooter and he has all the moves. He's not a dominating player because he's not a super rebounder and he's not the shot blocker you normally expect a 6-11 player to be but he's a quality person and he really wants to play.

"On a team with less talent, he'd score a lot more."

On this team, McMillen was the third high scorer last night.

He is not naturally aggressive. His aggressiveness is contrived, almost clinical, as opposed to the natural instincts of muscular players such as his own teammate, Len Elmore. But he backs down from no one and, as he has done with his life, hurls himself into the fray with good results.

McMillen is a brilliant student and has a chance to become a Rhodes Scholar. He is being pushed to run for the class presidency by fellow students, and opposing forces are mounting a "Stop McMillen" campaign that paints him as "The Establishment."

He comes by that naturally. He heads charity drives, works on the President's Council for Physical Fitness, speaks to kids' groups, plays basketball.

There is a constant tugging at him from many sides, not the least of which is athletics. There are still traces of those unrealistic expectations that he can singlehandedly shoot UCLA and the rest of basketball to shreds. He tries but he can't. He's special but he's no saint.

March 11, 1974

Tommy Burleson's Greatest Game

The taller you are in this game of basketball, the more difficult it is to reach the heights expected of you.

Tommy Burleson is seven feet, four inches tall – taller than anybody playing the game in this country – and he has been struggling for four years to attain the level of excellence dictated more by his towering frame than by reason.

He finally did it Saturday night in Greensboro. The fetters fell away and there he sat, his eyes glistening happily, surrounded by sports writers in the N.C. State dressing room.

His 38 points, 13 rebounds and furious defensive effort had carried the nationally top-ranked Wolfpack to a 103-100 overtime victory over Maryland in the ACC tournament finals. Burleson, the big kid from the mountains, was the hero of the greatest game ever played in the ACC tournament – and maybe the best game ever played in the ACC, period.

The moment, the very essence of these four years, came when Lefty Driesell, the coach of the losers, squeezed through the mob of writers, shook Burleson's hand and said, "Tommy, that's the best game I've ever seen a big man play."

Burleson felt 10 feet tall.

This was the way he had dreamed it might be someday but it never had been this way until now.

When he ambled down out of the mountains for his freshman year at N.C. State, he knew what a basketball was and what to do with it. He had played for Newland High and when there was snow on the ground at home he practiced on a hoop in the barn and at night his dad would roll a basketball to him to develop the big kid's hands.

But the elements of the city game, the refinements of competition with dudes on the block, were missing. He had a lot to learn.

There were games in which he got so wrought up in frustration, Coach Norm Sloan would sit him down on the bench until he could get his head straight. There was that burning embarrassment about the trouble with the pinball machines and the campus cop. There was that loss in the first round of the ACC tournament when he was a sophomore when he hit only seven of 24 shots.

There was the shadow of Maryland's big Len Elmore falling over his performances and the assertion by many that Lenny could eat Tommy's lunch any time they met. And finally, there was the day he learned that he, a seven-foot, four-inch senior playing center for the No. 1 team in the country, hadn't even made first team All-ACC.

None of that mattered much anymore as Burleson gloried in Saturday's victory. He could smile about some of it now. "I was so high for the tournament my sophomore year, I just about put the ball through the backboards."

Sloan said Burleson had accepted Elmore's election to the All-ACC team graciously. "I apologized to him," said the coach. "I told him it had to be a school, area, friendship vote that kept him off. He said, 'There are a lot of great players in the league.'"

Tommy wouldn't admit it had set him on fire for Saturday's classic, although he played it with a raging fury.

"I just wanted to play well," he said. "In four years at State, this is what I've been looking forward to, going to the NCAA playoffs, and it's finally come true. I didn't need anything to key me up for this one. Matter of fact, I was real relaxed today. I took my little sister Linda shopping."

Burleson's All-American teammate, David Thompson, helped Tommy play his career game. Thompson had so devastated Maryland in the past that Driesell had his guards helping to cover him. That took away some of Elmore's help on Burleson and let them play one-on-one.

Elmore was stunned by the results. "I didn't think anybody could score 38 points off me," he said.

Sloan felt the performance was vindication for Burleson's absence from the All-ACC team.

Burleson felt it was simply vindication for being seven feet, four inches tall.

March 10, 1975

David's Last Game

The collegiate basketball career of David Thompson of N.C. State ended dismally in Greensboro. The best who ever played in the Atlantic Coast Conference, possibly the best who ever played the college game, didn't score in his last 13 minutes and lost to arch rival North Carolina in the ACC Tournament finals 70-66.

Hailed as a three-time All-American and twice Player of the Year in the nation, the quiet kid from a dirt road outside Shelby, who had brought millions to their feet with his spectacular play, faded from the scene without a single ruffle or flourish.

The only cheers he heard when his college career had ended were those of the triumphant North Carolina fans. Nobody stopped him to shake his hand as he trotted off the court, his face expressionless.

Downstairs in the dressing room, you could hear the public address announcer and the crowd noises. Through the closed door came the muffled news that Carolina's freshman guard Phil Ford had won the tournament's most valuable player award.

"Oh, my God," said Thompson's senior teammate, Tim Stoddard. It was the third straight year someone else had won MVP. Thompson didn't seem to hear. He just kept on packing his gear.

He had played so hard against Virginia and Maryland in the first two games, his magnificent legs that lifted him and floated him around the court had finally succumbed to his unrelenting drive and cramped on Friday night. Saturday night, they failed to perform normally and he went out like a lamb.

North Carolina's worrisome zone defense, Walter Davis' harassment when the Tar Heels played man-to-man and his hurting, unresponsive legs combined to prevent Thompson from freeing himself for shots as he normally does. He shot poorly, seven for 21, and got only 16 points, 14 below his season average.

When it was over, the impact of Thompson's finale was not fully felt because it was thought the Wolfpack might accept a bid to the National Invitation Tournament. But in the dressing room, Thompson showed uncommon emotion when questioned about that.

"Hell, no," he said. "We don't want to go to the NIT. This team's too good for that."

The Wolfpack had been national champions last season. They had been chosen by many to repeat this season. But they never got their act together with any consistency. They missed tall Tom Burleson in the middle. They had their confidence shaken early in the season by a loss to Wake Forest and had it pounded to a pulp in a lopsided loss to Maryland. The only thing constant about the team was Thompson's excellence. He had some off games, of course, but he was always a factor.

When the Wolfpack beat Maryland in the tournament semifinals, some of the lost glory returned, and with it, renewed hope of repeating as national champion. When that hope was extinguished Saturday night, the Pack – tired, hurt, disgusted – decided to hang it up.

It had not been a happy season.

Coach Norman Sloan had complained bitterly at one point in the season that Thompson was being held and pushed by opponents and officials weren't calling it. Later, Thompson asked to be taken out of a game in the last few minutes, after the issue had been decided, because he felt the game had gotten too physical (he had been undercut on a jump shot) and he didn't want to risk injury. He said playing wasn't as much fun this year because of the pushing and tugging.

"Even when we won this year," said guard Moe Rivers Saturday night, "it wasn't really totally satisfying because of the officiating. Tonight, every time David shot, he was pushed, but at the other end of the floor, they called defensive fouls on him."

Thompson went out like a lamb – but like a man. When he had dressed, he went to the North Carolina dressing room to offer his congratulations and good wishes.

Now it's all over – the spectacular alley-oop shots with David soaring high to take a pass and drop it in the basket, a maneuver kids all over the state try to emulate now; the classic jump shot snapping nets; the clutch plays, like the tap-in to beat Maryland on national TV a couple of years ago; the brilliance against UCLA when the Bruins' reign was finally broken last year; the 57-point performance early this season; the 30 points in 27 minutes against Maryland last Friday night before he collapsed...

The memories are countless and they will linger. We won't soon see another like David Thompson.

February 20, 1982

The Gray Fox

They are a little late getting around to it, but the honors committeemen have named the late Everett Case to the national Basketball Hall of Fame.

What basketball is in this state today, what it is in the Atlantic Coast Conference and to some degree what it is in America, we owe to Everett Case, the Gray Fox of N.C. State.

It's appropriate, of course, that Case should enter the Hall of Fame but it's not necessary to his memory.

Ride past an inner-city playground and watch the kids playing hoops. Walk down any street in a suburb and look at the backboards standing at the ends of driveways. Drive down highways through the countryside and observe the baskets nailed to barns.

These are all monuments to Everett Case.

He used to tell us this would come to pass, that someday almost every house in North Carolina would have a basket. He was right and he was the reason.

Those great coliseums that have mushroomed out of the ground, some of them already aging out, are also his monuments.

Everett Case's high school teams won 726 games and lost 76 in Indiana, four times winning that state's championship. His service teams won 56 and lost five. In 18 seasons at State and two games into a 19th before he retired, his Wolfpacks won 376 and lost 133. That totals 1,159 victories and only 214 defeats.

That is one of the truly remarkable coaching records of all time. When he came to State, Case brought with him a wealth of talented players from Indiana. In his first 10 seasons, his teams had a 265-60 record, won 10 ACC and Southern Conference titles and seven Dixie Classics.

Two significant results have been attributed to the success at N.C. State of this smallish man who never played high school or college ball but had a touch of genius beneath his slicked-back silver hair.

Case gave the people of this state, particularly the vast agrarian segment with real or vicarious ties to what was then State College, a new source of pride where one was sorely needed. Today, our basketball remains one of the state's proudest qualities.

We owe that to Case, because his dazzling red and white teams, looking like death on a fast break as they stormed over one helpless victim after another, forced other schools to upgrade their programs to compete.

He saw to it that Reynolds Coliseum, on which construction had begun before World War II, was completed. The skeleton of steel had stood for years. When people began storming the doors at the outmoded old campus gym, Case called for the completion of the coliseum, but insisted that it be enlarged from the original plans.

It came out elongated, not the way a basketball arena should be laid out, but it quickly filled with wild-eyed fanatics and shimmering, deathless moments of glory.

Others looked at all this, watched Case's heroes regularly cut down the nets in a symbolic ceremony he had brought from Indiana, and knew they couldn't stand still. They had to try to compete. They hired new coaches, threw their programs into high gear and took off after the Fox. That was his other significant contribution.

They finally caught him, and in the end, the few years before he resigned because he was being wasted by cancer in his bones, they were beating him more often than he was beating them but his teeth had been pulled by the administration.

Part of it was his own fault. Case was a rascal. Twice his program was nailed by the NCAA for illegal recruiting. This can't be pardoned, of course, but Case had the good grace to admit to his sins and somehow that made them seem a little less ugly.

And then some of his players were caught up in the point-shaving scandal that struck college basketball in the early '60s. N.C. State decided it was time to gear down its program.

All of it – his own problems and the improvement of other teams – combined to end Case's reign. Shortly after he retired, he died.

He was buried on a hillside on U.S. 70. The day before he died, he told a friend that's where he wanted to be buried, "so I can wave to the boys and wish them luck when they go over to Duke." Everett Case had a profound impact on basketball in the South and on our lives, because the game is important to us. It changed our attitudes and our habits and made life a little better for us.

It's nice that he's finally in the Hall of Fame. Few, if any, deserve it more. But he was there in our hearts and minds a long time before they finally got around to making it official

April 23, 1987

The Impossible Dream

What had seemed, not very long ago, an impossible dream – an NBA team for Charlotte – came true shortly after noon Wednesday.

A couple of hours later, after the formalities and the mass press conference had ended, George Shinn, who had dreamed this dream and made it come true, found himself momentarily alone with another fellow from Charlotte. Shinn smiled a smile of sheer ecstasy and said, "Isn't it great?"

It is.

After two years of intense effort to bring a major-league team to a city that many gave no chance because of its size and its past sports failures, Shinn had spent a nervous Wednesday morning while the NBA Board of Governors pondered whether to award Charlotte a franchise.

At 12:10, he received a phone call in his attorney's room at the Helmsley Palace, the NBA's headquarters hotel. Come to Commissioner David Stern's suite immediately, he was told. Shinn thought this might be it, but he had thought that at 11 a.m., too, when he had been similarly summoned.

"When they called me the first time, I just knew they were going to call me into the room, put an arm around me and congratulate me," said Shinn. "But I didn't even get into the room. They just said there would be a press conference about 12:30. I was really discouraged. They made me come up there just to tell me that. They could've told me that on the phone.

"When they called the second time, it shook me up. I really had a feeling it was going to happen, but I had been nervous as the dickens. They kept making us wait and wait and it was really rough, it really was."

Shinn prolonged the agony by getting on an elevator that didn't go to Stern's floor. He rode to the top with several women ("I didn't want them to know I had made a mistake so I rode all the way to the top with them"), rode back down and got on the right one.

Stern met him at the door, extended his hand and said, "Congratulations, you determined little cuss." It was done.

Two years of work, two years on an emotional roller coaster, two years of clinging to hope when many dismissed the idea as folly, were over, and it had turned out right.

"First, I gave thanks and then I shouted," said Shinn.

He and the other new inductees from Minneapolis, Orlando and Miami were invited to have lunch with the other owners in a ballroom. "I asked if I could invite our other owners (Cy Bahakel, Felix Sabates and Rick Hendricks) to lunch," said Shinn. "I said, I think we've paid for it ($32.5 million).' They said sure."

As the press conference wound down, Shinn held a piece of paper in his hand. On it was written, "Call Gov. Jim Martin."

Shinn showed it around and said, "It's not often that I get a note like that."

"I don't think the majority of people in our area realize yet what getting this franchise means."

Max Muhleman, a public relations consultant who has helped steer Shinn from the birth of the idea to its culmination, said, "It was a miracle. I have to thank the Big Man. It was a miracle.

"No matter what people think it's going to be like, it's going to be better when they see this show come to town with their name on it.

"There's going to be an ACC kind of atmosphere. I know we're going to have some crowds of 20,000. It's going to be great."

Now that the quest has ended, Shinn said he is going to spend some time with his family, check on his other businesses ("They tell me the businesses are doing better since I've spent so much time away from them"), then visit some NBA franchises and ask owners, "What do I do to make my team successful?"

He added, "This is not a hobby. I believe in it."

We know.

Isn't it great?

November 28, 1983

Michael Jordan

What marvelous talents we've seen in these 29 years since the Atlantic Coast Conference was formed and the interest in college basketball in this area has flamed higher and higher.

Glittering names, dozens of them. Art Heyman, David Thompson, Charlie Scott, Phil Ford, Ralph Sampson, for a sampling.

Now, as he enters his junior season at North Carolina, there is no question that – based on sheer overall talent, sense of the game, nerve, effort and teamwork – Michael Jordan's name belongs up there with the best of the best, those select few whose names have been written across winter night skies.

In a 1982-83 season when Jordan was only a sophomore and the great giant Sampson was casting his long, dreaded shadow across the land in his senior year, the *Sporting News* saw fit to name Jordan its national player of the year.

Former coach and NBC analyst Al McGuire proclaimed him the No. 1 player in the country. Jordan was everybody's all-American. And Maryland's Adrian Branch paid the young Tar Heel a classic player's compliment, saying, "Guarding Jordan is dirty, dirty work."

Still Jordan works like some deep sub looking for playing time, like a dock hand bucking for a pay raise.

On the day after Carolina finished its regular season last March and Coach Dean Smith had given his players some time off, Jordan went home to Wilmington. His mother took away his car keys and took the phone off the hook to make sure her son rested instead of going out to find a game. He minded his mama, but the next day he was playing.

On the day after Carolina lost to Georgia in the NCAA East Region tournament, Jordan was in Carmichael Auditorium on the campus, playing in a pickup game.

There was work to be done.

After his freshman season, when all he did was play wonderfully and make the clutch basket that proved to be the winning margin in the NCAA championship game, Jordan got instructions from Smith to work on his defense.

He did. As a freshman, he never won the award Smith gives after each game for defense. Last season, he won it 12 times and Smith said he was three times better than he was as a freshman.

After another splendid year in 1982-83, in which he repeatedly made spectacular, game-winning plays, Jordan busied himself with more improvements like ball-handling and passing and defense again, at Smith's suggestion. And one of his own. Shooting.

He had noticed on game films – and some fans had written to ask about it – that his jump shot arched higher than his free throws. He was rainbowing his jumper.

Without a word about it from his coaches, Jordan changed his shot in the off-season. He had never won the week-long, pre-season shooting competition. He won it this year.

"I haven't seen a guy this talented work this hard," said Matt Doherty, a senior forward at Carolina. "His work ethic is intense, demanding, all business." Doherty smiled and said, "He doesn't need to work on anything. Maybe Coach is just trying to keep him humble."

Imitating Smith, Doherty said, "Michael, you've got to work on growing." He added, "Michael's grown an inch since he got here.

"Coming from New York, I've seen a lot of guys with talent but a lot of them are not smart. Michael has all the tools and he puts them to maximum use. It scares you sometimes."

Indeed.

Carolina, having already lost its first two games last season after winning the national championship the year before, trails Tulane by two points at Chapel Hill. Tulane has the ball out of bounds with only four seconds to play. Curtains again?

Two Green Wave players collide trying to catch the inbounds pass, Jordan scoops up the loose ball, whirls and tosses in a 30-footer to send the game into overtime and Carolina goes on to win.

Carolina leads Maryland by a point with only seconds left. Coach Lefty Driesell sets up a clever play that calls for his son, Chuck, a deep reserve, to drive the baseline for a layup. The play works. Chuck breaks free. But Jordan comes from the top of the key to block the shot and save the victory.

Virginia is closing the gap on Carolina. Sampson, 7-foot-4, shoots a five-foot hook. Jordan blocks it.

They play again. Virginia leads Carolina 63-60 with 1:07 to play. Jordan tips in a missed shot, then steals the ball, slam-dunks it, then beats Sampson for the last rebound and the Tar Heels have beaten the Cavaliers for a third straight time. In the first of those three, the ACC championship game of his freshman season, Jordan scored eight straight points at the end to lift UNC to a 47-45 win.

And then, of course, he hit The Shot that beat Georgetown for the NCAA title.

And despite all this, Jordan works.

It's always been that way since he was in junior high school. His dad, James, put up a backboard in the yard. The kids came to play and they called Jordan "Rabbit" because he was always hustling.

The talent most obvious to the average fan is his scoring. He's collected more than 1,100 points in two years, a school record, and averaged 20 per game last season. But that's only part of it.

Jordan soars ("There were times when I looked up and saw Jordan over my head," said Georgia Tech center Tim Harvey. "It was like watching Superman."), blocks shots, makes steals, sweeps up loose balls, hits teammates with crisp passes, rebounds – well, he does it all.

And spectacularly, so spectacularly.

What is not so obvious is his work on defense. In addition to playing his own man, he is free to go hunting, doubling the ball or the man with the hot hand. He stole the ball 78 times last season.

The only other players to whom Smith has given this freedom in his 22 years at Carolina were Dudley Bradley and Phil Ford.

Smith doesn't have to work at keeping Jordan humble, as Doherty jokingly suggested. Jordan looks at the championship, the victories, the honors, the attention and says, "Things have come so fast. It's like a dream. Sometimes I don't know if I'm going to wake up or live this dream out.

"I never fantasized about being an all-American. When I was in high school, a lot of people told me there was no way I could start for Carolina as a freshman. Some of them were my teachers who were alumni of State.

"I thought they were right. But I thought if I worked hard, maybe I could be the sixth player my first two years."

The fact is, he hadn't really been a sensation at Laney High until his senior year. That's after he grew six inches between his sophomore and senior seasons. And after he put a poster of ball handling drills on the back of his bedroom door and practiced them. And after he shot for hours on end. And worked on the other facets of his game.

Always, there was the work. "Michael was never one who thought he could get by without working," his dad James said.

Well, Jordan does take the easy way out sometimes. "I took a few days off from basketball this summer and played some golf," he said, a wry smile playing across his boyish features. "I shot 49 on the first nine, lost three balls and cheated a little. After a couple of days, I shot a 46 and didn't cheat as much."

Football

October 23, 1986

Still Choo Choo

Forty years ago, Charlie "Choo Choo" Justice was playing his first season of football at North Carolina.

Last Saturday, before the Tar Heels played N.C. State, Justice, 62 years old now, silver-haired and 25 pounds over his playing weight of 165, walked around Kenan Stadium on his way to pick up some tickets. Strangers passing by said, "Hello, Charlie" and nudged companions and said, "There goes Choo Choo."

Some four decades after he set a career total offense record that nobody at North Carolina has approached, Justice is still the most recognizable, most revered and most beloved athlete this state has ever produced.

Justice had come to sit in Kenan Stadium on Saturday with family and friends, but he found he was short one ticket.

He could have stood outside the gate and held up one finger, indicating, as others do, that he wanted to buy a ticket, but he said he didn't think he should do that. Nothing wrong with it for most people, he said, but people might not think it looked right for Charlie Justice.

He could have just told the people on the gate that he was short a ticket and they would have let him in. They know him. But he said he didn't want them to think he was asking any special favors.

He sent the others in and went back to the motel and watched the game alone on television, whooping and hollering as if he were in the stands. No problem. "I kinda like watching on television," he said. "I can see the replays. And I can say whatever I want to."

That's how it is to be Charlie Justice. Or rather, that's how Charlie Justice is.

Wherever he goes in this state, all these years after he helped bring joy back to a nation just emerging from World War II, Justice endures as a hero of almost mythic quality. It has its sweetness and its burdens, but neither has changed him.

Nobody every wore the mantle of athletic hero with more style and grace than Charlie Justice.

He and wife Sarah, who was his high school sweetheart in Asheville, live in a three-bedroom home on a spacious plot of land in Cherryville, where he and his son-in-law have an insurance firm. He no longer works full-time, and he plays golf a couple of times a week to a handicap that ranges between 12 and 14.

Sarah frets that he doesn't exercise enough and weighs a bit too much. He has had two bouts with heart trouble. But he looks fine and says, "I've had a good life."

He does a lot of public speaking. "It's amazing that people still want me to speak to their groups," he said. "I feel if they ask me, I ought to go if I can. They ask what my fee is. I don't have one. I just don't feel I ought to charge them to speak if they still think enough of me to ask me to speak."

He will be speaking to a statewide organization of auxiliary nurses in Charlotte next Monday. He likes that, he said, because the auxiliary nurses are like lineman in that they don't get a lot of recognition.

"I learned early to respect my teammates, that *we* did it, not I did it," he said.

"In my first game in high school, I touched the ball twice and scored twice, once on a 74-yard punt return and once on a 25-yard run.

"I was just 14 and I thought I was a big star. The headline in the paper the next day said, 'Justice Stars.' I got dressed that morning and went downtown to be with my buddies and enjoy this.

"I was walking down the street, and there was my big brother Jack leaning on a telephone pole, waiting for me. He said, 'Why don't you hang a sign on your back with your name on it so everybody will know who you are.'

" 'You think you're a star? Your sister could have scored those touchdowns with the blocking you had. Come on home and I'll show you what football is all about.'

"We went home and we blocked and tackled for three hours. When we finished, he said, 'Now don't ever forget who made you.' And I haven't.

"I get more satisfaction today out of my teammates accepting me, saying I represent them the way they want to be represented and telling me I've never let them down, than anything else that has ever been written or said about me."

Sometimes, Justice sits alone and reminisces about the glory days when he ran, passed and punted, returned punts and kickoffs, caught passes and played some defense, three times making All-America.

He watches a film of his spectacular performance in the old College All-Star game, and another film of what he feels was his greatest run, a 74-yard touchdown gallop against Tennessee on which he says he ran about 175 yards. Gen. Bob Neyland, the fabled Tennessee coach, said it was the greatest run he had ever seen.

Sometimes he thinks of the Heisman Trophy. He was twice runner-up in the balloting.

"That was the one thing I regret I didn't accomplish, winning the Heisman Trophy," he said. "When I was in high school and dating Sarah, we were riding around the night they announced on the radio that Frankie Sinkwich had won the Heisman. I told Sarah I wanted to win that someday.

"If I was going to win it, it should have been in 1948. I led the nation in total offense and punting, but Doak Walker (Southern Methodist) won it. In 1949, I might have won it if I'd played against Notre Dame in New York and had a decent day, but I was injured.

"I'd like to have won it, but then look at all the players who don't even get mentioned for it."

There is a warmth and softness to Justice that is reflected in his words.

He says, "I wasn't anything special, no different from a lot of ballplayers they've had at Chapel Hill." But, of course, he was. He was more exciting, more versatile and probably enjoyed playing football as much as anyone ever has. Pressed for his thoughts on why his fame has never so much as flickered, he says, "I was small. That was part of it.

"The war was over and everybody had been kinda cramped up and they were looking for something to give them a thrill. I ran a lot of different ways and showed a lot of enthusiasm.

"Duke had gotten all the recognition among North Carolina teams, the bowls and national rankings. Carolina had never had a national ranking, never been to a bowl game, never had much recognition. We achieved those things, and I got credit for it. I was supposed to be the one who led the Carolina people to it, put them on the map, but it wasn't me.

"Also, I was a native of North Carolina, and I stayed in North Carolina with the people, where they can see me. I think that's the reason people still look on me the way they do.

"I didn't have more ability than some, but I enjoyed it more."

More than the players, perhaps, but not more than the fans. In the foreword to a book entitled, *Choo Choo, The Charlie Justice Story*," Billy Carmichael Jr. wrote, "In North Carolina and to North Carolinians the world over, a never-to-be-forgotten number is 22 (Justice's number, long ago retired).

"Folks who don't know the number of the apostles or the number of Books in the Bible will tell you about 22. As long as there is a Chapel Hill, the number 22 will mean Charlie Justice, the Will-o'-the-Wisp of Kenan Stadium, the most thrilling athlete in the history of the University of North Carolina.

"... men will tell the Justice story over and over and over ..."

And now, some four decades later, we do. The memory still burns brightly, not only because of what Charlie Justice was, but also because of what he is now, as heroic in his golden years as he was in his glorious past.

December 26, 1974

Always Show Time

Before the echoes of the football season are lost in the cheers at Reynolds Coliseum, we ought to say another word or two about this wispy, freckled, bespectacled, pipe-smoking, fast-talking professor named Lou Holtz.

He teaches football at N.C. State. Guts football. Stick it in their ear football. Hit 'em where they ain't football.

In the 22 seasons it has been playing football, it's doubtful that the Atlantic Coast Conference has turned out any more entertaining football teams than the three Holtz has produced in his three seasons at State. And few have been as successful in terms of wins and losses.

In the three years prior to Holtz's arrival in Raleigh, State had won a total of only nine games while losing 22 and tying two.

In the three Holtz years, State has gone 8-3-1, 9-3 and 9-2-1 and has played in three bowl games, winning two and earlier this week tying Houston 31-31 in the Astro-Bluebonnet.

All eight of those losses marked against Holtz have been to bowl-bound teams.

If you wanted to make a case against the Little Professor, for Lord knows what reason, you could argue that he inherited a wealth of talented players when he came to N.C. State. To a certain extent, that's true, he did have Willie Burden and Charley Young and Stan Fritts and Roland Hooks and Bill Yoest, some people like that.

But Holtz also had on hand a lot of those players Penn State had rejected as too skinny or too slow, assorted other scraggly hand-me-downs and too many young, green players.

Holtz also inherited a program that was starting to suffer from rigor mortis of tradition. Three losing seasons in a row and two coaching changes in two years had not put the Wolfpack into a cheery frame of mind for Holtz's first team meeting and when they saw that little dude come in, more than one player said to himself, "No way, man."

But there was a way.

The Wolfpack busted down the doors getting out of the dressing room and when that first season was done and they had finally quit running and passing, Holtz's heroes had run up 409 points – 34 per game – and had routed West Virginia 49-13 in the Peach Bowl.

Last year, same story. A 9-3 record, 396 points, a 31-18 victory over Kansas in the Liberty Bowl.

Maybe Holtz did his best coaching job in that first year at State but I rather think it was this year.

There were some excellent players remaining, like Fritts, Hooks, quarterback Dave Buckey, offensive guard Bob Blanchard, defensive back Mike Devine, defensive tackle Sam Sennecca...but the offensive line, so critical to State's outscore-'em style of the previous two years, was a question mark.

This team had to be nursed along. It didn't really blend into the real thing until the last couple of games of the season, when Penn State and Arizona State were shot down in impressive performances.

It was a come-from-behind team, one that had an aggravating habit of falling behind early. The 'Pack was losing to Virginia 21-0 but won 22-21.

Though games such as that are rare, you might say they typify Holtz's teams. Just last Monday night, State was down 14 points with less than four minutes to play and tied Houston.

Professor Holtz got peeved at us sports writers for leaving some of his players off the All-ACC team and, in a vote held before State's comeback, for picking a Houston player as the star back of the game ahead of Buckey.

He didn't mention that his team – the most patched-up one he's had at State – finished 9-2 in regular season, best record in the ACC, and he didn't win Coach of the Year honors.

Maybe somebody deserved it more. Probably did. But nobody has made it more fun to watch than Lou Holtz since he showed up and the players said, "No way."

And we appreciate it, Lou.

September 19, 1977

Where's the Magic, Joe?

For the past 13 years, we have been accustomed to seeing Joe Namath wearing the green and white of the New York Jets. They called him Broadway Joe. He brought the young American Football League to maturity, passed the Jets to the Super Bowl Championship, packed the stadiums and achieved a level of glamor never enjoyed by any other quarterback. And then it all began to fade. The lights of Broadway went down.

Yesterday, Namath, 34 now and with knees stiff and scarred from injury and surgery, sought to start a new life with the Los Angeles Rams as another National Football League season opened in Atlanta. Clad in blue and gold and wearing the famed No. 12, he clutched at the lost glory but couldn't even outplay Scott Hunter, the Atlanta Falcons' second-string quarterback who was filling in for injured Steve Bartkowski, and Atlanta won, 17-6.

As the crowd of 55,000 made its way out of Atlanta Stadium, big Claude Humphrey, a 10-year veteran who stands 6-foot-5, weighs 265 and has a look of ferocity about him, stood in a corner of the Falcon dressing room and spoke in reverent tones of the man he had twice sacked for a total of 23 yards and had slammed in the ground several times after the passes were gone.

"Any time I get to Joe, it's a feather in my cap," he said. "It's still a big thrill to sack Joe, but I consciously go after him above the waist. I don't want to be the one who goes back there and rips his legs off. If possible, I stay off his legs. I get paid the same whether I hit him high or low. I don't want to hurt him.

"Namath has done a lot for the game of football, not just for the Jets.

"To hurt Joe would be like hurting Knute Rockne or one of the Four Horsemen.

"There's a magic that he carries with him that's good for football and I wouldn't want to be the man that finished him."

The magic of Namath, the glimmering star of stars, filled this bowl of humanity on this steamy Sunday afternoon. And at each passing situation, a murmur went up among the crowd while the Rams were still in the huddle. He completed 15 of 30 passes for a meager 108 yards and one touchdown and was sacked three times. Still every pass that fell to the earth was met with a mighty roar.

Reporters from four New York papers and most of the big west coast publications as well as an unusually large number of southern writers were on hand to watch the stoop-shouldered Namath debut with his new club. He gave them something of the past to see in the first quarter. He laid a long, perfect spiral into the hands of wide open Harold Jackson, but the normally sure-handed receiver bobbled it and lost a certain touchdown. Two plays later, Namath drilled the ball to Jackson again, on the same spot, and this time Jackson caught it and scampered over for a 27-yard touchdown. The extra point was blocked but LA had the lead and who knew how many more Joe might throw before the day was done? He had made this one look so easy.

But he never moved the Rams into threatening position again. Forgetting his presence and considering only his feats, he was a mediocrity. Hunter matched Namath's yardage exactly, while throwing 13 fewer passes. And he got the Falcons' running game going while the Rams never did.

After the game, Namath sat naked in front of his locker while reporters swarmed around him. His lower lip protruded, as if it had been slugged by Muhammad Ali. Someone asked what happened to it. Namath said, "Nothing, that's just a chew of tobacco."

He looked like anything but the glamor boy out of the popcorn and pantyhose commercials, the sleepy-eyed sex symbol on the posters, the slick talk show personality whose name rhymes with wee hours, scotch, and swishy blondes. His brown hair was wet and tousled. His face appeared gaunt. One of his eyeballs was red around the blue, where a hand or foot had penetrated his face mask. He looked tired.

Had he experienced any additional pressure, playing with a new team? He first said no, he had been with this team nine weeks, but then he said, "I've had the responsibility I've always had. Throughout the pre-season I felt I've had to prove I could play and yes, this was a money game. But as far as my position went, I felt it went okay. But teams win or lose games, not one guy. Quarterbacks get too much credit and too much blame. Assessing my own performance, well, we lost. What the hell, we lost."

A TV camera moved through the crowd of reporters and the lights went on. Namath looked up and said, "Hey, I don't have any clothes on, buddy. God dang." The camera man said he was shooting only from the waist up but Namath said, "Come back later when I have some clothes on. I'll be around."

He shifted his cud a little and said, "I was pleased to see Scott Hunter have a good game. You know he played at Alabama like me. He'd had a lot of ups and downs in his career but today he played a terrific game. I wasn't pulling for him, of course, but I'm glad he had a good game."

Down the hall in the Falcons' dressing room, Hunter was saying, "Joe's still got it. Did you see that one long one he threw? It must have gone 65 yards. He could throw out of a wheelchair better than the rest of us on two legs."

Namath's right knee was swelling as it always does when he plays or does something similar like running. Someone asked him, after all these years, with nothing left to prove, why he keeps taking the beating?

Namath looked up at the man with those sleepy eyes and said, "I love to play the game. That's why."

January 14, 1980

God and the Super Bowl

Does God care who wins the Super Bowl?

I went to the top to find out but you know how it is. You can never find a Pope when you need one.

Here it was just days away from kickoff and a question that had popped into my mind after a conversation with one of the Los Angeles Rams was unanswered.

Rich Saul, the Rams' center, had suggested that God determines the outcome of sports events.

I asked a fellow employee, Tina Robertson, to try to get Pope John Paul on the phone for me while I went for Billy Graham.

"Who's he play for?" she said. "Oh, that Pope Paul. Okay."

Within minutes, Tina walked up and said, "I've got the Vatican on the line. They say it's not possible to speak to the Pope and would you like to leave a message? You want me to try to get one of his assistants, a Cardinal or something, on the line?"

"Naw," I said. "I wanted to talk to the big guy."

Tina came back a little later and asked, "Why'd the operator laugh when I told her this was person-to-person to the Pope?"

I said I didn't have the faintest idea.

I called several local men of the cloth but they were out. I have no idea where they were. It was too cold to play golf.

I called Jim Bakker. I explained to a woman at the PTL Club what I wanted. She said she would find out if I could talk to Bakker that day and call me back by 1 p.m.

She never called back. Which raises another question – does that count as a fib?

I tried Billy Graham. Someone in Graham's office explained that he is leaving later this month for two months of meetings in England and has been devoting full time to that.

"I'm talking Super Sunday here," I reminded her. "This is big."

She said she'd pass the word to somebody who might or might not pass it on to Graham. I never heard from him. Too bad. He could've said some neat things like, "And Bradshaw shall come to pass..."

I went next for Father Guido Sarducci. Maybe you've seen him on Saturday Night Live. Real name's Don Novello.

Father Sarducci, billed as the gossip columnist for the Vatican newspaper, is famous for his insights on such topics as "The Last Brunch."

The person at NBC said Father Sarducci would probably love to comment on whether God cares who wins the Super Bowl.

She called back and said Father Sarducci had spent about two hours trying to write a commentary on the subject but wasn't satisfied with it and would have to decline, with apologies.

"He's been working on an album and he's kinda tapped out," she said.

"I understand," I said. "Billy Graham's kinda tapped out, too."

I was running out of religious leaders. I thought about trying for the Moslem viewpoint from Ayatollah Khomeini but Tina said, "Oh, no, I don't want any visitors from the State Department. Do it yourself."

I don't want any visitors from the State Department either.

I went for God. Not the real one. George Burns, who played Him in "Oh, God." Someone at Warner Bros. showed mild interest – so mild, I never heard from them again.

I know a fellow with a local Episcopal church who would give me a ready answer but I don't, well, trust him. During a prayer at a summertime service, he slipped in Tommy Lasorda's name along with other sick, troubled and unhappy souls. Obviously an L.A. fan looking for an edge.

I suppose the question will have to go unanswered, at least until Sunday. If the Rams beat the Steelers, then we'll know.

January 2, 1982

Tigers in Paradise

At 23 minutes before midnight, Nebraska threw one last desperation pass that fell incomplete and the horn sounded ending Clemson's 22-15 victory in the Orange Bowl.

The Tigers, unbeaten in 12 games, had assured themselves of their first national football championship.

Grizzled old Frank Howard, a legendary figure who coached for Clemson for 39 years before retiring in 1969, watched from the press box as the pass fell to the ground and a kind of glow came across his face. "That's it," he said.

"It's not the best game I ever saw, but it's the best victory we ever had."

That covers 86 years, a long time for any school to wait but especially long for folks who worship their football the way Clemson fans do. About three-fourths of the 72,000 brimming over in the Orange Bowl were obviously Tiger fans, most of them wearing orange clothing, some with their faces painted orange.

Long after their heroes had left the field, their band played on and they lingered, shouting, waving fingers in the air to symbolize their rank as No. 1, rejoicing in and savoring this magic moment that comes only to a chosen few, never to most.

There remains the formality of the voters anointing Clemson in the national polls today, but it is nothing more than that, a formality. It is assured. That will mark only the second time an ACC team has ever been accorded the honor in football and that fact was not lost on the Tigers.

As they ran through a tunnel from the field to their dressing room, they chanted, "ACC! ACC!"

A sports writer who has observed ACC football for many years watched the final moments of this fairy tale and said, "I never thought I'd live to see this. And they beat those SOB's from the Big Eight to do it."

National football champions come from the Big Eight, the Big Ten, the Pac 10, the Southeastern Conference or the Southwest Conference, not the ACC. They have coaches like Bear Bryant and Woody Hayes, not a 33-year-old like Danny Ford in only his third year as a head coach.

But Friday night, in that huge dish of orange with a national television audience watching, the ACC finally took its act to Broadway.

Despite its perfect record and its No. 1 ranking, Clemson had gone into the game a four-point underdog to Nebraska. There was a widely-held feeling that the Tigers were overrated, that they hadn't played a schedule that proved they were the best. There was a suspicion that they would succumb to the pressure.

But they left no doubt that they were better than the No. 4-ranked Cornhuskers. They played with fury, style and poise. In the final analysis, it was Nebraska that looked like a team bothered by the stakes. Clemson played like a champion.

Jeff Davis, the Tigers' star linebacker, said it:

"This team is special."

Perry Tuttle, who caught five of Homer Jordan's passes for 56 yards and one touchdown, said, "Before the game, Homer asked me how many touchdown passes I wanted. I told him, 'I don't care just as long as we win.'

"We picked up the paper this morning and read that we weren't going to win and a thing that said, 'Is Clemson really No. 1?' It seemed we were the only ones who believed in us.

"Now, the scoreboard shows we're the No. 1 team in the country. Now, no questions can be asked.

"It's such a great feeling. Every player dreams of this – being No. 1. Twenty years from now, I'll probably call up all these players and say, 'Thank you.'"

Ford gave credit to everyone but himself. He said he's always been proud of ACC football and while he's also proud of the league's basketball reputation, which has overshadowed football, he feels the ACC has proven it can compete with anyone on the gridiron.

"I'm so proud for our guys, our school, our people who have supported us for so long and for the ACC," he said. "Our teams have beaten some pretty big boys in the last few years, and now, they can't really say nothing. I have no doubts we're No. 1.

"How do I feel personally? I'm not a very personal fellow. I'm not worried about myself. When the last seconds ticked off that clock, all I thought about was our players, our school, our people."

A couple of Clemson fans who were not enthralled with Miami in the days leading up to the game visited the Metrozoo. They were looking at a bird and one said, "What kind of bird is that?"

The other said, "That's a bird of paradise."

The first fellow replied, "Long way from home, ain't it."

No doubt he changed his mind about 11:37 Friday night.

Suddenly, all those people splashed with orange were, indeed, in paradise.

December 16, 1982

The Bear's Magic

Word that Bear Bryant is retiring as head football coach of Alabama – make that head football coach of America; that's what he is – brought memories curling up like the smoke from one of his Chesterfields.

The year was 1975 and Bryant had come to Charlotte to promote a book John Underwood had written about him, entitled *Bear*. He was stopping at an old hotel and I went there to interview him and specifically to ask him one question, which we'll get to in a moment.

I phoned Bryant from the lobby and got him out of bed. He was barefoot and in his underwear when he let me into his room. Ordinarily an early riser, he had slept late.

Between puffs on his cigarette, he phoned room service for bacon and eggs, which he never got around to eating. He drank coffee and smoked as he fussed about forgetting his shaving cream.

I was struck by how gaunt, how old, Bryant's body looked as he ambled about, hunched over, complaining about the aches and stiffness that came with morning. I had never thought of him as being old because of the way he was and because of his face – a great face, weathered, craggy with the eyes of an eagle – and because of his voice, deep as an Arkansas well, raspy as a saw cutting through a pine knot.

He wasn't old – just his body was old – and he still isn't, although the calendar says he's 69.

Bryant has won more games than any other coach, 322, while losing only 85 and tying 17. He did it at Maryland, Kentucky and Texas A&M but mostly he did it at Alabama. The question I wanted to ask him was why his teams won more than most other coaches'. He said, "Because of the people I have with me. Players, coaches, managers, trainers, ticket takers, people that winning means a lot to. That's the only kind I'm gonna have around me. Many a person contributes to winning a ball game, if you think about it. You can go all the way back to the parents and the church.

"I think everybody in the organization – and I mean everybody – winning's got to mean something to them."

There was a great deal more to Bryant's unparalleled success than that, of course.

It goes without saying that he knew football.

For many years after he got into the profession, he was a physical, threatening coach. He said in his book, "...I've laid it on the line to a lot of boys. I've grabbed 'em and shook 'em and kicked 'em and embarrassed them in front of the squad. I've got down in the dirt with them, and if they didn't give as well as they took I'd tell them they were insults to their upbringing, and I've cleaned out their lockers for them and piled their clothes in the hall, thinking I'd make them prove what they had in their veins, blood or spit, one way or the other, and praying they would come through."

As Bryant's reputation as a winner grew, he also grew and the combination made him at once admirable and lovable. He finally learned that a player could quit football without being a quitter and that he didn't have to "be good or be gone." He realized he could no longer cuff his players around, force them to wear crewcuts, treat them like military recruits. He changed with the times, as a man and a coach. He wasn't too hardheaded to realize it when what he was coaching wasn't as good as what someone else was coaching and he would change.

He could recruit. A few teams probably have gotten better material year in and year out – Notre Dame, Southern Cal, Oklahoma, Nebraska – but Bryant got his share and made them better. Jake Gaither, longtime coach at Florida A&M, said of Bryant, "He could take his'n and beat your'n or he could take your'n and beat his'n."

He took no credit for his wins but always took the blame for defeat. He would beat a team and say that if coaching had been the deciding factor, the other team would have won. When he lost, he talked about his "sorry" coaching and about getting old and, lately, about retiring.

"There's nothing magical about what I do," Bryant said one day. "There's nothing like that. I'm just a big ol' dumb guy who coaches football because that's all I can do. I'm certainly not any smarter than anybody and probably dumber than most coaches."

There is something magical about the Bear, though. It's his presence. He fills a room or a sideline with it. You know you're in the company of a giant. Few people possess that quality. Those who do achieve. Most win.

Bryant may profess to be a big ol' dumb guy and all that but he has also professed something else:

"I ain't nothing but a winner."

August 30, 1987

Where Sweet Glory Waits

A good breeze had come up to cool the night and a slice of moon hung over one goal post.

For August, it was not a bad night to open the high school football season. A standing-room-only crowd of perhaps 3,000, which the public address announcer speculated might be the biggest ever at A.L. Barringer Stadium, had gathered to watch the Mount Pleasant Tigers open against the Central Cabarrus Vikings, a 3A team that had beaten the 2A home team 15 years in a row.

Benny Moose, Mount Pleasant High class of '66, now a phys-ed teacher at two Cabarrus County elementary schools, stood looking down on the football field where he once starred and said, "High school is a great time of life. Those were carefree days – no jobs, no taxes, no cares. The only thing on my mind for about 25 of every 24 hours was sports. And (boyish smile) sometimes girls. Being a high school athlete..."

He let the thought hang in the air, beneath the lights and above the neatly lined playing field, where sweet glory waits on football Friday nights. You would have to look far and wide to find a place where this uniquely American ritual is more richly performed than in Mount Pleasant.

This is a town of some 1,500 people. The school has 680 students. They are a blend of offspring from rural folk, Cannon Mills employees, transplanted Northerners and assorted others. Despite the disparity, the grown-ups and young alike are worshipful of high school football, filling stands at home and away with their numbers.

The stadium sits at the corner of N.C. 49, with its growling traffic, and Main Street, a leafy street climbing a few blocks uphill from the center of commerce.

From the home side of the grandstand, you can see a convenience store, a Hardee's, a motel, a mill and a lovely hillside, at the crest of which sits a fine two-story farmhouse.

Before the game, the school principal, Mike Burleson, clad in shorts, golf shirt, cap and loafers with no socks, said, "About 15 minutes ago, I got so nervous I thought I was going to be sick. It happens to me every year."

Charlie Fisher, class of '70, who sells timber, said, "We won four or five games last year. That's about all we expect of them. But people around here love it, I swear they do.

"We've got no chance tonight. Central Cabarrus High is about twice as big as Mount Pleasant, but we play this game every year for the gate. And we're real good friends. Central Cabarrus is only about 10 miles away. The families know each other. When we're not playing them, we pull for Central Cabarrus and vice versa."

Mount Pleasant coach Bobby Cloninger, who once played for the team he now coaches, told his team, "Don't give them any blue plate specials," but the Tigers did. Natrone Means, a sophomore playing in his first varsity game for Central Cabarrus, returned the opening kickoff 88 yards for a touchdown.

The thousand or so Central Cabarrus fans went wild. The Mount Pleasant fans groaned.

While the action boiled on the field, nature took its course along the fringes.

The adults sat in the stands, those who could find seats. The kids played on a grassy hillside behind one goal post. Once, a daddy had to go down the hill to fetch a young'un who, oblivious to the pounding thrusts and counter thrusts on the field, frolicked in an end zone.

And the students, most of them, cruised on foot behind the stands. The boys, looking their James Dean best, checked out the girls and the girls, makeup just right, hair carefully fashioned and perfume trailing behind them, checked out the boys. From time to time, a couple stepped out of the flow of traffic and shared marathon kisses.

A veteran huntsman tried to recall if he had ever been so bold in his youth and concluded he had been a teenage wimp.

Mount Pleasant generated a nice drive to tie the score at 6, David Rowland gunning a 17-yard touchdown pass to Endra Black.

The P.A. announcer told the crowd that one lucky program holder had won a bottle of dandruff remover shampoo. The crowd snickered.

Central Cabarrus surged ahead 12-6 before halftime on Chad Polk's 6-yard dash. In the third quarter, a strong Mount Pleasant drive died by inches at the 24. A penalty set Central Cabarrus back to the 19. From there, Means, a 6-0, 200-pounder with speed and a sense for open spaces, raced 81 yards for another touchdown. That ended the scoring, the final being 19-6. A desperate drive by the Tigers fell short at the Vikings' 7 in the fourth period.

When it was over, the two teams formed lines and passed each other, shaking hands as the P.A. announcer said good night and told the folks to drive carefully and "get up Sunday morning and take these kids to Sunday school."

As Cloninger walked off the field after shaking hands with Central Cabarrus coach Larry Mason, his 5-year-old daughter, Anna, ran up and hugged him. "That puts it all in perspective," he said.

Nobody hurried to get out of the parking lots. The students usually cruise the Burger King at Carolina Mall in Concord or park at a couple of service stations nearby after games, but they were going to a dance in the school gym this night.

Benny Moose's words were true to the mark. High school, he had said, is a great time of life.

September 6, 1987

The Irish

Glory's mantle cloaks thee,
Golden is thy fame...
– From the Notre Dame alma mater.

On Friday nights before football games at Notre Dame, the pep band parades around the campus, gathering up students behind it in wild reverie.

They move into Stepan Center, an assembly hall. The football team is there, along with several former players, seated on a stage.

The coach is introduced, the students and alumni in town early for the game raise a cheer that could split a boulder and arc rolls of toilet tissue across the room, and the band plays the Notre Dame fight song. The fight song of all fight songs. Dante's Inferno with music.

Then the coach talks about the next day's game, and when he's finished, the bedlam begins anew.

Some players and former players speak and as each is introduced and after each has spoken, the crowd goes insane, streamers fly and the band plays the song again. By the time it's over, innocent bystanders are ready to suit up and the band's lips hurt.

On Saturday, fans stroll through the quad before the game, some stopping to buy food or drink from little stands set up by students here and there. There is a good, faint smell of smoke from the cooking fires. The trees with their changing leaves give the splendid quad the feeling of a multicolored tent.

Near the Hesburgh Library, there is a statue of Moses with one hand raised, forefinger extended. The students and old grads call it "We're No. 1 Moses." On another part of the campus, a statue of former university president Rev. William Corby with hand upraised has been dubbed "Fair Catch Corby." And towering above the stadium is a 132-foot mosaic of Jesus with upraised hands. This, of course, is "Touchdown Jesus."

And in the stadium, the presence of Knute Rockne and the Four Horsemen and the Gipper and a thousand others who have worn the Fighting Irish colors is felt, and on a gray day, if you've had a nip or two against the chill, you might even see them.

I've been to football games across the nation, including many at the stadiums of the traditional powers, but nowhere have I had the feeling I get at Notre Dame.

This is where college football lives. This is its home, not Oklahoma or Miami or Texas or Arkansas. Tradition? This is where tradition was invented.

This season, Notre Dame football marks its 100th anniversary. It's a time for all of us who have had so much as a passing acquaintance with the game to share in the celebration and raise the echoes.

In a way, it's our team, too, America's team. Whatever our allegiance, Notre Dame always has been there in our consciousness to be admired, but how sweet the victory if ever we've had a team come away a winner over the Fighting Irish.

Notre Dame football is and long has been a symbol, the symbol, of excellence in collegiate sports.

Notre Dame's first game was played Wednesday, Nov. 23, 1887. The Irish lost to Michigan 8-0 in South Bend, Ind. They open this season Saturday at Michigan.

Notre Dame hasn't lost many since that first one. It has the best winning percentage in the game, .755, at 651-198-40.

The legendary Rockne accounted for a great many of those wins. In one span of 13 seasons, his teams lost only 12 games. It was during that time that Grantland Rice, writing about the Notre Dame-Army game in 1924, penned his famous lead, "Outlined against a blue, grey October sky the Four Horsemen rode again. In dramatic lore they are known as famine, pestilence, destruction and death. These are only aliases. Their real names are Stuhldreher, Miller, Crowley and Layden."

After 100 years of playing the game, the Irish have losing records against only five teams, three of which they played only once. There was a period a few years back when they played a relatively soft schedule, but that's no longer the case. This season, as befits their heritage, the Irish play Michigan, Michigan State, Purdue, Pittsburgh, Air Force, Southern California, Navy, Boston College, Alabama, Penn State and Miami.

Notre Dame for many years had a policy against bowl games. Since the ban was lifted 18 years ago, the Irish have played in 12 games, winning eight.

They have been designated national champion 17 times by at least one recognized selector. Six of their players have won the Heisman Trophy.

A couple of other things: Notre Dame doesn't redshirt. And over the last 18 years, only six players who remained in school for four years failed to graduate. Thirty-one players have been named academic All-America.

And so, with glasses hoisted high, we say:

Cheer, cheer for old Notre Dame,
Wake up the echoes cheering her name,
Send a volley cheer on high,
Shake down the thunder from the sky....
– From the Notre Dame Fight Song.

February 1, 1988

Killing All the Demons

In the moments between the third and fourth quarters of Super Bowl XXII, Washington fans sent a lusty chorus of "Hail to the Redskins" into the cool evening air at Jack Murphy Stadium.

At midfield, the man wearing number 17 for the Redskins raised his fists and shook them several times in joyous celebration. Not at anyone, not with anyone. Alone for a moment in a crowd of 73,000.

There was still a quarter of Super Bowl to play, but Washington had the pathetic Denver Broncos by the throat, and Doug Williams had killed all his demons. Free at last.

Williams, 32, will be remembered as the first black quarterback to play in the Super Bowl, which was basically the only distinction accorded him coming into a game that had John Elway's name on the marquee.

But Williams showed the world how insignificant that bit of information really was.

He passed for more yards than anyone – Namath, Unitas, Bradshaw, Montana, Staubach, Theismann – who ever played in a Super Bowl. And he engineered the biggest single-quarter explosion in the history of NFL post-season games, five touchdowns in the second quarter, as the Redskins put away what would be a 42-10 victory.

We must pause to add a footnote here. Williams and his record-busting Redskins were operating against a defense that was disgraceful, a team whose performance was described by its own coach as embarrassing.

Denver came into the game a 3 1/2-point favorite, but after taking an early 10-0 lead, it was as soundly beaten as any team ever has been in the Super Bowl, never mind what the scores say.

Elway, who was compared not with Williams but with the greatest quarterbacks of all time in the pre-game evaluations, could get nothing done against the Redskins' defense after the first quarter. He finished with only 14 completions in 38 attempts, and three of those were little underhanded shovel passes. The Redskins' scheme smothered him with pressure and blanketed his receivers.

When the last minute had ticked away and Williams, voted the game's most valuable player, had waded through the crowd mobbing him on the field, he repeated what he had said all week: his first concern was playing football, not trying to prove he could play despite his color.

His coach, Joe Gibbs, said, "Hopefully now we're at the point where people are looking at players as players and not at their color."

Williams' stats ought to be noted because they're pretty, if for no other reason. He was 18 of 29 for 340 yards and four touchdowns, with one interception and one sack.

Washington's explosion was a shock. Elway had thrown an 80-yard touchdown pass on Denver's first offensive down, and gotten the Broncos a field goal and 10-0 lead with more heroics.

He became the first quarterback to catch a pass in a Super Bowl. Steve Sewell took a handoff and then tossed it back to Elway, during the drive to the field goal.

That was typical of Denver's early play. The Broncos were wide open, jazzing it up, almost toying with the Redskins.

But then Washington's defense came alive, and that was that for the one-dimensional Broncos.

Williams, who had left the game on the preceding series with a twisted knee, came back out and blew the game open. He did an Elway, hitting Ricky Sanders on first down for an 80-yard touchdown.

"That seemed to get us going," said Redskins guard R.C. Thielmann. "It was like a dream land. Everything Doug threw and everything that we blocked went for big yardage. It's unlike Redskin football to score that fast. We're used to seven-, eight-minute drives, not going 80 yards in a minute."

When the half ended, Washington had scored five touchdowns, needing only 18 plays with a possession time of only five minutes, 47 seconds.

Williams, who limped through the second half from the early knee injury, graciously and accurately dealt much of the credit to the running game, which featured rookie Timmy Smith's record 204 yards, and defense, which featured pain.

But this one will be remembered as the one in which a quarterback, who was supposed to be washed up, couldn't throw touch passes and didn't play well in the big ones, killed all the demons. Throwing long, short, hard and soft – whatever it took.

For all the Redskins' splendid play – and they were splendid – this one was his.

Golf

July 1985

Billy Joe

Of all the people in sports with whom I have crossed paths over the years, most of whom I admired and enjoyed and some of whom became my friends, my favorite remains and will almost certainly remain Billy Joe Patton.

I almost added, "a golfer from Morganton," but that no more describes Patton than "a writer" describes Mark Twain.

The time and place of our most frequent encounters undoubtedly has something to do with the joy that Patton's name evokes, as it did these past few days when, at age 64, he was playing in the N.C. Senior Amateur at Charlotte Country Club.

The time would be the years between the mid-50s and the mid- 60s when he was in full flight as our most exciting and colorful amateur golfer, and the place would be Pinehurst, where he had some of his finest moments.

There are two reasons I mention all of this now. One is that the North and South Amateur, which Patton won three times, begins Monday in Pinehurst. That brings memories of sweet days covering the North and South in the softness of springtime with its sunshine and soft perfume from blossoming shrubs, and the longleaf pines and the elegance of that lovely village gushing back.

The second is that a young man who appeared to be in his mid-20s dropped by the office a few days ago to talk some golf and when I mentioned the name of Billy Joe Patton, he said, "Yes, I've heard of him."

Heard of him, that's all? Well, of course. The years slip by so rapidly, we often forget that a generation has passed and that visions that are still so vivid in our minds are not shared by the young.

Patton is a treasure that ought to be preserved, so let me tell you about him. But how, in so little space and time?

First, let's get the numbers out of the way. Patton won three North and South Amateurs (one of the country's most highly regarded amateur tournaments), two Southern Amateurs and several lesser tournaments. He won 20 consecutive matches at Pinehurst against stiff opposition at one stretch. He played on five Walker Cup teams and six other international teams. He twice led the U.S. Open after 36 holes, finishing as low amateur in both, and was twice low amateur in the Masters. He is in two halls of fame and in 1982 won the Bobby Jones Award presented by the U.S. Golf Association in recognition of distinguished sportsmanship in golf.

But that is relatively lifeless information.

This was Billy Joe:

In 1954, he led the Masters after one round, was tied for the lead after two, fell five shots back after three but then played himself back into it early in the final round with some brilliant golf, including a hole-in-one at the sixth. But he was a daring player whose fast swing and go-for-broke attitude regularly put him in honeysuckle and behind trees throughout his career. (Nothing he couldn't handle, usually, because he had marvelous imagination and an ability to extract himself from peril that I've never seen equaled.)

He chanced reaching the green in two on the par-five 13th hole on that final round at the Masters, when he was galloping neck-and-neck with no less than Ben Hogan and Sam Snead, and found water. He walked off the 13th with a double bogey. As he went to the next tee, he noted the dejection in his huge gallery and said, "Let's smile again."

Another visit to water after a long-odds gamble on the 15th did him in, and he finished one shot behind Hogan and Snead, who tied for the championship and played off the next day, Snead winning.

Playing Labron Harris in the semifinals of the U.S. Amateur at Pinehurst, Patton found himself two down at the 13th. He had about a 6-foot putt for birdie to win the hole. To snap himself out of the doldrums into which his game had fallen, he went into his golf bag, pulled out a pair of bent-up glasses that looked like he had sat on them, which he had, and a beat-up cap, and put them on. Then he holed the putt.

He won the next hole to even the match but then, his game being like the wind, he hit an awful shot, lost the hole and eventually the match.

Once in the North and South, playing extra holes, Patton found his tee shot on the second hole, which runs alongside a road, in a downhill lie in heavy rough. He had no chance to reach the green with his next shot.

As he dug in to whack at the ball, a car stopped nearby and a woman asked one of the spectators if he knew where she could find a room.

Patton, hearing this, never looked up.

"Just wait a few minutes and you can have mine."

After he had won the Southern Amateur on the same Pinehurst course in 1965 at the age of 43, when he knew twilight was settling over his days of glory (it was his last significant victory), he climbed into his convertible and began the drive back to Morganton with the top down, alone.

"My wife thought it was just another tournament I had won," he said. "My kids felt about the same way. But that victory did something to me. I was alive.

"After I accepted my trophy, I got in that car and drove out of Pinehurst. When I got on the highway and there was just me and the pine trees shooting by, I let out the damnedest yell you ever heard. I kept shouting and driving. I let it all out."

Let it all out. That was always Patton's way. Smashing long drives, finding them in the trees, studying what seemed to be a solid wall of lumber in front of him and then ripping, twisting, climbing shots through the trouble, onto the green and knocking the putt in for birdie. He played swashbuckling golf, happy golf, splendid in its result; golf that substituted soul for mechanism, golf that had dramatic uncertainty to it, golf to which bystanders could relate.

His saving grace was a putter that loved him. He has often said that back when he was young, nobody could handle a 6-footer the way he could. He just didn't think he could miss.

Once in the North and South, his approach to the 18th sailed over the green and came to rest on asphalt near the clubhouse, a good 100 feet from the hole. He chose a putter, rolled it along the asphalt, through a swale, onto the green, six feet from the hole. And made it to save the match.

Along the way through his glory days, down all the fairways and through all the brambles and brush, he chatted amiably with the gallery. He loved crowds. They ignited him. Ken Venturi once said of the Masters, where Patton played 13 times and almost always finished well, "If they locked the gates and didn't let anybody in, Billy Joe couldn't break 80."

And the galleries loved him, as much at the time, I believe, as they loved Arnold Palmer.

There was a joy to his game that few playing at the upper level of golf could equal.

All of it – his scrambling, his nerve, his down-home gabbing with the spectators, his passion, his grace, his humor – all of it made him the most delightful and endearing person I've ever come across in sports.

At this time of the year, I always think of him and feel good for having been there when he was.

November, 1960

Boy Wonder

It takes his elders a little while to adjust to the idea of having wisdom spill from his cereal-ad face like notes from a tenor sax, but Jack William Nicklaus, 1959 United States Amateur Champion, is a man among golfing men and every bit as mature as you might expect a rising senior at Ohio State University to be. You need sit with him only long enough for the first impression of brashness – the result of an undiluted frankness – to steal away unnoticed and you find that he has not spent all of his life just learning to hit a golf ball as well as he does. He has a good idea of what counts, how much of that he wants, and how he is going to get it.

Incongruously, a Little League quality to his rusty, high-pitched voice and a kid-next-door stamp on his round, tanned face give Nicklaus the air of a fellow who is even younger than his 20 years. But one facet to this kid is patently clear and that is that as the youngest player to win the Amateur in 50 years, he is in the formative stages of what many respected observers feel will be one of the great golfing careers of our time.

With the 1959 United States Amateur Championship, a North and South Amateur, two victories in the highly-regarded Trans-Mississippi Amateur, an International Four-Ball Championship partnered with former British Amateur king Deane Beman, a march to the quarterfinals of the 1959 British Amateur and assorted other titles and achievements behind him, Nicklaus is already a major force in the game.

This early blossoming by a slightly pudgy Columbus, Ohio, youngster who isn't even old enough to vote has raised, on the one hand, a question and, on the other, a slightly premature but nonetheless natural comparison.

The question:

Is Nicklaus planning a career as a professional golfer?

The comparison:

Nicklaus looks like a good candidate – a great candidate – to challenge the feats of the immortal Bobby Jones.

It is in discussing these two subjects that the maturity of the Nicklaus mind reveals itself.

When the question regarding Nicklaus's plans to turn pro or remain amateur was put to him, it was done with care. To simply ask him, "Jack, are you planning to turn pro?" would have been a waste of time.

The United States Golf Association's code governing amateur status decrees that a statement of intention to become pro is as obvious an act of professionalism as is accepting prize money. For this reason, many an amateur has said no when he meant yes, simply to protect his status until he could win a big title and cash in on it by going pro.

It was with this is mind that Nicklaus was told, "I'm going to ask you if you plan to turn pro or remain an amateur. Before you answer, let me say this. If you plan to become a pro, just say 'Let's drop the subject' and it will be forgotten, for good.

"If, however, you plan to remain an amateur, we can print it. But let's make one condition. If you think there's a chance you will ever turn pro, please say so and let's forget about it."

Nicklaus appeared to bristle for a moment and then he said, "You can print this or you can forget it – I will never become a professional golfer.

"First, let me explain that I can play all of the golf I want to play without becoming a pro. I think the ideal situation would be to work eight months a year and have four months off to play golf. That may sound like a dream, but I hope to make it a reality.

"My father, Charlie Nicklaus, owns three drugstores and is planning to build some more. He also has some real estate holdings. He has worked hard for these things and I feel that his efforts have not been directed entirely toward making our family comfortable for the present. He has tried to build up something for my sister, Marilyn, and me. He will be retiring soon and the businesses will be ours. My sister and I will be financially well off.

"I think it would be a rotten trick on my part," he continued, "if I should throw away the things my father has worked so hard to provide for me. That is one real reason I will never play professional golf."

To prepare himself to take over for his father, Nicklaus is working toward a degree in pharmacy. Meanwhile, he is testing himself to see if he really likes pharmacy and will be active in it or if he will pursue some other profession and limit his drugstore activities to supervision. The test is as an insurance salesman, a position he assumes in his free time. Right now, he thinks he may remain in insurance.

"I don't care to be on Wall Street," he says. "I just want enough money to live comfortably, play golf and give my family the things they want."

That family presently consists of the former Barbara Bash, an Ohio State coed who became Mrs. Nicklaus in July.

Although he did not say it, it is reasonable to assume from Nicklaus's great admiration for Jones that he wishes to remain an amateur in the hopes of matching at least a part of the Grand Slammer's glorious record as a non-pro. He knows Jones personally and has a respect for the man that equals his respect for the golfer, although their association got off to a poor start.

Jones was so taken by young Jack that he promised at a banquet prior to the 1955 National Amateur at Richmond that he would come out the next day and watch Nicklaus in action. True to his word, the great man put in his appearance at the 11th hole of Jack's match with New Yorker Bob Gardner. Only 15 years old and playing his first Amateur, Nicklaus was so anxious to impress, he lost the 11th, 12th and 13th holes and eventually lost the match one-up.

Despite this rough start, Nicklaus and Jones have developed a mutual admiration. Jones saw his young friend play at least part of every round during the 1960 Masters. "When people ask me about my goals in golf," said Nicklaus, "I answer with a question. What does everybody in golf set as a goal?

"The answer, of course, is Bobby Jones. I don't see how anybody can handle himself as well as Bobby Jones has. He knew when to quit. If he hadn't quit when he did, some of his luster might have been lost, but as it turned out, nothing can ever be taken away from him. He's fantastic. He is the greatest golfer who ever lived and probably ever will live and he is one of the greatest persons.

"That's my goal. Bobby Jones. It's the only goal."

And it is a distant one, but some of the top men in the game think Nicklaus can reach it. Whenever you as the touring pros who have seen him play, "What's your impression of Nicklaus?" they will almost invariably mention his name and the name of Jones in the same breath.

Probably the best analysis, one which pretty well sums up the feelings of the experts, was submitted by a fellow amateur, Billy Joe Patton. Patton's credentials as a critic include competition in the Walker Cup matches, captaincy of the Americas Cup team, and competition in major amateur and open events for many years.

Said Billy Joe, "If Jack plays in five National Opens, he's got to win at least one of them. He's that good. He is in a class by himself as an amateur. He has gone off and left the rest of us and we aren't likely to catch up," said Patton. He's a super driver, a great long-iron player and a terrific putter. He putts like Harvie Ward did when Harvie was at his peak.

"Nicklaus is, right now," Patton said thoughtfully, "probably the greatest amateur since Bobby Jones – and he'll get better."

Nicklaus almost made Patton look like a prophet when he came roaring down the homestretch of the National Open championship last June with a strong shot at winning the title. If he had, he would have become the first amateur to win the Open since Johnny Goodman in 1933. But shaky putting on the final two greens left him just short of Arnold Palmer's 280 and he had to settle for a second-place 282.

Jack Nicklaus began playing golf at the age of 10 and before the year was out he had won his first title – a club junior event. He has been winning ever since, knocking over the Ohio Amateur at age 16 and the National Jaycee Junior Championship at 17. Then he really began to show his stuff by taking that first Trans-Miss, in 1958. It wasn't until last year, though, that he felt he became something more than just another amateur.

The tremendous power, the accuracy of his irons and the magic of his putter had long been there, but something which he feels is almost – if not equally – as valuable was acquired when he played in five professional tour tournaments – the Chicago, Buick, Western, Carlings and Motor City Opens.

"That's where I learned most of my golf," said Nicklaus. "I gained a wealth of knowledge just talking with the pros, seeing how they play the game and playing in such keen competition. I would recommend that any amateur golfer planning to play competitive golf try the tour for awhile. I was a mediocre amateur before playing in those five tournaments. Now, at least, I can hold my own."

It was during this swing that a second major point in the development of the shiny new Nicklaus was reached. "I had always been a hooker," he said. "It was one of my worst faults. It kept getting me into trouble.

"Last year, after the Western Open, I went home pretty discouraged but also pretty determined. I was sick and tired of hooking my tee shots. I was hooking myself out of contention. Driving should have been one of the strong points of my game, because I have always been able to hit the ball a long way, but it was one of the weakest points."

Nicklaus spent hours on the practice tee. He diagnosed his ills – closing the clubface at the top of his backswing and letting his left knee sag at impact. He made minor adjustments in both cases, found the route from tee to fairway and drove it relentlessly into his mind and muscles with arduous practice.

Now he unleashes his tremendous power with confidence and feels there is no reason why he should ever drive the ball out of the fairway more than twice a round. Except when he did it intentionally, Nicklaus didn't drive out of the fairway more than a dozen times during the National Amateur last year.

With this problem conquered, Nicklaus has turned his attention to his short-irons. As Patton said, "If there is a weakness in Jack's game, it is those short-iron shots. But I hesitate to call it a weakness because he can still hit them better than you or I can. It is just that his short-irons are not as sharp as the rest of his game."

Nicklaus recognizes this. He calls the short wedge shot "the hardest shot in golf" and dreads it doubly when it must be carried over trouble.

There appear to be no major mental hazards for him to clear. His approach to tournament golf is 100 percent positive. He practices hard before a tournament but says, "I never practice well. I don't concentrate well in practice. Generally speaking, I don't know what I'm doing until I get onto the golf course."

His emotions before a tournament vary, he said, according to how well he is playing at the moment and how he has fared in that particular tournament in the past. "I try to get myself charged up for every tournament," he explained. "Sometimes I start getting myself mentally right for as long as two weeks before the start of the tournament for an event like the Masters.

"I thought I could win the Masters this year," Nicklaus went on. "I was playing that well before the tournament started. It doesn't bother me that I'm competing against players like Hogan and Snead. I have a tremendous amount of respect for them and I know I am a long way from doing the things they have done, but a player has to have a certain amount of cockiness to be successful and I have some of it. I don't mean conceit. I mean the belief that you can win. If a fellow believes he can do something and has the ability to do it, it may take years but he will eventually get it done."

Nicklaus feels the most valuable asset a tournament player can possess, once he has the talent for hitting the ball, is a clear head, the ability to retain his composure in the face of adversity and continue to think properly. "A person must have a certain amount of nervous tension to be successful in competition," he says. "Call it spirit or natural temper. If he can really get mad and contain it inside, he can make that work for him, give him drive. Unfortunately, I have not yet learned to do that. One of my ambitions is to learn to contain that natural temper – not destroy it, but let it work for me.

"I have made, say, a seven on a hole and had people tell me, 'Now don't get mad.' You have to get mad or you'll never play again. It should push you to do better things, though, not simply cause you more trouble. So far, it has gotten the best of me."

Nicklaus feels his golfing fame has not altered his campus or home life appreciably, except in one respect. That is the demand on his time. "Naturally," he said, "it is nice to be widely known for worthwhile achievements, but it forced you to do many things which you don't like to do and those things take up time you want for other things. Public appearances are a headache. I hold mine down to a minimum. I just don't like speech-making and that sort of thing."

It appeared, for a moment, that there was, after all, a touch of the very young behind that face, but the mature Nicklaus chased away the idea by adding, "It's all so new to me now. I suppose that's why I rebel against it.

"I hope, if I continue to play well, I will learn to like it."

August 10, 1975

Andy Hardy Tees Up

Playing golf with Mickey Rooney is like playing polo in a dune buggy with a flash flood bearing down on you.

There was no particular reason for haste when Rooney, Howard Niven and I teed off at Myers Park Country Club, but after we had negotiated four holes in half an hour, letting the movie star set the pace, I gasped, "Do you always play this fast?" and Rooney replied, "Usually faster.

"I can take one look and know what club I need. When I get to my ball, I'm ready to hit. I don't need all this looking back and forth from the ball to the green and all these practice swings. I pick a club, walk up to the ball and hit it, that's all. Who needs all this other stuff?

"If I'm going to fast for you, we'll slow down."

"No," I protested through parched lips. "I like to play fast." I didn't tell him I was getting stomach cramps.

We finished the first nine holes in one hour and five minutes. Niven and I went for water while Sonny Kyle, an assistant pro, loaded his clubs onto a cart to play the back nine with us. Kyle is a fine player but he really slowed us down. It took an hour and 15 minutes to play the back nine.

When we pulled up to the clubhouse at the finish, the golf carts steamed, whinnied and shook like plow horses that had just run the Derby in two minutes flat.

Rooney, the pros' pro of the entertainment world, was in Charlotte doing *George M* at the Summer Theatre, but between curtains, he was storming the city's golf courses. He played Quail Hollow Country Club earlier and the layout proved too long for him.

"Would you believe I was six feet, three inches tall before I played Quail Hollow?" he said. "Now, I'm only five-two."

He played the championship tees there, of course. He won't play the regular tees. He says that's not really playing the game.

Rooney wore tan checked trousers, a yellow shirt, love beads and granny glasses as we played Myers Park. He took off the beads and pulled an orange cap down over his thick, gray hair for the game.

Word swept through the clubhouse that the 49-year-old performer was preparing to play. It happened to be ladies' day and they swarmed out of the clubhouse to watch him tee off. They applauded vigorously when he smacked his tee shot down the middle. They were deafeningly quiet when I hooked mine into the trees.

Thankfully, the gaggle of ladies stayed behind as we set out on our cross-country cart race. On the second hole, a gang of screaming youngsters was spotted bearing down on us yelling, "Mickey, wait for us!" and "Mickey, we want you!" but a club official overtook them and herded them back to the clubhouse.

Rooney, who has been golfing for 25 years and says he would play day and night if someone would turn on their headlights, is no bad swinger. He stands well back from the ball, spreads his feet wide in a closed stance and knocks the devil out of the ball. For a fellow his size, he has unusually good power.

The greens had him mystified, though. He could never get the feel of them or solve the problem of reading the break, except for one long putt he holed for a birdie on the par four 13th. ("Even a blind hog finds a barrel of hominy sometimes," he remarked.)

He shot an 89 from the blue tees but he's a good 10 strokes better than that. He has shot as low as 68.

Rooney plays with all of the enthusiasm of Andy Hardy, chatting constantly, pausing only briefly to hit or wait impatiently for someone else to play.

He talks a negative game. He muttered to himself, "I'm not a bad golfer. Not bad, I just stink," and after one of several double bogeys, he commented, "Not bad for a rank amateur – and I mean really rank. If I don't improve, I'm going to put my clubs away – until tomorrow."

He complained that his clubs were too light and once, after a shot fell short, he blurted, "Hit the ball, you midget!"

When it was over, he sipped a ginger ale in the clubhouse and said, "I love this game. A lot of people play it better than I do but nobody loves it more. I can't get enough of it."

Which may explain why he (cough, gasp) plays so fast.

April 10, 1975

300 Acres of Madness

There is little about this town to suggest that anything more troubling than a yawn occurs in Augusta on these soft spring days. Broad Street hums smoothly with downtown shoppers. The gin mills and tattoo parlors that cater to the soldiers from Fort Gordon sit dark, awaiting the night's trade. The suburbs are like old lace, with narrow, leafy streets, their dogwoods and azaleas in bloom. Black kids play their games on the sidewalks outside their crumbling tenements.

But on the western outskirts of this quaint, gentle old Scarlett O'Hara-land, there are 300 acres of madness.

The Augusta National Golf Club looks placid enough. Rolling. Brilliant green. Thickets of great pines reaching for the sky, with splashes of red and white flowering shrubs and trees at their feet. At the end of the magnolia tunnel that leads into the grounds, an unimposing white clubhouse rests at the crest of a hill. You can sit on its veranda and through the early foliage of a giant Georgia hackberry entwined with wisterias and a huge live oak, see a half dozen of the holes of this famous course ebbing and flowing as the verdant land falls away down to Rae's Creek. And you can just taste a mint julep and hear some mammy saying, "Yas'm, ma'am."

But there is no peace here this week. The Masters began today. It is the queen of all golf tournaments and the promise of riches and everlasting glory mingle with the sweet treachery of the course to torture the mind of every man who sticks a peg into the ground.

As *Sports Illustrated* author Dan Jenkins wrote, "It'll stir your grits."

There is something about this golf course that is bewildering to the best players on earth who come here each spring. Exactly what it is has never been satisfactorily resolved, which is why it is so maddening.

Every man arrives here with this own special idea of how to go about winning. Men who play together week after week on the tour have theories that are in direct conflict.

They begin preparing for the Masters mentally and, in some cases, physically weeks and months ahead. Ben Hogan used to go to Seminole in Florida and practice for a month before coming here because that course is similar to this one in many ways and the weather was good. Jack Nicklaus, a four-time winner here, invariably comes in a week and a half in advance to prepare, although he says he starts getting ready mentally when the year begins. Many, on the other hand, think it's better to play a tournament the week before the Masters to stay mentally tough.

No man playing the Masters for the first time ever wins it because of the subtleties of the course that must be learned and the magnitude of the title.

Lee Trevino, who has won the world's other three major championships, quit trying for two years because he said he didn't hit the ball high enough and couldn't hook it and therefore could never win here. But Arnold Palmer is a low hitter and he has won it four times and Nicklaus rarely hooks it and he has won it four times.

Nicklaus convinced Trevino he should come back and he did. Even though Trevino has one of the half-dozen best games in the world, he has altered it this week from his basic fade to a hook.

"You've got to hook it here," says Sam Snead. Right, agrees Billy Casper. Others, though, say no. Bob Murphy said he tried hooking it for 27 practice holes this week but in mid-round gave up on the idea.

Some players didn't even go onto the course for a final practice round yesterday, hoping a day of rest would be the secret. Others, though, were out there grinding, trying until the 11th hour to puzzle this thing out. They putted at invisible holes, trying to guess where the flags would be and studying the baffling breaks of the greens.

It's a relatively open course with no genuine rough along the fairways. it's not unusually long, though it plays long. And it's in perfect condition. So what makes it so impossible to solve? Nicklaus did it once for four days, sledging it to its knees with scores that moved the late Bobby Jones, one of the founders of the tournament, to say Jack had "played a game with which I am not familiar." But the next year, Nicklaus won with a score that was 17 shots higher.

"It's club selection," says Gay Brewer. "It's the weather," says someone else. "It's the pressure," says Gary Player, the defending champion. "On the last nine holes you can shoot 32 or 42." Billy Casper says you've got to be long but George Archer isn't and he won.

Bert Yancey has built a mock-up of the course to study at home but has never won here.

And so it goes.

Each man took his own theories out there with him today, wrapped lovingly around his hopes. Someone will win, of course, but that won't necessarily mean he has solved the mystery of this 300 acres of madness.

Undated

The Marker of Gum McClure

At his death, James Ernest "Gum" McClure left five golf trophies, some rich lore, a lot of friends and a scar on our consciences.

One of the trophies, undoubtedly the last he won, reads, "1975 Griertown Open, Senior Division." One of them reads simply, "Champion 1969."

We don't know what he won but we know it wasn't anything of consequence. Some say he won a couple of tournaments on the black golf tour, in Atlanta and Asheville, but that wasn't the real thing. When McClure was in his prime, black men weren't welcome in any golf tournaments except their own and there weren't many of those.

McClure was in his 70s when he died. He had been living with his sister, Mary Lou Bost, for the last couple of years, with that dreadful leftover time to kill after his wife had died and he had become too old to work and felt too poorly to play golf.

McClure raised a family doing yard work and caddying. "We laughed about that," said Mrs. Bost. "I told him he never held a steady job in his life because he wanted free time to play that golf. They say he was good at it, too."

He was good at it.

"Gum" caddied for and played with the late touring pro Clayton

Heafner many times and Heafner said, "If he had been given the opportunity, he could've made it big as a tour player."

"Gum," who acquired his nickname for his ever-present wad of chewing gum, started Jim Black in golf, and several years ago, Black made it to the pro tour that McClure never knew except as a caddy.

"Jim could've been a real good tour player," said Black. "He had more shots than anybody I've ever played with, one of the greatest pairs of hands I've ever seen."

"Gum" was also one of the best one-club players anywhere, something he learned as a kid.

"I learned how to play the whole golf course with just one club when I first started out," McClure once said. "Back then, there was no such thing as a whole set for us. Somebody would give us an old club and three or four of us would play a round with it. Maybe it would be a putter.

"Then somebody would give us another club and we'd use it to play the whole course. We'd copy the swings of the best players we saw. That's how I learned to play."

And that's how "Gum" came to play the notorious gambler that day in 1965 at Revolution Park in Charlotte. The gambler had been in town for a few days, playing the local sports. Someone asked him how many holes he would spot an "old man" and he said none.

Suppose the old man uses only one club, they said, would you spot him half a stroke a hole?

The gambler whipped out his bankroll, threw it on the ground and said, "Bring him on."

"Gum" was summoned from the clubhouse. He ambled down the hillside carrying a putter he had borrowed. Using only the putter, "Gum" birdied the first hole, played the first five in even par, won every hole and nonchalantly walked in.

He could use the whole set of clubs, too. Although he ordinarily played only once or twice a week, between yard work and caddying, he hung around 68 or 69 pretty regularly on courses such as Revolution Park.

One day Black, home for a visit from the tour, shot a 63 at Hillcrest in Charlotte. Not good enough. McClure shot 62.

His nine-hole scores at Hillcrest and Revolution included 29s and "a whole gang" of 30s.

"We got to laughing not long ago about Jim when he was a kid," said Mrs. Bost. "We lived on a farm and all of us worked it except my older brother, Fred. He worked at Charlotte Country Club.

"Every day, Daddy would send Jim to the club to take Fred his lunch and he'd tell Jim to come right back. But every day, Jim would stay at the club and caddy or slip around and play some golf. And he'd get a whuppin' every evening.

"One day, I asked him, 'Jim, why don't you come on back home? I can't stand to see you whupped every day.'

"And he said, 'Now, don't worry about it. It don't hurt no longer than it takes to get it.'

"He just wanted to play that golf. He was willing to take a beating to do it."

In that respect, he never changed. He labored with his hands and then carried the clubs of white men he could beat with just one of those clubs, to make the money to support his family and play that golf.

In another time, he might have been a star. As it is, he's merely a legend.

March 24, 1976

A Round with Arnie

What's it like to play golf with Arnold Palmer?

I'll tell you what it's like. We played yesterday, the King and I. I outdrove him once, on the 16th hole, by a couple of yards, but I was so accustomed to hitting first, I didn't even notice it until after I had hit my second shot. I blew my chance to say, just once, "You're away, Arnie." And maybe snuff my nose and hitch up my pants like you know who. I'll never forgive myself for that.

Palmer and I played Quail Hollow Country Club in Charlotte with Harry Nicholas, executive vice-president of First Citizens Bank & Trust Co., and Tommy Byrne of Wake Forest, the former Yankee pitcher. Billy Booe, the Kemper Open tournament director, had set up the game to give Palmer a look at the new trees lining some of the fairways and the new bunkering on several of the holes where the $250,000 tournament will be played in June. I saw a lot more of the trees and sand than Palmer did, or at least from closer range.

I've been writing about Arnie since he was an amateur at Wake Forest. I had breakfast with him the Sunday he won his first Masters title in 1958. We've socialized a bit and our paths have crossed hundreds of times at golf tournaments. So playing a friendly 18 with him is not going to bother me, right? Wrong. Bad wrong. I was more than nervous before we teed off and for the first two or three holes I was scared. Don't ask me why because I don't know. But my caddy, Calvin Miller, said he understood. "I was nervous, too, " he said, "and I wasn't even carrying his bag."

There's something about having a man who has won four Masters titles, two British Opens, one U.S. Open and about five dozen other tournaments standing there watching you that makes you feel like you're swinging a shovel with broken arms. All those smart-alecky things you've written about Miller Barber's swing ("He looks like a cave man killing lunch") and about Doug Sanders' swing ("He looks like a motorcycle having a wreck") flash through your mind and you think, "Lordy, I wish Miller Barber was here to hit this one for me. Or even Mrs. Barber."

All of which is quite presumptuous, of course. I don't think Arnie was all that concerned about the condition of my game. He would say nice things about my good shots but very diplomatically pretend not to be paying any attention to the bad ones. And by the end of the first nine, I was fairly comfortable and enjoying the game immensely, although I must confess it gave me a bit of a start when I played a punch shot from beneath some trees on the 11th hole and Booe, who was spectating, said, "I think you got Arnie on the leg with that one." Actually, it wasn't even close, Arnie said when I reached the green. "I always jump and run like that. It's an affliction called fear."

Palmer did not play very well but next to the rest of us, he looked like he was shooting 50. He three-putted three times, made only one putt of any size all day, hit an occasional wayward iron and had a couple of drives that didn't satisfy him. He shot a three-over-par 75.

That, of course, is not very stylish for Arnie, even from the Kemper tees which makes the course seem about 10,000 yards long. His spirits seemed to rise and fall with each shot, but generally, he seemed to be enjoying the round.

When he hooked his approach into the sand on the fifth hole, he said to himself, "Now, why did you do that? I know why I'm doing it.

The left side is not strong enough..." When he hit a marvelous drive on the sixth, he said, "Now that's the way to hit a golf ball."

On the par five 10th, Palmer studied his approach shot and asked Nicholas how far it was to the pin, which was on the backside of the green. Nicholas said it was 95 yards. Palmer disagreed. "I think it's 120 yards," he said. "But I'm gonna hit this shot 105 yards, and sort of split the difference."

He knocked the ball onto the green but short of the flag. He and Nicholas paced it off. Palmer had hit the ball 105 yards, exactly as he has said he would. It was another 12 yards to the pin.

"That's why he's in the business he's in and I'm not," said a smiling Nicholas.

Palmer will not play in the Heritage Classic this week or the Greensboro Open next week. He has played in only six tournaments so far this year and has missed the cut in three of them. That's three less tournaments than he has ever played at this stage of the season.

"I said early this year that if I wasn't playing well, I wouldn't play much before the Masters. I still think I can win a tournament. The day I don't think that, I'll quit. And I'll tell you, I've come damn close to it a few times this year. Seriously," he said.

"I get real encouraged when I'm practicing but then get on the course and play like I'm playing today and I get discouraged again. I lose patience with myself. My problem is not making bogeys. I'm just not making birdies in two rounds and missed the cut. Before, I would make 10 or 12 birdies in two rounds. I now I'm not hitting the ball well but I'm not hitting it so badly that I should miss three cuts in six tournaments."

Oh, by the way, if you want to know how Arnie and I came out, he nipped me by 12 shots. He beat me out of five bucks but I guess that's not much to pay to play golf with the King.

June 1978

The Little Round Man

This one is about "the little round man," one of the great men and great – but honest – con artists I have ever known.

His name was Fred Corcoran. He was a short, stout man with slicked-back gray hair who always stood with his hands clasped behind him and always sat with them clasped on his rather ample stomach.

He was always at the major golf championships and a lot of the lesser ones and he always seemed to linger on the fringes, sitting on the clubhouse veranda at Augusta talking to Gene Sarazen or standing near the scoreboard at Oakmont chatting with Dave Marr. Always available but unobtrusive. And the single best source of golfing information on the premises, including the tour handbook.

If you were the average golf fan, you might pass him by without knowing he was a giant of sports. He managed that without ever becoming much of a celebrity. But he had such a powerful influence on golf at one time, when he was tournament director for the Professional Golfers Association of America, that he is generally credited with bringing the tour from rags to riches, expanding it and starting the upward climb of purses that now total $9 million.

Corcoran was also the driving force behind the International Golf Association that stages the World Cup matches. He helped launch the women's tour. He was active in producing the Westchester Classic, once the richest tournament on the PGA tour.

As the first of the sports agents, he had in his stable, among others, Sam Snead, Tony Lema, Ted Williams, Stan Musial and Babe Didrickson Zaharias. He never had signed contracts with them, preferring to deal on a handshake.

Corcoran organized the Golf Writers Association of America. Last year, he was inducted into the Golf Hall of Fame. I mention all this now because Fred Corcoran died last week at the age of 72 in a hospital in White Plains, N.Y., and because he gave me – and others – more than just material for writing.

From time to time, Corcoran, who traveled the world as easily and as regularly as we might drive to the office, would invite eight or ten golf writers to go with him to places like Ireland and Scotland and he would take care of the tab. Junketing was acceptable at the time.

I doubt that I would ever have made it to Ireland or Scotland or England if Corcoran hadn't included me in a couple of his trips. I might never have seen St. Andrews, the cradle of golf. Corcoran talked our way into the Royal & Ancient Room in the clubhouse, which is for members only. On one wall a small sign commands, "Silence."

Once there, he smooth-talked a club official into opening the door of the wall safe in that room, where all of the major golf trophies of Great Britain are stored. The gold and silver treasure was literally stunning in the brilliant lighting of the safe.

If it were not for Corcoran, I might never have played the Old Course and stood shaking on the first tee as I felt the presence of the spirits of great men.

And I know I wouldn't have become almost certainly one of the first men ever to be served a picnic on a bearskin rug from the trunk of a limousine parked behind the ninth green at St. Andrews. Arranged, of course, by "the little round man," which we called him behind his back.

Had it not been for him, I might never have fallen in love with Ireland, traveled its lovely countryside, played its golf courses, kissed the Blarney Stone. I might not have sat drinking with the others well into the night in a saloon in Limerick, making up limericks, or stood alone on a grassy little hillside in Killarney gazing in wonder at the still, silent beauty of a misty lake.

Had it not been for Fred Corcoran, I might never have played golf at Prestwick, on the course where the first 10 British Opens were played a century ago.

We were to have lunch there but the gentlemen were requested to have neckties and we had none with us that day. We had on golf shirts. Corcoran disappeared and returned a few minutes later with a handful of bulky plaid neckties, which we tied on with our red shirts.

Had it not been for Corcoran, I might not have traveled to Troon to see the British Open, miss my ride back into town and wound up having a glorious time with two inebriated Scots who somehow got me onto the proper buses, though one of them kept falling out of his seat into the aisle when we made a curve.

I hurt to think that I might have missed the long hours in the evenings in Glasgow listening to Corcoran and an old pal of Damon

Runyon's, the late Harry Grayson, tell wonderful stories about golf and boxing and baseball.

And had it not been for Fred Corcoran, I might never have stayed at the grand old Savoy Hotel in London, from which we ranged out to see all the wonders of that great city. And on Sunday afternoon, we rode in chauffeur-driven limousines out into the countryside to the estate of a wealthy acquaintance of Corcoran's and ate strawberries, drank tea and played croquet, just like Englishmen.

All along the way, "the little round man" fussed like a mother hen at us for bringing golf bags bigger than the pros carried, for oversleeping, for insisting on staying an extra day in London, for running up big tabs in restaurants and bars. And all along the way, he was working his wonders.

"Yes," he had said into the telephone, "I think we might be able to work in a trip to London on our itinerary, although we are pretty solidly booked. Incidentally, one of the fellows coming along stayed in the Savoy during World War II and asked if we might stay there on this trip, if we come. You can arrange that, can't you?"

He was the fellow who had stayed there during the war. And of course we were going to accept the invitation to London. It simply was not Corcoran's nature to let on anyone was doing him a favor.

Our golf clubs and luggage put us about 400 pounds over our limit for the airliner. "Hell, you don't need those damn clubs," said Corcoran. Old Tom Morris (or somebody) shot even par on the Old Course in a 50-mile wind with three clubs."

But the silver-tongued little man arranged not only to have the excess baggage fee set aside, but got us all into the first class cabin at no extra cost. Jack Nicklaus took the same plane. Tourist.

Many of us owe a lot to Fred Corcoran. We'll never be able to pay it off now. But surely he's happy. If "the little round man" couldn't talk his way into Heaven, I'm afraid there's not much hope for the rest of us.

June 14, 1980

America's Guest

George Low probably doesn't really exist. Chances are, he's a creation of Damon Runyon when the author was in one of his more imaginative moods and Runyon died without ever telling us any different, leaving Low to wander forever around golf courses where tournaments are being played.

If you've ever been to the Kemper Open in Charlotte, you've probably seen Low without realizing it. He's 66 years old, his shoulders hunched, his gray hair combed neatly back and his blue eyes seeming to see nothing except the thoughts running through his mind.

From time to time, he moves from one place to another in a slow, shambling walk – never far from the clubhouse – but mostly, he sits in golf carts he finds idle in some shady spot, smoking and sipping a beer. The pro golfers wave to him and speak. He nods back to them. Then someone will sit down in the cart with him and they will talk awhile.

George Low is the self-proclaimed greatest putter who ever drew back a blade and he has spent a great part of his life proving it to anyone who doubted it and could pay the price to find out. He has also been to the putter what Pablo Casals was to the cello, exhorting his pupils – who have included some of the best golfers – to quit playing the notes and make music.

"I could putt for the cash as good as anybody who ever lived," said Low yesterday afternoon as he lazed in a golf cart outside the Quail Hollow clubhouse. His voice is gravelly and when he talks, it reminds you of Phil Harris.

"I could do anything that required hand-eye coordination – pitch coins, bowl, shoot baskets. I learned to putt at Carnoustie in Scotland. My old man retired and went over there for three years. I'd putt all day on that big old practice green."

He looked up at the practice putting green, where several of the pros playing in the Kemper Open were working on their strokes. "I haven't practiced one iota in a year," he growled. "I had a broken wrist. These guys could beat me now but they're scared to try."

Low played the tour himself until 1974. He was the first pro to beat Byron Nelson in 12 tournaments the year Lord Byron won 11 in a row.

Freddie Haas, an amateur, won the tournament but Low won the top top prize, $2,800 in War Bonds. Nowadays, he groused, they get $2,800 to play a one-day outing on a Monday.

Exactly what Low does for a living is unclear. Ask him and he'll tell you with a twinkle in his eye, "I'm in the mining business. I mind my own business."

He had a line of putters out and claims Jack Nicklaus has won about 95 percent of his tournaments with one of them but said the distribution firm didn't do a good job of peddling them. Now, he's about to bring out some new putters with a new company. He has been known to make a sporting buck on the putting greens and he charges an undefined but worthwhile amount to work with anyone who has the talent and who can afford the money and the time.

But Low has been described in a *Sports Illustrated* article as "America's Guest," a man who is allergic to tabs. Asked about that, he just grunted and mumbled something, obviously piqued about it.

Low is the first to admit he can't help anyone who doesn't have the touch. Touch. It's an almost religious word with him.

"You can have a million bucks and your old man wants you to play the violin," he said, "but if you don't have the touch, you'll never learn. Same with putting. Some people have it and some don't. Jack Dempsey could tear your head off but he'd freeze trying to hit a golf ball. A lot of baseball players make good golfers, better than average, because they have touch.

"It's like a broad. You ask her to throw a ball. If she gives it that shove, you can't help her, but if she rears back and really throws it, you can. Same with guys. If they throw like girls, Dick Tracy couldn't help them."

Ask him who's the best putter on tour today and he'll tell you, "Jack Nicklaus is the best putter, day in and day out. Some guys may have fewer putts in a round but they aren't hitting as many greens as Nicklaus. They're chipping up close and one- putting.

"The most pathetic fellow out there is Orville Moody. If I could putt for him, he'd win tournaments. There's probably not five players out here who can beat him tee to green. But I can't even stand to watch him putt."

What about nerves? "Hell," he said, "I'm old enough and been drunk enough that my nerves ought to be jumping all over the place but it's mind over matter."

Low admits he has been beaten more than once in putting contests but he says, "Some hotshot would come along and beat me one time and quit. If they stayed with me any length of time, I'd grind 'em down. I could putt for the cash.

"I did lose a marathon match one time in Pinehurst. Ky Laffoon and I started putting in the afternoon and kept on until after dark and he beat me. Turned out the s.o.b. was half Indian and he could see in the dark and I couldn't."

November, 1980

The Goose and the Golfer

A Washington physician was found guilty of killing a goose out of season with his putter at Congressional Country Club last year. He was fined $500 by a federal magistrate.

The doctor pleaded innocent. He claimed his approach shot injured the goose and that he put it out of its misery by whacking it on the head.

Witnesses, however, said that he attacked the fowl in anger when it honked just as he was stroking a four-foot putt on the 17th green.

The man was, in my opinion, innocent by virtue of temporary insanity, regardless of whether it was a case of euthanasia or hunting out of season.

It's common knowledge that golfers suffer periods of insanity, a condition brought on most often by missed putts, hooked drives and shanked wedges.

If the good doctor had asked, I could've paraded people to the stand to testify to this fact, most of them playing partners of people who three-putt frequently.

We who play the devil's game can't justify the lengths to which the doctor went, if he's guilty of goosicide as the court found, but we can find some small measure of understanding in our tortured souls.

Golf can bring bile welling up in the gentlest man, can transform a reasonable human being into a wild-eyed maniac.

Dave Kindred, writing on this topic in the *Washington Post*, hauled out this quote from author Arnold Haultain, written in 1908:

"It is a game proverbially provocative of reprehensible expletives."

And the most common cause of the reprehensible expletives is the short putt that misses the mark, especially one that loses the match.

Someone once asked Billy Graham what he thought when he missed a short putt and he declined comment. Dean Smith prides himself on never using profanity but golf sometimes exasperates him to the point that he begins spelling a dirty word through clenched teeth.

I've seen a man miss a short putt, hurl the offending club into the woods, fall to his knees and commence to tear at the turf around the hole with his bare hands, growling like a crazed animal.

We, his playing partners, simply stood by, nodding our understanding.

I've seen a man attempt to set a golf course on fire. After three-putting eleven consecutive greens, he stalked over to the edge of the woods and tossed lighted matches into the fallen leaves.

The most notorious angry golfer was probably Lefty Stackhouse, also a tour player. If his thought processes malfunctioned on a shot, he might punish his head by ramming it into a tree trunk. If he got too much right hand into a shot, he might place the offending hand on a ball washer and pound it with his putter or shove it into a thorny bush until the flow of blood indicated it had been sufficiently punished.

Ky Laffoon, who played the tour at a high and consistent level of anger, once missed a short one, stuck his putter into a pond and screamed, "Drown, you s.o.b.!"

And Laffoon has been known to tie his putter to the back of his car and drag it down a highway to make it pay for its recalcitrance.

Tommy Bolt, who earned the nicknames of Thunder and Terrible Tommy with his lightning fury, once looked heavenward with teeth gnashing and fists clenched after missing a little putt and snarled, "Me again, huh? Why don't You come down here and play me? Bring your kid, too."

His playing partners edged away from him, in case the Big Shoulder Turn in the Sky decided to show Bolt some real lightning fury.

I've played many a round with a man who swore that cows lowing in the distance and dogs barking in neighboring yards were out to wreck his game and he cursed them appropriately. He insisted it was no coincidence that a buzzard happened over just as he was preparing to hit across a pond.

Haultain writes of golf, "The frailty of the human mind is shown in utter nudity, not hidden under cover of agility or excitement or concerted action...and so these exposed men make excuses to cover their failings...the nature and number of which must assuredly move the laughter of the gods."

Laugh, gods, if you will, but then you've probably never had a goose honk just as you were stroking a four-footer.

If, in fact, that provoked the doctor to club the goose, well the man undoubtedly was not thinking clearly. Even the most fanatical of us will admit that what he did was dreadful. He overreacted.

He should've just kicked its butt.

March 12, 1981

Fiery Temper, Big Heart

Every year at this time, the memories of the big ol' bear- like man with the molten lava temperament, the velvet touch and the golden heart come pushing through like spring flowers.

Clayton Heafner.

He made Tommy Bolt look like a Sunday school teacher. He made Tom Weiskopf look like a Boy Scout. He strewed broken golf clubs and purple prose from coast to coast but the big redheaded Charlottean could be as gentle as a mother's kiss with a wedge or a putter or a fellow in need.

He was notorious for his temper but with it, he could play. People who played alongside him on the tour, like Sam Snead, say he was one of the best.

He had lost some use of a foot. The toes would drag when he walked. He wore a metal spring device to make the toes lift when he stepped.

He hadn't played golf in months, maybe years.

But Heafner had a talent that could survive even these things, that joint that made walking a chore and the inattentiveness to his game.

He had put together a one-day pro-amateur tournament at Eastwood, the golf course he bought as a place to settle into business after his retirement from the pro golf tour. When the tournament came up one pro short, Heafner said, "Get my clubs. I'll play but I'll have to ride a cart."

He duck-hooked his drive off the first tee behind an equipment shed no more than 100 yards away. Rather than thrash around in the bushes looking for it, Heafner took a stroke-and- distance penalty, reloaded and hit his third shot before he ever left the first tee.

He shot 66 and won the tournament.

He was almost a great player.

As a rookie on the tour in 1939, he shot a 66 in the third round of the U.S. Open, which then had a double-round finish on Saturday. Besieged by newsmen, fans and equipment representatives, Heafner not only missed lunch, he had no time to relax. He shot 80 that afternoon and finished tenth.

In 1949, he missed a six-foot putt that would have tied him for the Open title and finished second to Cary Middlecoff. In 1951, he shot a final round 69 in the Open but Ben Hogan shot a 67 to beat him.

Heafner won six titles on the tour. In 1948, he won money in 22 of 24 tournaments and averaged only 70.43 strokes per round, second only to Hogan's in the race for the Vardon Trophy, emblematic of the tour's best scoring average.

He was named to the U.S. Ryder Cup team three times and never lost a match in that international competition.

That's how close Clayton Heafner came to greatness – he almost won two, maybe three U.S. Opens and almost won the Vardon Trophy.

The stories of Heafner's temper tantrums would fill a book. Some have melded together over the years but that's okay. Stories ought to get better with age.

My favorite is this one, and I suspect it is a blend of two or three:

Heafner became fed up with his game during a round and, after driving under a tree, told his caddy, "Go pick it up."

A woman in the gallery said, "You can't do that. I bought you in the Calcutta pool."

"Okay," said Heafner, "leave it there," and stalked off the course.

He was so angry, he wrenched the steering wheel off his car and had to drive into town turning the steering column with his big paw, the way you might turn a doorknob.

After he left the tour, Heafner enjoyed sitting around Eastwood telling stories, playing gin rummy or betting a little tad on matches others played on his course. He never lost that temper, though. Some people say he ran off half the customers at Eastwood with his gruff manner. Not true. A third, maybe.

He died on New Year's Eve in 1960, five days after suffering a heart attack.

September 17, 1981

Slammin' Sammy

The year was 1936.

Joe DiMaggio was a rookie with the New York Yankees. Paul Muni and Louise Rainer won the Academy Awards. James J. Braddock was the heavyweight boxing champion. Jack Nicklaus wouldn't be born for another four years and television sports wouldn't be born for another three. Count Basie brought his big band sound out of Kansas City.

And Sam Snead won his first "official" professional golf tournament, the Virginia Closed Pro.

Sam Snead – formerly known as Slammin' Sammy Snead, still known as The Slammer – is bidding for another tournament title, the World Seniors Invitational at Quail Hollow Country Club. He may not win it – it's been awhile now since he won one – but if he doesn't foul a plug or drop a valve, he should be a reasonable contender and if he holes a few putts, he could win it. He's still that good.

At age 69.

Golf is a game that can be played for a lifetime but not at the level Snead has played it and still plays it. At his age, most guys sit in rocking chairs and nod a lot. Those who play golf generally have trouble getting in and out of the cart and swing at the ball like Queen Elizabeth to keep their joints from flying apart.

Snead still has a walk that is so jaunty, Jim Ferree once said, "he could walk on eggs and not break any." He's so supple, he can still kick a leg up and touch the top of a doorway with his foot.

The Slammer doesn't bunt, he swings for the fences. He can still knock the flagstick out with a 3-iron, drop a wedge onto the green like a butterfly with sore feet and make a few putts with his sidesaddle style, his only concession to time. Just two years ago, he shot his age – 67 – in a regular PGA tour event one day and the next day bettered it with a 66.

His triumphs alone made him one of the half-dozen or so greatest golfers in history and put him into the Hall of Fame. His ability to sustain his excellence for so long makes him one of the most remarkable figures ever in sports. Independent record keepers say Snead has won 135 tournaments. Snead says 101 of those were staged by the PGA (now the TPC) but the TPC credits him with only 85 official titles. Okay, 85. They can go ahead and carve that one in stone. Nobody's going to touch it.

And the swing, held up for most of our lives as the textbook, hasn't changed appreciably. *Golf Digest* this month features sequence photos of Snead's wins in 1937 and 1981. They look identical, fluid, simple, wonderful.

Snead's strongest competitors during his prime – if that can be defined – were Ben Hogan and Byron Nelson. Both disappeared from tournament golf many years ago, but the Snead legend continues to build. There he was Wednesday, Old Man River in a straw hat with a fancy band, pulling on his spikes, getting ready for a final tuneup for the World Seniors Invitational.

There are no secrets to longevity in the game, he was saying. No diet, no eight-hours-sleep-a-night routine, none of that. Just that golf swing he was born with and has never tried to change and a career with no interruptions.

"It's like everything else," he said. "You've gotta keep your hand in. You can't quit and expect to come back as good as you were."

For most of his years, he played almost every day. In the last few years, he has gradually cut back. His tournament schedule has been reduced to about a dozen and a half a year, maybe four or five on the regular circuit, the rest on the senior tour.

Next year, when he's 70, he says he'll probably play the expanded 16-tournament seniors schedule and "maybe scratch around a couple of days at the Masters."

There was a time when a poor score would turn Snead into a major storm with thunder and lightning. Not any more.

"I guess I'm gettin' kinda used to it," he said, smiling. "I used to want to break clubs and chew somebody out but I figure now I'd better enjoy it and go on about my business."

Snead says his career as a tournament player would have ended many years ago if he had continued to putt upright, in the normal fashion. His putting had eroded to the point that he had the yips.

The same thing happened to Hogan but Hogan simply quit playing in public. Snead wanted to continue playing tournament golf. He started straddling the line and putting. That was soon outlawed. He changed to side-saddle, an awkward but effective style in which he holds the club out to his side, his left hand high, his right hand down near the clubhead. He stoops to conquer.

"That kept me in the game," he said.

Among his titles are three Masters, three PGA's and a British Open. You'll notice – as the world has noticed for so long – that there's not a U.S. Open mentioned there.

Snead was runnerup in that one four times, a contender many times more but could never win it, even when it seemed he had it locked up. It's such a well-worn story, it hardly seemed appropriate to bring it up but Snead himself mentioned it. He seems to have come to an understanding with himself about this glaring void.

"Nobody's had any better life than I have," he said, "and the Open thing, it just looks like that was in the cards from the start."

Bob Toski says he thinks the secret to Snead's longevity lies not in his athletic coordination but in his desire, his competitive spirit. Toski says he's never seen anyone who enjoys golf more and delights more in winning than Snead.

"Yeah," said Snead, "I still enjoy it but it's like it always was – I enjoy it when I play well and I don't enjoy it when I play bad."

Which means he usually enjoys it.

How long will he keep going? Well, famed columnist Jim Murray wrote, "The legend of Sam Snead defies belief. It smacks more of a sound stage than a fairway. It's not a career, it's an eon. It is now running neck-and-neck with the Ice Age as an historical era. He's a living fossil. He may be the first man in history to birdie a hole posthumously. Look for a news story 45 years from now that goes:

"'Samuel Jackson Snead, 99, died on the 14th green at Humidity

Hollow Golf Course yesterday. This seriously affected his short game, but he still managed to par in the rest of the way for a net 69 – 53 living and the rest posthumously. If rigor mortis doesn't set in, he will still be an odds-on favorite at tee-off tomorrow.'"

That was written 15 years ago.

June 21, 1982

The Immortals

With a swing of his club as gentle as a mother's kiss, Tom Watson opened the gates of golfing greatness and ran through arms raised to the sky, ecstasy glowing on his boyish face.

Watson, 32, hit a stunning little pitch shot that he estimated to be only 16 feet long – and that the great Jack Nicklaus described as "impossible" – out of high rough from a downhill lie into the cup on the 17th hole.

The birdie two, which sent Watson racing around the green in wild celebration, effectively ended a memorable battle with Nicklaus, who had made a dramatic bid for his 20th major championship and appeared perhaps to have won it.

The birdie left Watson needing only to par the last hole to win his first U.S. Open. He did better than that. He played the par five 18th, bordered on the left by the Pacific Ocean and on the right by out-of-bounds, cautiously but still birdied it to win by two shots with a two-under-par 70 for a 72-hole total of 282.

"I won it on the 17th," he said. "That shot meant more than any other shot of my life."

With three British Opens, two Masters and 25 other titles behind him, this triumph, achieved on the beautiful but harshly demanding Pebble Beach Golf Links under appropriately grim skies, confirmed what we have suspected for the past few years. Watson belongs among the great players the game has known.

This Open earned a special place in the annals of the game, as well.

Watson began the day four under par for the tournament, tied with Bill Rogers for the lead. Eleven players were within four shots of them. Nicklaus was one of those 11, three shots off the pace after rounds of 74-70-71.

The stiff breezes that so often blow off Carmel Bay to toss and turn the golfers' shots was absent on this cool Sunday. But the course, which winds through forest and along the bluffs above the bay, and the smothering pressure that accompanies the national championship conspired to produce a rare drama.

Nicklaus, bidding for an unprecedented fifth U.S. Open title, knew he had to work his way into the thick of the chase early. He did that by recovering from a shaky start – a bogey on the first hole and a missed opportunity for a relatively easy birdie on the second – by reeling off five straight birdies from the third through the seventh holes. The crowd thundering at his heels was going mad.

Watson and Rogers, meanwhile, were holding their ground and others – defending champion David Graham, Bruce Devlin, Lanny Wadkins, Dan Pohl and Bobby Clampett – were close.

But one by one, as fate would have it, the others fell away, leaving the stage to the two best in the game today, Watson and Nicklaus.

As Nicklaus walked to the 15th green, where a birdie putt awaited him, he told his son, Jackie, who was caddying for him,"Well, there are only two of us in it now." He made the birdie to catch Watson.

Nicklaus had reasonable birdie chances on the last three holes but had to settle for pars. He said, nevertheless, after he had finished to a long, standing ovation from the throng beside the last green, he thought probably he had won because Watson, who had just bogeyed the 16th, had to par in to tie him.

"When I went into the tent to sign my score card," Nicklaus said later, "I saw on a TV monitor where Tom had hit his tee shot (a two iron) on the 17th and I thought, "Well, he's going to have to birdie 18 to catch me because there's no way he can make par on 17 from where his ball is.

"I didn't see him knock the ball into the cup. All I saw was him running around the green and I thought he was doing that because he had barely missed.

"I thought, I can't believe anybody holed it from there. I still can't. It was impossible."

Watson didn't think so. He had already holed a 25-foot putt to save par on No. 10, a 20-footer for a birdie on No. 11 and an astonishing 35-footer from the fringe for a birdie on No. 14 that was traveling so fast he would have had a long comeback putt had it not gone in.

"I looked at my lie on 17 and saw that it was sitting only about half-way down in the rough (which was about eight inches high)," said Watson. "I saw that I could get the leading edge of the club under it so I knew I could get it out okay.

"My caddy, Bruce Edwards, said 'Now you get this close,' and I said, 'I'm not gonna get it close, I'm gonna make it.'

"I opened the face of the club, sliced across it and when it landed, I said to myself, 'That's in the hole.'"

If Watson didn't think he was in serious trouble, he was a minority of one. Rogers, paired with Watson, said later, "I'm in a state of absolute shock. It's just amazing to see something like that. I'll remember it as long as I live.

"You could have stood there with 100 balls and tried to pitch them with your hand and you couldn't have done what he did. I've seen the man do things like this before but never in a major championship.

"And it wasn't just that shot on 17, either. He made some great putts on 10 and 11, and the one on 14, well, humans can three-putt from where he was."

Both Nicklaus and Watson said they enjoy these confrontations at the summit that they've had on a number of occasions.

"I can't imagine a better scenario than battling with Jack Nicklaus at Pebble Beach," said Watson. "When it got down to Jack Nicklaus and Tom Watson, I drew upon some old memories. They were fond memories because I won (specifically, he said, the British Open in which he played Nicklaus head-to-head in the final two rounds and shot 65-65 to Nicklaus' 65-66). In a small way, and maybe in a big way, they helped me to win today."

When Watson had holed a 20-footer for the birdie on 18 that iced his victory, one of the first people to greet him as he left the green was Nicklaus.

Laughing, Watson said later, "He shook hands with me and said, 'I'm gonna beat you, you little s.o.b.' Then he congratulated me and told me he was proud of me."

Nicklaus, 43, said, "I do enjoy these confrontations with Tom and I'd like to think there'll be a few more. I played a good championship, one that was certainly good enough to win except for one fellow."

Nicklaus' closing 69 was his 27th sub-par round and his 22nd sub-70 round in Open competition, both records. This was the fourth time he has been runnerup, equalling the record held by Sam Snead, Bobby Jones and Arnold Palmer.

For Watson, who earned $60,000 for the victory, it was a first but one that he said "makes me feel my career is one plateau higher."

No question about that.

December 7, 1982

A Love of the Land

Barron Connell is out of the hospital now, back at his home behind the fifth tee and seventh green at Larkhaven Golf Course. He likes the view. He has always loved the land, had a feel for it, particularly the eastern part of Mecklenburg county where his family roots are deep. He's farmed it and shaped it and looked after it.

In fact, just a few weeks ago, he went back to the place near Arlington Baptist Church where he and his buddies used to camp when they were kids, to a spot near the old swimming hole, and bought burial plots for his wife and himself. He already had plots in the city but he thought about it and decided he wanted to be buried out there where he's at home, where his friends and relatives are buried.

Connell thinks about those things now because he's 68 years old and the day before he was supposed to have surgery two weeks ago, the doctors performed a biopsy and decided the cancer was inoperable.

In a reflective mood recently, Connell looked back over the years before retirement and said, "I was just a shy country boy. I wasn't outstanding in any way."

That's not really how it was. Connell did something that would catch the fancy of anyone who admires an adventurous spirit. He went to the library and got an instruction book, cranked up his old red-bellied Ford tractor and built a golf course, Larkhaven, out along Camp Stewart Road.

You just don't do that, especially not that way. But he did.

Connell, a compositor for The Charlotte News for 20 years and later product manager for Carolina Linotype Co., had played golf maybe three times. He read that the owners of Carolina Golf Club were thinking of selling their course for industrial development or for conversion to a private club. He had this lovely piece of land he'd bought in 1943 for $47 an acre and had dairy farmed for several years, and it was sitting idle.

He checked the courses in nearby towns and learned that much of their play came from Charlotte. With the loss of Carolina as a public facility, Connell figured another course could succeed, even as far out as Camp Stewart Road.

And there was already a "clubhouse" there, the Connell home at the time, which was well over 100 years old.

Connell borrowed the instruction book and sought assistance from U.S. Golf Foundation consultants and he and teenaged son Butch set about building a course in 1957. Two years later, the first nine opened and in 1963, the second nine opened.

"We built 99 percent of it with that one tractor," recalls Butch Connell, 39, who would later win the conference high school golf championship playing for East Mecklenburg. "Sometimes Daddy and I would be out there until 9 or 10 o'clock at night. The next morning, he'd be back out there. I'd go to school, then come home and work some more.

"The neighborhood kids got 50 cents an hour for helping us. I got to eat at home.

"Because we didn't have the money or the equipment to do anything else, we laid the course out basically the way the farm was contoured, so we didn't have to move any more soil than was necessary. When we built the greens, we didn't use any of the modern methods and soil mixtures. Our greens were built of plain dirt. We've reworked them since and were the first public course in the area to have Tifton 328 grass and later bent grass."

Butch Connell says he thinks the big reason his father built a golf course went beyond money. "Our family's always kinda been in love with the land," he said. "Daddy had talked about building some fishing ponds on the property but I think he decided on a golf course partly because he was thinking of the beautification of the land. It was about half swamp before we built the course."

Although Barron Connell probably didn't realize it at the time, the idea of a man, his son and a tractor designing and building a golf course was preposterous. Golf courses are built with big money, designed by professional architects, fashioned by an army of dirt movers. It's an exact science and an expensive one.

Larkhaven is obviously not the product of any architect's or agronomist's genius. The touring pros could find a hundred things wrong with it. But it's a pleasant place to play. And it's a tribute to something fine in a man.

They say the cancer is such that Barron Connell may die of old age before it takes him but you never know about those things. Connell says it's okay. He's in better spirits than Butch has seen him in for several years.

"I feel good about the whole thing," said Connell. "Not a lot of people live to be 68 like I have."

And not a lot of people have the spirit, the vision, the determination or the stamina to build a golf course the way he did. He says he wasn't outstanding in any way, but that was outstanding.

September 19, 1983

Video Replay

When I get into my car, an alarm goes "bong, bong, bong" to remind me that I haven't fastened my seat belt. When I fly on a commercial airliner, a person checks a computer to tell me which seat to take once I'm on the plane. And the plane itself is capable of taking off, flying to its destination and landing, all on computer command, I'm told.

I know all about the addiction of youngsters to computer video games. At airports, terminal doors slide open automatically without being touched. You don't even need a gun to rob a bank anymore. The job is already being done by computer.

The computer age makes me uneasy. I've never won a serious argument with a zipper, much less an electronic gadget. But whenever I felt threatened, I could escape to the golf course.

Except for arranging starting times at large resorts, and, of course, the ringing of cash registers and the operation of golf carts, golf has been spared the onslaught of electronics.

Until now, that is. Any day now, thanks to Burington, Inc. of Elkhart, Ind., it's going to be possible to rent a Video Caddy, a videotape recorder attached to your golf cart that will film your shots during a round and allow you to see an instant replay on a 7 1/2-inch color screen right there in the cart. It's already available for purchase by anyone with $2,350.

I maintain it's the worst idea since the invention of the triple bogey.

It already takes about five hours to play a round on a busy day. With the introduction of the Video Caddy, we're talking about a move into prime time since rounds will probably last well into the evening hours.

I can see it now. Ol' Wally's going to focus his videotape recorder on his ball, get set to hit and think, "I wonder if my hair's combed."

While he's trying to hit, the other members of his foursome will be standing behind him, waving at the camera. You know they will. Television has demonstrated that there's not one in a thousand Americans who can resist waving at a live camera. If there's an ounce of ham in ol' Wally, which there is in most of us, sooner or later he's going to be standing there over a shot, a smile is going to creep across his face, and he's going to drop his club, start humming *Me and My Shadow* and go into a soft-shoe right there on the tee. Then one of his partners will barge in front of him and start doing Cagney or Bogart ("Play the front nine again, Sam") and then sing *My Way* with a big finish that can be heard all the way to the clubhouse. Keep in mind that the Video Caddy also records sound.

Wally will hit a shot that looks like a rat running an out pattern, and he'll race over to the cart to watch the replay. He'll say, "What was wrong with that swing?" and somebody in his group, looking over his shoulder at the screen, will say, "It looked like Phyllis Diller falling down the stairs. But you had good extension."

Think of what will happen when ol' Wally takes his wife, Gladys, out to play and brings along the video:

GLADYS: Now don't point the camera at my bad side.

WALLY: Which side is that?

GLADYS (she swings, hits a wormburner about 35 yards): What did I do wrong?

WALLY: You mean other than the fact that you wore high heels so your legs won't look pudgy? Well, let's look at the replay.

GLADYS: Oh, I didn't know you could get *General Hospital* on this thing.

WALLY: That ain't *General Hospital.* That's us arguing.

GLADYS: Oh, what's that? It looks like an EKG.

WALLY: That's your backswing. Now, you tape me hitting and we'll study my form. I'll show you how it's done and it'll be right there on tape for you to study, a truly classical swing in the mold of Johnny Miller hitting to the 18th at Oakmont.

WALLY (he swings and flushes a covey of quail): Now, how does that look on the screen?

GLADYS: I'd say it was more in the mold of Rick James getting down on *Super Freak.* No, actually, it looked more like a wreck scene on *CHiPs.*

WALLY: How'd you like to play the title role in a videotaped movie called *Murdered With a Pitching Wedge*?

GLADYS: Honey, you know you're not worth a darn with a pitching wedge. You think we could pick up *Days of Our Lives* on that thing?

September 14, 1984

Living Legend

Out on the rolling green velvet of Quail Hollow Country Club, there was the real thing. Famous names like Barber, Sifford, Bayer, Thomson, Goalby and Wall, some of whom have accounted for a chapter or two of golfing history, were battling in the opening round of the WBTV World Seniors Invitational golf tournament.

But one of the largest galleries was gathered around the practice putting green.

Arnie (it is redundant, isn't it, to use the last name, Palmer?) was playfully rolling 15-footers, trying to make three in a row. "Ok," he would say, "now I'm gonna make 'em all." He would make two and one of the onlookers would urge him to try it again. One woman told him he was standing in the wrong place.

He seemed to be enjoying it. No, he *was* enjoying it.

He was done for the day. He had opened with a one-under-par 71, not bad, not especially good. He could have been on his way to his home on the 15th fairway for some privacy, but that's not Palmer's way. He likes to hang around golf courses and putting greens and clubhouses. After all these years, he still loves it. He's in no hurry to get away. He doesn't need it anymore. He wants it.

When you probe the enduring fascination of Arnold Palmer, that might be one of the answers. The galleries sense that, from the moment he pulls into the parking lot until he leaves, he enjoys it. It's not just a day's work with him.

That is remarkable. Since he became our most revered sports idol back in the late 1950s, Palmer has had more people tugging at him than any other figure in athletics. The galleries want autographs, the press wants interviews, friends want conversation, his army of lieutenants wants a word with him about some deal that could add to the tens of millions that he – the corporation – reportedly earns each year.

He is almost never alone. Some who know him well say he doesn't like being alone. Perhaps it's just habit. When he had finished his press conference after his round Thursday, he headed off to get some lunch. Nobody left with him, no aide, no writer, no fan. He walked a few steps and looked back over his shoulder as if he were surprised that he was for that 100 yards alone.

And it was a peculiar sight.

Palmer took a week off last Christmas and he and his family went to Snowmass, Colo., to ski. It's the longest he can remember being away from the crush of people who want a signature, a conference, a glimpse, a smile. It's the only real vacation he has taken in years. Once many years ago, recalls Doc Griffin, his man Friday, Palmer spent four days on an island in the Bahamas. "He was miserable," said Griffin. "There were no telephones."

"I have my own little ways of getting away when I want to," said Palmer. "I can play golf at Latrobe (his club in Pennsylvania) and nobody galleries there. (Golf with his buddies, that's getting away for him.) It's just not something I really want to get away from."

It's difficult for him to walk 50 yards without being asked for an autograph. He may have signed more autographs than any man in history.

"That's good," he said, changing shoes in the clubhouse, getting ready to go off and talk another business deal. "I don't mind that. It's become a part of my life.

"I look for the people out there on the golf course. They keep me fired up to do the best I can. It's not something I take for granted. It still excites and pleases me. And I know a lot of them. They're my friends."

I watched Palmer play a few holes Thursday in part because I'm like everyone else, I like to watch him play, but also because I wanted to have another look at him out there to consider again what it is about him that has set him apart from the rest, that has made him our most captivating sports figure.

You could do a book on it, of course, but one thing that struck me again was that he just looks right. When Arnie stands up to a tee shot he looks right. He looks like a man who is going to knock the dimples off that ball and caution be darned. He looks like a man, in the truest sense of the word.

When he hits a poor shot he winces and the wince looks right. When he smiles at someone in the gallery, the smile looks right. It melts women and gives the men something to tell friends about at the office the next day.

He wins an occasional seniors tournament, but it has been 11 years since he won on the regular PGA Tour. But just last year Sears brought out a new line of clothing carrying his name. He regularly has to pass up lucrative offers because he doesn't have the time. Everyone still wants a piece of Arnie.

He still finds time to have a beer with the guys in the clubhouse, famed players in their own right but men who look on him with reverence and would fight for him if he needed them.

What is it about Arnie? Why is he still The King? He's just, well, he's just right.

April 14, 1986

A Grand Day for Nicklaus

For a good while now, we've been lamenting what we had lost in professional golf, the true glory of great players battling down the stretch for a grand prize, cheered wildly by people who cared deeply.

And then there was Sunday.

Jack Nicklaus won the Masters again.

They have played this queen of tournaments for 50 years now but never has there been one more golden than this.

Forty-six years old, without a major championship since 1980 or a victory of any kind since 1984 and in the process of being dismissed as a serious challenger, Nicklaus summoned some classical golf out of his scrapbook to make this perhaps the most glorious day the game has ever known.

It was certainly the greatest achievement in golf of the man generally recognized as the best who ever played.

Six shots behind with 10 holes to play, Nicklaus began a run that crumpled the will of most of his competitors, including the steely Seve Ballesteros, and reached far enough to withstand last-hole threats by Tom Kite and Greg Norman.

Nicklaus birdied the ninth, 10th and 11th holes, but still found himself three behind Ballesteros.

But Nicklaus, the Golden Bear, had tasted blood, which, on reflection, may have been lacking when his game was on the wane.

When Ballesteros scored an eagle-3 at the 13th, his second eagle in six holes, Nicklaus was still four shots behind. But then he eagled the par-5 15th himself and followed with a birdie – very nearly a hole-in-one – on the par-3 16th, which he described as the most exciting place in golf on Sunday afternoon with its huge gallery of fans clustered there in an amphitheater of azaleas and pines.

With the thunder of the crowd echoing in his ears, Ballesteros cracked at the 15th. Going for the green in two from a comfortably short distance, the Spaniard hit a dismal iron shot into the water in front of the green and bogeyed.

Though he left that green tied with Nicklaus, Ballesteros was finished, as his shockingly poor first putt and resulting three-putt bogey on the 17th hole attested.

Nicklaus played those last 10 holes seven under par, despite a bogey on the 12th hole, shooting 30 in the last nine and 65 for the day to win his sixth Masters.

What a day this was, for us and for Nicklaus, crammed with marvelous golf not only by him but appropriately by his competitors as well, and teeming with drama and giddy excitement every step of the way. He has now won 20 major championships, 18 of them as a professional, and 89 titles overall, but he said he had never heard cheers like those he heard Sunday.

"The sound walking from green to tee was actually deafening, unbelievable," he said.

Several times in those last few holes, he said, tears came to his eyes as he lived again the sweetness he had known so many times but so rarely in recent years, sweetness so many of us thought was lost forever.

"I get pretty emotional," said Nicklaus. "I sort of welled up four or five times coming in and I told myself, 'Hey, you've still got some golf left to play.' "

A friend had taped a newspaper story on the refrigerator of the house he was sharing with Nicklaus early in the week. It said he was through and people who are 46 don't win the Masters.

"All week, I kept thinking, done, through, washed up, huh?" said Nicklaus.

Sunday morning, one of his sons, Steve, phoned and asked, "What do you think it will take, Pops?"

Nicklaus told him 66 to tie, 65 to win.

Steve said, "That's the number I had in mind. Go do it."

Another of Nicklaus' sons, Jackie, caddied for him. He said Jackie kept telling him, "You'll get another birdie" and "Get one more" and, aware of one of his dad's putting problems, "Keep your head still."

When Nicklaus holed out on the last hole, he embraced Jackie and, when he finally got a moment, went and hugged his mother. She hadn't been to the Masters since 1959 and had said she'd like to come back one more time.

It was all so perfect, this grand day for Jack Nicklaus and for us.

As darkness fell over Augusta National Golf Club, Nicklaus mentioned the fast greens, tough pin placements and emotion and said, "This is a young man's golf course."

Sunday, he was young again. And so were we.

July 1, 1986

Pinehurst

I have been coming to Pinehurst for more than 30 years now, usually on business, occasionally to see how my feeble golf game will hold up against one or two of the area's splendid courses.

Despite my familiarly with this town that residents still prefer to call a village, I never set foot on these premises that I don't feel a spell cast over me.

Pinehurst grows and suffers the clutter of condominiums here and there. The annual spring and fall influx of golfing tourists, lured by an ever-increasing number of courses, escalates into the large thousands. But somehow Pinehurst manages to retain its charm.

You drive out of the throbbing cities and through the nondescript little towns and trail pickup trucks down highways past sprawling farms, and then suddenly you're in Pinehurst, a thousand miles away from where you just came.

Author John P. Marquand, one of its many famous residents over the years, wrote, "Pinehurst's greatest attribute is its friendliness and calm. Even on the most crowded days of the spring season, when individuals are struggling feverishly for starting time on the golf courses and when the hotels have run out of reservations, peace never wholly leaves Pinehurst. It never loses the spiritual lack of haste or the impression of leisure and repose and hospitality that its founder designed for it."

If there were a hall of fame for golfing resorts, Pinehurst would be one of the original inductees, and if there were a hall of fame for golf courses, Pinehurst's No. 2 would be one of the first to be honored.

I've tried to reason out what it is about this place that is so endearing. It's beautiful, of course, a Mona Lisa of fair land, and placid, and it embraces the game with a motherly hug.

But there's more to it than that.

There's a special feeling here, something spiritual. Ghosts walk here, some ghosts of the living, some ghosts of the dead. Some came to play golf, some to live, some simply to enjoy the salubrious air and the peace that lies over the place.

You walk the fairways of No. 2 and are aware that this is where Ben Hogan won his first professional championship. Legendary figures like Walter Hagen, Jim Barnes, Tommy Armour, Francis Quimet, Harry Vardon, Bobby Jones, Babe Zaharias, Patty Berg, Gene Sarazen, Bryon Nelson and Sam Snead have walked these same paths. Jack Nicklaus won here as an amateur. And on and on it goes.

It's a place that has been home or a vacation destination for people like John D. Rockefeller, John Phillip Sousa, Annie Oakley, J.P. Morgan, Will Rogers, Warren Harding, Al Smith, Gloria Swanson, Eddie Rickenbacker, Bette Davis and Gen. George C. Marshall.

And it's a place so rich with stories, you could fill a book with them – stories ideally recounted over an amber glass at, say, the tiny bar in the Pinehurst Inn in the heart of the village, a hall of fame saloon for golfers.

I'll tell you one, found in the March 30, 1922, issue of the *Pinehurst Outlook* newspaper.

P.G. Wardell and a friend were playing at Pinehurst against two Detroit clubmates, and there were high wagers on the match.

But Wardell's caddy was driving him mad. The caddy dropped the bag of clubs just as Wardell was putting, dropped clubs on Wardell's feet when he lifted them from the bag, stepped on Wardell's ball in a sand trap and generally behaved in such a way that Wardell felt compelled to dismiss him at the 11th hole.

Wardell's friends had played a trick on him. When the caddy removed his wig, Wardell recognized him.

The caddy was Edgar Guest, whose homespun poems were syndicated nationwide a half-century ago.

And then there's the one about...

August, 1986

The Boys at Eastwood

When a hot air balloon landed on the 18th fairway at Eastwood Golf Course recently, regulars who have played there over the years gave it only passing notice. Not much that happens at Eastwood surprises them anymore. They probably figured it was just another guy trying to win a bet, maybe laying even money he could get down in two from 1,000 feet up.

When you've seen a golfer playing from the clubhouse roof, another throwing the ball around the course with a basket-like container called a cesta that is used by jai alai players, another hitting his shots while standing in a golf cart and a professional wrestler playing the course wearing his mask, you tend to shrug at a balloon landing on the fairway.

There is an Eastwood Golf Course in every city and town of any size. They just have different names. If you've ever bought a sleeve of X-out balls, played in sneakers, Hawaiian-print shorts, black dress socks and no shirt, or lied about your handicap, chances are you've played an Eastwood. If you've ever eaten pool hall chili, parked your delivery truck behind the clubhouse where your boss couldn't spot it from the road or hit a wayward shot into the bay of a service station, chances are you've played an Eastwood.

Eastwoods are not country clubs. They are public courses with a special come-on-in, have-a-beer clubbiness of their own; places where much of the clientele becomes a part of the fixtures; places where if you can't make a game you lack imagination.

Eastwoods have a never-changing odor, a blend of steaming hot dogs, cigarette smoke and beer; an aroma that is as pleasant to the regulars as a Thanksgiving kitchen.

This particular Eastwood is hunkered on 124 acres in northeast Charlotte, so close in you can leave work downtown on the pretense of going to the doctor and be on the tee in, oh, 20 minutes. If it weren't for the Gulf station behind the 10th green, you could say it sits at the intersection of The Plaza and Eastway Drive. When you're hitting your tee shot on the 11th hole, you must contend with the bustle of traffic along The Plaza some 10 yards away and in the shopping center across the street. Away from that corner, though, it's a pretty little 18-hole course; short, relatively flat and in remarkably good condition for the amount of play it gets.

The clubhouse is a one-story concrete block structure that looks as if it could have been the first motel ever built. It's painted white, with a ground-level porch that is little more than a concrete walkway covered by a roof supported by wooden posts.

It has a locker room, but the lockers sit in dimly-lighted disarray, some along the walls, some in the middle of the bare floor facing in various directions. Only about half a dozen are used.

Augusta National it ain't.

The regulars sit in the grill room, which accommodates several vinyl-topped tables. They arrive early and sit drinking coffee or if they work the night shift – or even if they don't – beer. It's not unusual to see several empty cans cluttering a table by 9 a.m.

Some sit there for hours on end. Willie Worrell, who presides over the place as manager and pro with a megaphone voice and a crusty good humor, calls the sitters "heatsuckers" or "airsuckers," depending upon the season. If it's winter, he'll bellow at them to "quit suckin' up my heat, get out there and play." In summer he'll bleat at them about sucking up his air conditioning when they ought to be paying their fees and playing golf.

It is in the grill room where the games are made. Everyone, of course, is looking for an edge. This fomented "The Great Vaseline War," which caused Worrell to chew more vigorously than usual on whatever imaginary thing he chews. (We pause here to point out that the real names of some of the players will not be used, to protect the guilty; we will substitute nicknames.)

A fellow called Slick played for who-knows-how-long, and at what profit, surreptitiously applying Vaseline to the faces of his clubs. This reduced friction and allowed him to hit the ball straighter and with more distance.

The others eventually found him out, but his life was spared. Rather than feed him a jar or two, they simply began using it themselves. But it got to be a bother, dipping into the jar and smearing the stuff on their clubs and then cleaning their hands. They solved that by putting globs of Vaseline on the sides of their carts, and just wiping the clubs across the glob when they needed a fix.

Worrell finally had to have a sign painted and put up in the clubhouse decreeing that no more Vaseline be put on the carts because other customers were complaining that it was getting on their clothing and some were demanding that Worrell pay their dry-cleaning bills.

This wasn't the biggest problem management had encountered, however. "The Midnight Axman" was the biggest.

The fifth hole is a par 4 with a slight dogleg to the right out about where a good tee shot comes to earth. At one time, long hitters could carry the corner of the trees and drive the green. Try as he might, and he always tried, Bush Hog could not quite carry the trees with his tee ball. He could get a running start, jump three feet off the ground and swing like a turbine blade and still he would find himself in the thicket.

One night, he went out and, using either a hatchet or an ax, chopped down four small hickory trees – leaving a clearing about 15 feet wide and high enough that he could hit a wedge through it. Jack Horton, who managed the club at the time, figured it took the man at least an hour to do the work.

The felled trees were found a little way back in the woods. The limbs had been trimmed and the area tidied up. "Whoever it was didn't want the wood," opines Horton.

Horton and everyone else knew who did it, but couldn't pin it on the night stalker. Besides, they understood. He just did something all of them have wanted to do from time to time. Bush Hog just bought himself more trouble, though. Horton planted six good-sized cedars in the opening and built a long sand bunker beyond them.

A few of the Eastwood crowd have been superior players. One, who shall be called Noel, has played for large sums of money around the country, sometimes against famous players, and earned the reputation at one time of being the best money player in the land. Indeed, when the late Titanic Thompson, probably the most famous golf gambler ever, came to Eastwood several years ago to add to his bankroll, he was so impressed with Noel that he took him to distant places to play well-heeled suckers.

As you might imagine, then, Eastwood regulars have not been climbing over the tables begging Noel for a bet. He's had a hard time getting a game and this has led to some rather bizarre events, some of them having to do with golf.

Once, during a discussion of gambling nerve in the grill room, Noel blustered that he would have his head shaved for $100. Eyes met eyes, heads nodded and the money fell on the table. Noel, never one to welsh, went across the street to a barber and had his head transformed into a cueball.

Noel has done all that can be asked of a man to get a bet, and more. He has thrown his tee shots with a cesta, like any common jai alai player. He has played the best ball of six others, winning one side and losing the other. He has played two men, he from the back tees and they from the ladies' tees; he let them play captain's choice, allowing them to tee up anywhere, including in bunkers. He has played every shot in a round other than those close to the green with a paper cup over his ball.

One fellow, Lefty, lost to Noel every time they played, no matter how weird the bet. "Play me again," Noel told him, "and I'll use your clubs." Lefty was left-handed. Noel had never played left-handed, just hit a few balls that way.

"Okay," said Lefty, "but if you beat me left-handed with my own clubs, I'll never play golf again."

He never played again.

Noel didn't always win. He lost the front side to two men one day, spotting them the ladies' tees, and they refused to go out for another nine. They were blue from the cold. The temperature was in the high 20s and the wind was wailing. They'd had enough. Noel hadn't. He offered to play in a bathing suit if they would try him again. As much as they wanted to see that, they declined and sat in the grill room sucking up Willie Worrell's heat.

Another of the better players, Cool, who later left town when he was charged with drilling holes in air conditioners (the better to sell homeowners new ones), became legend one day.

Cool bet he could hit three balls off the clubhouse roof and make a par 3 on the 10th hole with at least one of the balls. The green lies about 200 yards from the rooftop.

He made two pars.

They've played Eastwood hitting all but the short shots while standing in a golf cart. They've played it with nothing but a putter. They've played it by throwing a ball all the way around. They've played from the first tee to the 14th green and then back to the 10th. They've done that a lot. Noel once negotiated the perils from the first tee to the bottom of the cup on the 14th, a distance of about 1,000 yards with trees and ponds along the way, in five strokes.

Clayton Heafner, for whom the annual Eastwood tournament is named, owned the course for many years before his death in 1960. He had twice been runnerup in the U.S. Open and twice played on the U.S. Ryder Cup team. His sons, Vance – now a PGA Tour player – and Mike, and his daughter Donna now own it. Both Vance and Mike have won the tournament named in honor of their father.

This competition can be a severe test of a man's nerves at times. Such as the Sunday when Bob Bryant had a 10-foot putt on the final hole to win it. The big crowd following him didn't bother to stand off to the side of the green. A number of them walked out onto the green, encircled him and his putt and loudly placed bets as to whether or not he could make it. Now, that's pressure. But he made it.

Heafner ruled Eastwood with a mailed fist. He had a temper that could keep a 2-iron from talking back. "Clayton had a temper they wrote about," says Horton. "He'd cuss out the President of the United States as soon as he would a caddy."

Heafner wouldn't put sand in the traps because he figured when someone hit a shot from one of them, 25 cents worth of sand flew out.

He was tough, but he also had a soft heart. He staged a pro-am once and when three amateurs wound up without a pro for a partner, it upset him. He was having health problems near the end of his life, one of which required him to wear a spring-like mechanism to make the front of his foot lift when he walked. He hadn't played golf in months, maybe years, but he said, "Get me a cart and I'll play with them."

He duck-hooked his first tee shot behind an equipment shed but shot 66 and won the tournament.

Maybe you know Eastwood. Not this one, perhaps, but an Eastwood in your town. A place where you can get the latest line on the ball games. A place where you can drink beer in the morning and not feel uncomfortable about it. A place where you can take off your shirt and beat the ball around for 18 holes and maybe never lose one of your X-outs. A place where they'll ice down some beer in a plastic bag for you to take onto the course.

A place where the carts look like they were at Tobruk, and have a little Vaseline on them. A place where you can sit around and "suck" some heat or air conditioning and argue about who plays whom and how many ups you get and talk loud and tell lies and laugh.

A place where you can have a good time. Plain and simple. A damn good time.

January, 1987

The Greatest Match Ever Played

It began, as so many golf matches do, in the amber glow of cocktail party conversation. Of course, most contracts struck at times like that have all too often produced regrettable mismatches. What grew out of this evening in 1956, however, was a classic battle between Ben Hogan and Byron Nelson, both barely edging past their primes, and the best amateurs of their day – perhaps the best players – Ken Venturi and Harvie Ward. It was the finest golf match ever played.

That's a tall claim, considering that the game has been played for centuries and that history does not record its "friendlies." But consider also this: Four players of such rich talents played a course with the strength and beauty of Cypress Point and among them produced 27 birdies and an eagle.

Rise up ghosts, if you will, and top that.

Because we must rely on the memories of the competitors for details, the exact margin of victory is unclear. Nelson believes his twosome won 3 and 2. Venturi says his side lost only 1 down. Hogan and Ward remember the confrontation but few of the particulars.

"I remember playing the match and how excited Ken and I were to be playing Hogan and Nelson," recalls Ward. "I know we played some fantastic golf that day, all of us, but I don't remember much else about it."

An inquiry to Hogan brought this response: "I have tried to reconstruct this in my mind but have found that as one gets older the memories get dimmer, especially details of something which happened almost 30 years ago. I feel sure you can rely on the information given you by the others. Please understand."

The accounts given by Nelson and Venturi vary slightly and neither can recall how some of the holes were played, but what they recount provides us with enough information to satisfactorily reconstruct the event.

Let's set the stage.

Hogan and Nelson were both in their early 40s. Ward had just turned 30, Venturi was 25. Though Hogan and Nelson, both Hall of Fame players, were edging past their prime at the time, they were still among the best players on earth.

Hogan had won 62 tournaments on the United States Tour. At one stage of his career, he had not finished outside the top 10 in 14 years in either the Masters or U.S. Open and in 18 of those 28 tournaments he had finished no lower than fourth. He had won four U.S. Opens, two Masters, two PGA Championships and one British Open and, as evidence that he still had a firm grip on his game, had been runner-up in the 1955 Masters and U.S. Open and would be runner-up in the 1956 U.S. Open.

Nelson had to his credit two Masters, two PGA Championships

and one U.S. Open title, as well as the most remarkable two years in recorded golfing history. In 1944, he won 13 of the 23 tournaments he entered and in 1945 won 18 of 31, including 11 in a row. In 1947, he had virtually withdrawn from competitive golf but, proving he was still a player to be reckoned with, he returned to win the French Open in 1955.

In those days, amateurs did not race out of college and onto the pro tour as they do today. Venturi and Ward had finished with school and were employed by a San Francisco auto dealer, Ed Lowery.

Several weeks after the match, Venturi, who had played on the 1953 U.S. Walker Cup team, would threaten to become the only amateur to win The Masters, finishing as runner-up after leading by four strokes with one round to play. He would turn pro later that year and eventually win 14 tour events, including the 1964 U.S. Open, before physical problems drove him off the tour.

Ward, though an amateur, was widely regarded in the 1950s as one of the finest players in the world, with a game that one writer described as "flawless expression." He won the British Amateur in 1952 and was runner-up in '53; won the U.S. Amateur in '55 and again in '56; was a three-time Walker Cupper and finished fourth in The Masters in '57.

Here, in Nelson's words, is how the match came about:

"Ben and I were in California to play in the Bing Crosby Pro-Am. George Coleman, a wealthy businessman from Oklahoma, had a home in back of the lodge at Pebble Beach. He had a cocktail party one night before the tournament and invited my wife, Louise, and me and Ben and his wife, Valerie. As usual, Ben and Valerie didn't go.

"Kenny and Harvie had just gotten through playing for the San Francisco city championship and Kenny had beaten Harvie.

"Before dinner that night, George and Eddie Lowery got to talking. George always liked to kinda kid Ed about Kenny. George asked Ed if he'd thought Kenny would beat Harvie.

"Ed said, yes, he had bet on Kenny. His next remark was, 'Those two kids could beat anybody in the world.'

"George said, 'Think so?'

"Ed said, 'Yeah.'

"George said, 'Pros included?'

"Ed said, 'Yes, anybody.' And he wasn't drunk, by the way.

"George said, 'How much would you bet?'

"Ed said, 'How about $5,000.'

"George said, 'All right, I'll take it.'

"The next question to George was, 'Who are your players going to be?

"George said, 'I'm gonna take Nelson and Hogan.'

"Ed kinda gulped but he said, 'Well, okay, I'll still take it.'

"I said, 'George, you'll have to call Ben. I don't know if he'll play.' Ben was a friend of George's and said he would play, but he wanted George to make a starting time at Pebble Beach to throw people off because he didn't want a lot of people around. When we teed off, there was hardly anybody watching but word got around and before we were through, we had a bigger gallery than the tournament had."

By the time the match began, Lowery and Coleman had time to think over the bet they had made "after they had had a couple of belts that night," and reduced the ante to $50. The players didn't bet a dime, just pride.

"We didn't challenge them," said Venturi. "We just wanted to play with them together." He recalls that the mood was "light" as the pros and amateurs swapped blows.

But there was magic in the air that day.

While early holes are lost in the mist of time, both Nelson and Venturi recall that at the end of 10 holes, Venturi and Ward were nine under par – and one down. Hogan had holed a 60- to 70-yard wedge shot in the 491-yard 10th for an eagle three.

"There was not a missed shot in the whole round," said Nelson. "It seemed like we were tying every hole with birdies."

He wasn't far wrong. Only three holes, the first, eleventh and fourteenth, were halved in par.

Nelson believes the match was closed out at the famous wind-swept par-three 16th, which plays 233 yards over the Pacific Ocean. He chose a driver and almost sank his tee shot. He finished 10 to 12 feet past the cup and holed the putt for birdie. But he remembers that the four played out the round.

As Venturi recalls it, "We halved every hole from the 10th and were one down going to 15. Ben and I birdied the 15th with twos. Harvie and Byron halved the 16th with twos, and then they halved the 17th with (birdie) threes.

"On the 18th, I had a birdie putt of about 12 feet, straight uphill, and I made it. Ben had a birdie putt of about 10 feet, with a right to left break, to win the match.

"Byron said, 'Come on, Ben, knock it in.'

"And Ben said, 'Don't worry, I'm not going to be tied by a couple of amateurs.' He knocked it right in."

With all the birdies and the eagle, the foursome suffered only one bogey. Hogan shot 63, nine under par. Venturi shot 65. Nelson and Ward had 67s. The best ball of the four was 16 under par on a golf course that ranks among the most challenging in the world.

"It was the best golf I've ever seen," said Venturi. "And that's the only team who ever beat Harvie and me. We would have challenged the world. Come to think of it, that was about what we did."

May 19, 1988

God Help Us

The day dawned cloudy and threatening, but shortly before some 50 Charlotte-area ministers were scheduled to tee off, the sun came out.

How do they do that?

Seeing this, I thought about asking one of them to say a word of prayer over my putter, the blackest of sinners, before we set off in the Hankins and Whittington Funeral Service Clergy Golf Outing. (I was a guest soul.) But I figured God had his hands full answering the silent prayers of his 50 chosen. Still, it couldn't hurt hanging around with preachers. A little divine intervention might rub off. You never know.

I picked up some tees in the golf shop and remarked to the attendant, "Guess I'll have to watch my language today."

A minister standing at the counter said, "I curse."

I told him one of the other ministers had said, "We don't curse on the golf course when we miss a shot, but where we spit, grass will never grow again."

"Yes, I've heard that," he said. "But I curse."

Now there was an honest preacher.

I curse, too, but I was determined that not one epithet would cross these lips on this day, and I did pretty well. I got all the way to the third hole before firing off my first "dammit." Luckily, my companions, walking the straighter path, were out of earshot, in the fairway.

One of the ministers, Ron Downs of the Southland Christian Church, hit an iron shot into the water. Grady Faulk, an old football player and now pastor at Stough Memorial Baptist, noted the immersion and said, "You made a Baptist out of that one."

"That water will put the fear of the Lord in you," said Thurman Stone of Calvary Church, and he didn't even smile when he said it.

Faulk and I, sharing a cart, were rapidly being brought to our knees by the golf course, playing what he called "Catholic golf – a-cross here, a-cross there."

"Let's start playing some golf," he said, and I agreed. Faulk then told our companions that we had "made a covenant."

We cleaved to our covenant for a few holes. During that stretch, one of my "oh, hell" shots was heading out of bounds when I beseeched it to return to the fold, promising that all was forgiven. Damned...uh, darned if it didn't hit a tree and bounce back into the fairway.

"Either a monkey threw it out, or the Lord had mercy on you," Faulk philosophized. I suspect it was a monkey. Not even God can reason with a hook.

Brother Faulk said he had played golf only about four times in the past several months but added, "I'm going to repent and start playing a little more."

Preachers talk like that. They are shameless.

Preacher joke:

A philanthropist staged a golf tournament for men of the cloth and promised to donate $50,000 to the church or synagogue of the winner's choice. A Catholic priest phoned the Pope, explained how much his church needed the money and asked if Lee Trevino could be ordained just long enough to play in the tournament.

"By all means," said the Pope, "ordain him."

The tournament was played and that evening, the Pope phoned and asked, "Well, how did Father Trevino play?"

"Very well," said the priest. "He shot a 68."

"Wonderful," said the Pope. "When do you get the money?"

"I'm afraid that's the bad news," replied the priest. "We don't. The Jewish synagogue won the money. Rabbi Nicklaus shot a 66."

Play in the ministers tournament was slow, ample evidence that the shepherd had been tending their flocks, slow enough to, well, make a preacher cuss. As we came to the end our travail, Faulk, a wry smile on his face, intoned, "I have fought the good fight, I have finished the course. Epistle of Paul the Apostle to Timothy."

I said, "The Lord will get you for that."

As I prepared to leave, I noticed that my car had a flat tire. The ministers had all gathered in the clubhouse for a little fellowship and repast. No one was around to hear all those oaths I had saved up.

Thank God.

Boxing

June 14, 1983

The Face of a Fighter

The face in the crowd was unmistakable. Overhanging brows laced with scars, broad nose, pouty lips, defiant chin. The classical face of a fighter. Waban Thomas's face.

Come on out to the house sometime, Thomas said, and we'll talk.

It's a big white house with a garage, a barn, a pickup truck, a fish pond, a stand of trees and plenty of room for Thomas to grow his garden. It's a friendly, warm kind of place as befits this big warrior who has known so much violence but has put it all behind him and is as gentle and caring a man as you'd ever want to meet. He lives in semi-retirement with his wife, Doris, and their daughter, Dawn.

He's 55 now, gray at the temples, too heavy around the middle. He retired from his job as a dock loader at a motor line and now works a couple of days a week as a security guard. "I'd go back to work steady if I could find a good-paying job," he said. "I'm strong, I can lift heavy stuff and I work fast."

What he would really like to do, he says, is move back to his birthplace, Calabash, and work in the seafood business with his brothers and sisters and other relatives there. He goes there lots of weekends. It's where he got his name. Waban was the name of the tugboat his father captained when the son was born. Hence the nickname "Tugboat."

Waban Thomas was one of the most exciting and successful fighters Charlotte ever had. Not the most stylish. Exciting. He could take a punch that could knock down an apartment building and keep coming in. He wasn't stylish but nobody had more heart.

He would take five punches to land one. He fought in a crouch, stalking, always stalking, absorbing the blows on that craggy face and his thick, hairy body to get within range to throw one of his devastating punches.

Defense was not one of his strong suits. Durability was. And punching power. As best he can figure, he fought 239 times, 42 to 45 of those as a pro, and lost a total of only 24, four times winning the Carolinas Golden Gloves heavyweight championship. In those 239 fights, he took blows round after round that would have floored a bull.

"I didn't pay much attention to it," he says now, sitting in front of a fire in his den. "I always just said, 'Let's get the show on the road.' If a man got into the ring with me, he had to fight."

There is no hint that the punishment of the '50s and '60s – and one bizarre interlude in the '70s – has harmed Thomas.

"I feel good," he said, playfully throwing short hooks with his left and right from his easy chair. "I feel ready to go. If I had it to do over, I'd be a fighter. Yeah, boy, I loved it."

Thomas's career was a series of fights with guys wearing street socks and wrinkled bathing trunks in Spartanburg or Camp Lejeune or Raleigh, when he had to get up the next morning and go to work on the loading docks at the trucking company. But it was laced with enough glamor that he can sit now and enjoy his memories and the sweet lament of the opportunity that just barely danced away.

He fought Bob Baker, a big name, in the rain at Memorial Stadium in Charlotte and lost a good fight.

He fought Charlie Norkus at Camp Lejeune, broke his right arm on Norkus's head in the seventh round but finished the 10-rounder and lost a split decision.

"If I had won that one," he says now, "I would've gotten a title shot. I never got the big chance. Something always went wrong."

In February, 1967, Thomas, faded at 36 and weighing 205, was called to fight a 22-year-old hotshot named Buster Mathis, who weighed 234, in Houston. Thomas had four days to get ready. He lost in the first round, hitting the canvas four times before the fight was stopped. That ended his career.

Until 1977.

Thomas and Neil Wallace had fought the most memorable fight in Charlotte ring history in 1957, Thomas winning in the eighth round by TKO. In a return bout in 1967, Thomas had won again over the man he says today is the best he ever fought.

In 1977, 10 years after Thomas's last fight and 20 after Wallace's, they fought again. Thomas was 47, Wallace 51. It was vulgar, obscene, in a way, but in another, it was oddly beautiful, two old fighters who had never lost that instinct, battling like aging lions, relentlessly fighting each other and the years in a fascinating brotherhood bathed in blood.

They went eight rounds before it was stopped. Wallace won. Both came out gruesomely battered and splattered with crimson.

"Waban was the anvil to Wallace's hammer," quoth Snooks Howard, poet, philosopher, dog trainer and ex-pug. "Waban was the personification of the fighter as a gladiator."

And Waban Thomas says, "Maybe I'm prejudiced, but I don't think fighters are as tough as they used to be."

May 20, 1975

For Whom the Bell Tolled

The big man moved across the newsroom and, though it had been a long time since one of them had come by, you knew this was an ex-athlete looking for a handout. You can tell. There is something about their structure and manner, something about the way they move. And the shabby clothes. And the head hanging a bit to hide the embarrassment.

This one was especially worn. His clothing was threadbare, torn in places.

He was a handsome man, though the face bore the burden of the years now, with furrows washed in it by trouble and time. He looked like a sad country song.

He introduced himself but the name didn't ring a bell. Said he was an ex-fighter. He needed 45 cents to catch the bus home, he said. If I could spare it, he'd try to pay it back. I gave him some money and he thanked me, started to say something else – maybe to recall a fight he had won in a lifetime of losing – but turned and walked out.

When he was gone, I wished I had given him more and had asked him to sit and talk awhile.

There is something about prizefighters. Tragedy in one form or another stalks them. It's often trouble with the law or liquor or women. They don't turn loose of their past as easily as other athletes. They dream of comebacks from oblivion and revel in lost nights of glory. Their sport has withered. They are living ghosts.

The Charlotte colony of ex-pugs and managers and trainers and hangers-on has thinned, unreplenished since the pro sport died in the city many years ago.

They were an odd and colorful lot.

There was the welterweight who liked to use the telephone. To call strange women. That affinity earned him a prison term. When he got out, he drifted out west, changed his name, billed himself as a longshoreman and got some pretty good fights. He got one with Gaspar Ortega in Tucson. Ortega was the champ but he lost the first two rounds to our guy before putting him down in the third. The papers in Tucson said it was a game performance by the "longshoreman."

He drifted back here and telephoned me. He was very handy with a phone. He wouldn't identify himself. He was bad about that. He said he wanted to book himself a match here, wear a mask and fight under an assumed name like "The Masked Marvel" or something.

The reason he wanted to hide his identity, it turned out, was that he had felt the crowd's contempt when he lost his stomach and wouldn't finish his man when he had him hanging on the ropes in a bout a few years earlier. He felt he had to make restitution for that but said nobody would come to see him fight if they knew who he was.

The bout never came off and he got into trouble with telephones again.

There was a big ol' lovable heavyweight, a terrific puncher and a popular pug in his time, who fell in with some people who were running guns.

He maintained he didn't even know of his involvement, and maybe he didn't. He finally worked himself free of the trouble.

And there was the old turkey-necked manager they called Honest Jawn. He lost his mind and did some crazy things but until he died, he still loved to sit in a rocking chair near the ring at the old Sportsmen's Club Gym and watch the young hopefuls work out.

One of the occasional performers in the old, smoky rings here has gone down on one of an assortment of offenses and wound up in the penitentiary. Another was nailed on a truck heist charge.

Not all have been in trouble with the law, of course. Waban Thomas, perhaps the most popular and successful heavyweight to come out of Charlotte, has finally tucked away his dreams of yet another in a long series of comebacks and is leading a quiet, normal life, working on the loading dock of a freight line.

And the last time I heard from Joe (Golden Boy) Lassiter, the classiest boxer we had, he was running a pool room.

But they never forget the ring, once they've known it. They cling to those moments when the only light in the place was shining on them. They talk of what might have been, of big money bouts in Miami or New York that they had been promised but never got, of how they might have won the title with a break or two.

Bartender, bring us another beer...

December 15, 1977

Return Match

It was anything but a classic and yet it will be remembered for a long time by the 1,520 people who came through the fog and mist to the coliseum last night to see Waban (Tugboat) Thomas and Neal Wallace fight again. It had been 20 years since they had met in what is generally remembered as the greatest fight ever staged in this city.

Thomas is 49 years old and Wallace is 51, as well as could be determined. Wallace hadn't fought in 20 years, Thomas in 10. It didn't figure to go more than two or three rounds but it went eight before the ring physician looked at Thomas' pulverized face and stopped it, awarding the TKO to Wallace, who had lost both the "greatest fight" and the return bout in 1967.

They had lost most of what they had when they were in their prime but neither had lost the fighter's instinct, whatever it is that makes a man keep standing and moving in on weary legs and slugging through the thudding blows and the screaming pain. In that respect, it was every bit the fight the first one had been so very long ago.

Though they were looking into each other's face and seeing the eyes swell and the blood flow so freely that Thomas' trunks and referee George Diehl's shirt and Wallace's body were smeared with crimson, they kept boring in, their gloves landing with sickening thuds, hoping the other would go down and end the savage spectacle.

Later, in his dressing room, filled with well-wishers who had come to hug him and tell him what a great fight it was, Wallace said, "We remind me of game chickens. They fight to the death but they love it. Being human beings, we have more compassion, more feeling. I'm sure Waban loves me the way I love him. But I know Waban's tough like I am and I know he can take it like I can, so I didn't feel any urge to quit hitting him. I was looking to knock him out."

Thomas said he had not lost any of his old fighting instinct, either. "I felt the same as I used to," he said, "but I couldn't throw my punches. I wanted to keep going when they stopped it. But ever since I started training, I'd had trouble with my arms. I trained too hard at the start and my arms started troubling me. My arms went down and I could never get the strength back in them again. I saw a doctor every day and took therapy but it didn't help. Maybe if I'd gotten a postponement, I'd have gotten my old power back again but they had everything set to go tonight so I figured I'd go ahead and fight."

Their legs appeared to be in good shape for men of their age but their bodies and faces showed the years.

Long, intensive training had not taken the sag out of Wallace's chest. Thomas, always bulky, was very heavy around the waist and the thick coat of hair on his chest and shoulders and back had turned grey.

Everything – their punches, their bobs and weaves, their flat-footed steps – had slowed with the years and as the rounds wore on, the weariness of this young man's game showed in their slumping shoulders and their faces.

Their faces ... the very sight of them made you wince every time another blow landed and for all the admiration you felt for these two old warriors looking for their lost glory, you kept hoping one of them, either of them, would fall and it would be over. You knew they didn't belong in the ring and yet there was a spell-binding fascination to this weird spectacle.

Thomas' face, which looks like a clenched fist with its overhanging brows that have been lacerated by leather a hundred times or more and its broad nose and pouting lips, began to bleed almost from the start. First there was a cut on his left cheek, then a cut over his right eye. Then Wallace began to bleed from his left nostril.

As they fought on, Thomas, employing his old familiar style of crouching and lunging with his long punches without regard for blows that rained on him, bled more profusely. When it was over, his face was a horrible mess. Blood seeped from his nose and the corner of his mouth. The bleeding from his eyebrows had been stanched but both eyes were puffy. Everywhere you looked on his face and even around his neck and shoulders, there were ugly red splotches where veins had burst and the blood had risen to the skin. He looked like he had walked into a propeller.

Wallace did not look a great deal better, though he had made more of an effort to avoid being hit than had the ever-advancing Thomas. Wallace's eyes were puffed. There was a big lump under the right one and the left was surrounded by broken veins.

Wallace was cheerful, smiling, talking about fighting again. Thomas was somewhat more subdued but he summoned up a half-smile and said, "It was Neal's time to win. You can't win 'em all."

He said this would be his last fight. "Neal ought to quit, too," he said. "If he keeps fighting, he's gonna get hurt."

Wallace was right. It was like watching game roosters fight to the death. You knew what you were watching was wrong, that these two aging men searching for something from their youth in the thud of their gloves and the flow of their blood should not be doing this. You wanted to turn away but you couldn't. There was a pathetic glory to it that will linger in our memories. And maybe, with it all, it was worth it for in that blood-spattered ring, these two old warriors had halted for a few moments the hateful encroachment of age for all of us.

February 27, 1979

The Tomorrow Man

This is about Burgess (Snooks) Howard. He probably won't like it.

He doesn't like most newspaper writers. He has what he calls a "cold contempt" for most of them because they "write a good lead paragraph, then quit trying."

Howard is a writer himself, largely unpublished. He is gifted, but the world has not yet accepted him as one of our great talents, which is a source of bafflement and frustration to him.

He has worked for "about 14" newspapers on general assignment and sports but that was a long time ago, shortly after he quit boxing.

Now he writes novels, two so far, and poetry and country and western lyrics by the hundreds.

"Pick a word out of the dictionary," says Howard, "and I've written at least a few paragraphs about it."

He writes at night. During the day, he is the self-professed "best dog trainer in the world," ("I can train a dog to use a commode, then flush it; to sing *Dixie* or walk a narrow plank.")

He also admits to being the world's greatest newspaper photographer, the world's greatest teacher of boxing and the most perfect Leo who ever walked, among other things, adding with a shrug, "If you don't believe me, try me."

Howard had kind of slipped out of earshot for several years while he plied various trades around the country. He surfaced in Charlotte again awhile back. And now the mere mention of his name fetches up memories.

Howard is a relic but a well-preserved one at 54, with a powerful build and a face that has stood up well under the wash of the years and the thump of fists. ("I've had probably 80 street fights since I was 16 years old," he mentions, for no apparent reason, "and I've lost only two.")

He is a delightful relic of our fistic past, a Runyonesque character lingering from the 1940s and '50s when boxing was a staple of our sports fare, when you could find a fascinating soul with a bent nose on every street corner.

When the sweet science was populated with guys like Honest Jawn Allen, the trainer who always had "the next champeen"; Doc DeNeaux, who operated better outside the ring than in it; Golden Boy Joe Lassiter, the classiest of them all, who died early, running a ratty poolroom; Tugboat Waban Thomas, who moved like his nickname but never backward; Neil Wallace, a big ol' warmhearted bear of a guy who let himself get messed up on a gun-running rap; D.C. Smith, a one-legged trainer; Early Hamilton, who was taught to box by a nun in an orphanage...

Snooks Howard belonged to this colorful era and contributed a chapter to it. He was an early-day, white Ali, posturing, predicting, singing his own praises, particularly with regard to his body and "one of the best left hooks in the world."

His style was cramped somewhat by frequent defeat, which today he estimates came about half the time in his 131 pro fights.

Howard blames his lack of conditioning for many of his defeats. "I always got tired in the fourth round," he said. "I wouldn't train for God."

Boxing ceased to be a major part of Howard's life in 1953 and he since has had little use for his skills and his well-turned muscles except those times when he worked as a collector for a loan company and as a bouncer at P.J. Clarke's famous watering hole in New York or when someone thought to preserve the virtue of womanhood about the time Snooks was making his move.

Along the way, he has tried a lot – steelworker, short order cook, bellhop, truck driver, newspaperman, photographer, public relations, bartender, TV salesman, waiter, busboy, men's clothing salesman, women's shoe salesman, night watchman, drummer and unpublished novelist, among other things.

He has written a 160,000-word novel about a public relations man who is a former fighter but the novel has met with repeated rejection. Howard says it's because of ethnic remarks in the manuscript, inter-office politics and, in three cases, women editors over 40 who resented the fact that his hero is over 40 but keeping company with a younger woman.

"I've done most everything and people have told me I'm a genius at some of it," says Howard. "But this is not the last stop, baby. There is no last stop until they put you in the ground.

"There are still things I want to do – train dog trainers, hunt for pirates' gold, run a discotheque, be a motorcycle mechanic (he rides one), hang glide, see another Hawaiian sunset, and, yeah, I wanta write me another book.

"I was born in 1924, but I ain't 54. I have few regrets. Let yesterday stay with yesterday's sorrow. I'm a tomorrow man. I can't wait for that old scrambled egg sunrise in the morning.

"Every morning I look out the window and whether it's sunny or raining, I say, 'Thank you, Lord, baby.'"

And well he should.

Lord, baby, has blessed Howard with the body of a fighter, the tongue of a con artist, the soul of a poet and the ability to train a dog to flush a commode and sing *Dixie*.

Well, the rest of it is fact. The part about the commode and *Dixie*, we'll just have to take Snooks' word for it.

October 3, 1980

Even the Greatest Must Yield

Muhammad Ali fooled us again, as he has so often in 20 years.

"I am the master of illusion," he had said earlier in the week. And he was.

But this time, he fooled himself as well.

Fighting to win the heavyweight title for an unprecedented fourth time on a sultry Thursday night in an arena set up in a casino parking lot in Las Vegas, a city flashy enough to mirror his image, The Greatest learned that time waits for no man, not even him.

We had thought it might.

Against the champion, Larry Holmes, he was the 38-year-old man who had nothing left but his bravado, and even that evaporated into the desert air as his former sparring mate easily destroyed him with hundreds of punches that found the mark.

It ended with Ali sitting on a stool in his corner after 10 rounds. He had always had the pride, courage and craftiness to make a fight last, even when he lost, and he might have tried to continue this time – against all reason – had his manager, Herbert Muhammad, not stopped it.

It was a dreadful way for it all to end for Muhammad Ali, the man who had brought a glow to the sport unlike anyone ever had. Sitting there, with the millions of people he had charmed looking at him, all he could do was stare at the ring floor.

He didn't protest when his handlers stopped it. He knew he was finished. He looked so old.

Ali spent virtually all of the 10 rounds trying to protect himself from Holmes' left jabs that were like a cobra striking his face and body time after time and Holmes' left hooks that rocked his head. Ali rarely punched. He threw a few jabs and occasionally tried a right hand counter over Holmes' jabs, but these were token efforts, harmless.

Yes, Ali had fooled us again, made us believe that after two years of inactivity and after training almost 40 pounds off his body, he was still young enough and strong enough to fight and perhaps beat a 30-year-old man.

He had brought the betting odds down to near even money. He had orchestrated a fight that produced an estimated two billion viewers in 60 countries, some $50 million and a record live gate of $6 million.

It had begun so grandly. The crowd, drawn by the fascination of this man to a 24,000-seat arena built just for this fight, glittered with personalities like John Travolta, David Hartman, Sylvester Stallone, Norm Crosby, Kris Kristofferson, Cathy Lee Crosby, Frank Sinatra, Tom Jones, Ken Norton, Sugar Ray Robinson, Roberto Duran, Sugar Ray Leonard and the beloved Joe Louis, who was pushed up to ringside in a wheelchair.

Ali entered the ring first, to the familiar chant of "Ali! Ali!" He was grim as he waited five minutes for Holmes to show, but once Holmes had entered the ring, he was the old Ali, jawing and making faces at his opponent, pretending to try to get at Holmes and leading the "Ali" chant.

And in the early rounds, Ali taunted Holmes, as has been his style. Though he did nothing to demonstrate that he could harm Holmes, Ali said to the champion as the second round ended, "Are you ready? Are you ready?" And after the third, he walked with Holmes to his corner and said, "You are through."

But all the while, Holmes was smashing his fists into Ali's face and body, finding openings in the aging warrior's cover that others before had found so impenetrable. And Ali shut up. He knew he was in trouble.

In the fifth round Holmes did a little dance, something like Ali had done so many times.

In the eighth, Holmes was clearly in command and in the ninth, he caught the toothless lion with an uppercut that stunned him and sent him reeling into the ropes. Ali somehow summoned enough of his old skills to survive, but couldn't fight back and in the 10th, he threw no punches, just stood there, looking very tired and beaten, his face swollen and cut. The crowd booed. They booed Ali, who wouldn't fight because he couldn't.

As Ali sat sagging on his stool after the 10th, Pat Patterson, working Ali's corner, called from the ring apron down to Herbert Muhammad, seated on press row. Patterson said, "What do you want to do?"

Herbert Muhammad, who had spent most of the fight looking at the concrete beneath his feet, unwilling to watch what was unfolding in the ring, said simply, "Yeah."

Patterson relayed the message to trainer Angelo Dundee and Dundee told the referee, "That's it. Stop it."

The referee walked across the ring and lifted Holmes' arm and an era ended.

Always in the past, when things have gone badly for Ali, we have known he would find a way, if not to win, at least to survive. He had tricked us so often, we thought he might be tricking us again, he might be setting Holmes up for something.

But not this time. The magic was gone He had nothing left.

All of us eventually yield to time and Muhammad Ali had, too.

As he sat staring at the ring floor, something he had said earlier in the week floated through the air.

"When I retire," he had said, "you're going to miss me. There'll never be another like me."

Racing and Running

May 22, 1974

When Petty Was a Kid

If there is a glamor figure in the monstrous noise, grimy hands and blurring speed of stock car racing, it is Richard Petty. They call him Sir Richard and King of the Road and things like that. He poses for sunglasses ads and does TV commercials for mobile homes. There has been a movie about his life. He has clean features and good teeth and a heavy dash of Presleyian charm. And most importantly, he wins.

At the age of 34, Petty has won more races than any stocker past or present – despite being shut out through the years at Charlotte Motor Speedway, where he'll be running his red and blue (make that red and Petty blue) No. 43 in the World 600 Sunday.

His daddy, Lee, sitting in a golf cart at Tega Cay after his daily round, pondered his son's success and said, "Richard was just born into racing."

Indeed, a great race driver helped to deliver Richard and his brother Maurice, chief mechanic on the Petty cars. That would be Lee, three-time national champion.

"Back then in Level Cross, women didn't go to the hospital to have their babies," he said. "Both my boys were delivered in the home we live in right now and I helped the doctor with both of them.

"We've never moved. Now, Richard lives in a house beside us and Maurice lives across the road."

And the three own Petty Enterprises, Inc., a rich racing operation right there at their back doors.

"Richard and Maurice were real close brothers," recalled Poppa Lee, puffing on a pipe. "They and their cousin, Dale Inman, who does most of the hard work on Richard's cars now, used to play together back in the hills around Level Cross all the time. They raced wagons, bicycles, anything they could find that would run.

"When they were about 10 years old, my wife and I started taking them with us to races.

"Kids weren't allowed in the pits but they'd sneak in. They'd get thrown out and pretty soon, they'd sneak back in."

And so, racing came naturally to Richard. When he had finished high school (where he played football and baseball), Lee offered to send him to college but the youngster's mind was turned to race tracks, not classrooms. That meant a four-year wait until he was 21 and eligible for NASCAR competition. He spent the four years working in Lee's pits, listening, looking, learning.

"I gave him a car when he was in high school," said Lee. "I guess it was a hot rod. I understand he did a lot of challenging with it on those dirt roads around home. I never did tell him 'Don't do this, don't do that.' His momma had brought him up to know right from wrong.

"When he was around 18 or 19, I was doing a lot of testing for General Motors and we'd go to an old track and while we were there, I'd let him run some.

"In his first few races, you could tell he had learned an awful lot from just watching."

Richard's first race was in Columbia, SC. Lee didn't see it. He was racing somewhere else. He remembers though, that Richard didn't appear nervous before leaving for Columbia.

"I've got a lot of respect for the way he seems so calm before a race," said Lee. "I always got nervous but he's taught himself to control his nerves before a race."

Maurice also took to driving when he was 21 but eventually decided he was better suited to build engines than race them. Before he gave it up, though, the veteran Lee and the fledgling Richard and Maurice sometimes found themselves racing against each other.

"Now, that was some headache," said Lee, chuckling at the memory. "There I was trying to win a race and at the same time looking out for them. When you're racing with your sons like that, there's a certain amount of anxiety about it. I was always anxious about everyone on the track but when your sons are involved it's different."

Petty said as early as 1960, he could tell Richard was a driver of unusual skill.

"You could see how he moved a car around in traffic, how he anticipated what the other fellow was going to do," he said. "He had the knack. And I think he learned to utilize drafting at Daytona faster than anybody else. He's a good one.

"But looking back on his boyhood, I'd say he was pretty normal."

May 27, 1983

Ol' Pops

I never drive into the grounds at Charlotte Motor Speedway without thinking of Curtis Turner.

They called him Pops, because that's what he called everybody whose name he couldn't remember. When Turner was driving race cars and helping to make CMS come alive, there were a lot of nicknames in the stock car fraternity – Fireball, Little Joe, Speedy, Junior, Tiger, Banjo, Tiny, Buck – sobriquets that spoke of rugged, earthy men in a rugged, earthy sport.

Some of them lived as recklessly as they drove, and recklessness was a trademark of the old dirt bullrings and the sprawling new asphalt tracks that were growing out of cotton fields and red clay as the sport began to take off and flourish back there in the 1950s and '60s.

None lived more recklessly than Turner, although Little Joe Weatherly probably got a tie with him because they were running mates.

Both are dead now. So are Fireball and some of the others.

Pops, what do you think of this thing now? Did you ever imagine that big stars like Burt Reynolds and Loni Anderson would show up for a race at the track you and Bruton Smith willed to life, staying one step ahead of your debtors until the speedway was born, then losing it to them?

Could you ever, in your wildest imagination, expect to see the mayor host a black-tie affair as part of the World 600 celebration?

Big name movie stars. The glamor back in your time, Pops, was provided by buxom girls in bathing suits with ribbons across their buxomness proclaiming them Miss Modified or Miss Rack and Pinion or some such.

And how do you like the way the place looks now? It's pretty. Did you ever think you'd see a pretty race track? One with flowers and grass and street signs in the infield and a driver's lounge and air-conditioned boxes with seats that cost the customers more than you won in some races at the bullrings when the promoter didn't run off without paying you? And all those grandstands and crowds that have reached 130,000?

Pops, remember when both you and Bruton announced at about the same time that you were going to build superspeedways here? I don't know whose idea it was first but you two tried to out-slick each other for awhile there and then threw in together and made it work.

Well, you got the track built, anyway. Then you lost it in bankruptcy. Well, I guess you know Bruton went off for a long time, made a lot of money in auto dealerships and then suddenly reappeared as the majority stockholder in the speedway. He got it back and that seemed to be the right thing, considering the battles you two fought to get it built.

He's the one who's responsible for most of the class you see around the place now and he and his right-hand man, Humpy Wheeler, are responsible for the huge crowds and the acceptance the sport is gaining, although you guys, you and Little Joe and Buck and Fireball and all them, had already ignited the explosion of spectator interest with your driving.

I remember when you got back into racing after Bill France suspended you for not knuckling under to him and you drove at your racetrack for the first time. I asked you how it felt to come back there as nothing more than a driver and you just shrugged and said it didn't bother you.

Not much bothered you then, Pops. Life was just a long- running party for you. We still laugh about the time you and Little Joe started racing in the streets in rental cars and banged into each other the way you did on the tracks and tore those cars up pretty good and then drove them into a motel swimming pool.

And the time you were flying your plane over a little town in South Carolina and decided you wanted a drink of liquor and landed on the main street to go see a bootlegger just at the time church was letting out.

You guys were something, Pops.

Remember when Buck Baker got mad at some ol' boy, some

hometown hotshot, for running into him at a dirt track somewhere and pulled his car over and waited for the guy to come around the track again, then rammed him? Buck said he had to fight his way out with a tire tool after that.

Those were crazy days, Pops. There was you and Junior Johnson and Fireball Roberts and Speedy Thompson and Little Joe Weatherly and Tiny Lund (one of you said Tiny drove a car so hard and wrecked so often, if you had given him an anvil, he would've broken it).

And there was Lee and Richard Petty, Nelson Stacy, Fred Lorenzen, Jack Smith, Lee Roy Yarbrough, Marvin Panch, Joe Lee Johnson, Jim Paschal, Bobby Johns, Rex White, Bobby Isaac, Ned Jarrett, Tiger Tom Pistone, Jimmy Pardue, Darel Dieringer, to name a few more.

It was more dangerous back then. The cars hadn't been refined and you didn't have all the safety features they have now. There were no fuel cells in the cars then and fire was the greatest danger in a wreck. That's how Fireball bought it. Jarrett and Lund stopped on the track and pulled him out. He fought a good battle with his burns for a few weeks but lost. It's still dangerous. There are still some fires. But it's not like it was then.

Maybe that – the knowledge that you might die on any Sunday – made you live the way you did.

Well, I didn't mean to get serious on you, Pops.

They're running the World 600 again Sunday. It'll be a far cry from that first one in 1960 when you guys barely got the asphalt poured before the race and it chunked so badly, there were potholes in it.

This is going to be a spectacle, big, stylish, glittering with celebrities, rich in prizes, a showpiece of sports.

I hope you enjoy it. You and your pals helped make it happen. And, Pops, when it's over, what do you say we have a drink?

May 25, 1973

The Last American Hero

This was the cocktail party after the premiere showing last night of The Last American Hero at the Capri Theater. Junior Johnson, whose slam-bang life in moonshine and stock car racing inspired the film was all dressed up for the occasion, wearing plaid trousers, a navy blue sport coat, a white shirt and a tie that he jokingly said might be the first necktie he'd ever worn.

He looked like he belonged on the veranda of a country club, but the years of growing fame, the wealth accumulated through driving and building racers, the warmth of attention the film has brought him haven't changed ol' Junior that much.

At 41, the graying legend still has the mountains in his shy manner and his language and his blood.

The movie deals to a great extent with Johnson's whisky- running adventures. He is not embarrassed by that long chapter of his life in which he hauled his daddy's illegal products ("A little pleasure at a dollar a pint") in fast cars that thundered through the night along the dirt roads around Ingle Hollow.

"I don't have no regrets about my past," said Junior, leaning against the wall, talking above the noise of the cocktail party. "I wouldn't turn around and do it another way.

"My only regret is that my daddy served so much time for making whisky but as for my own life, I don't have a regret. Making whisky was the only way people around home had of making a living. It was a way of life. Everybody did it. It wasn't a gangster-type life at all and when you got caught, you never resisted. You knew you'd done wrong."

They nailed him at his daddy's still one day and he did 11 months and three days in jail but the lawmen never caught him hauling liquor.

"That was one race you couldn't afford to lose," he said, his round, tan face crinkling up in a big smile. "It was a challenge, too. You was loaded and they wasn't. I reckon a load weighed as much as 1,500 pounds."

Someone asked Johnson if running from the lawmen and outwitting them by such means as listening to their calls on the police radios excited him.

"Fast cars excited me," he said.

His daddy wanted him to get out of the liquor business and when a car owner who knew of Johnson's driving skills fetched him from behind a plow one day and hauled him off to drive in a stock car race, he found a new profession.

"I'd never even seen a stock car race," he said, "but I wasn't scared. I think Gwyn Staley won it and I was second. It was at North Wilkesboro, I'd say about 1949 or '50."

Johnson roared off from that beginning to win every major NASCAR title and two national championships. He was famous for his fearless, all-out style.

He was reckless to a fault, just as reckless on the tracks at Daytona and Darlington and Charlotte as he had been on the backroads of Wilkes County.

"My worst habit as a racer was that I didn't give the car a chance. I drove it to death. I either broke it or drove it too hard. I either finished first or I didn't finish," he said.

His last season behind the wheel was 1966 and he went out gloriously, winning the prized Southern 500 at Darlington, a title that had eluded him through his 15 years of racing. He had career winnings of $500,000. He said he never feels the desire to drive again.

He is a highly successful car owner-mechanic now. Bobby Allison drove Junior's car to 10 firsts and $278,000 in prize money last year. Cale Yarborough will be at the wheel of Johnson's car in the World 600 in Charlotte Sunday.

Johnson's attitude toward his hell-bent racing style has changed now that he's the investor. "When you're a driver, the only thing you've got at stake is a pair of goggles and a helmet," he said. "But now I take $100,000 worth of equipment to every race. Believe me, it pays to finish second."

Which proves Johnson has changed a little, after all. But not too much to spoil the image.

May 16, 1974

The Simple Life

Tony Waldrop recently bought himself a yo-yo. A couple of days later, the great miler walked into a library on the University of North Carolina campus yo-yoing.

"All of a sudden," he said, "I could feel people staring at me, like, 'Tony Waldrop shouldn't do things like that anymore.'

"It has always been my philosophy that if you have a yo-yo in your hand, you yo-yo."

That he was a senior, a sophisticated college man and in the midst of a streak of sub-four-minute miles that has now reached 11 and turned the track world on its ear doesn't prevent Waldrop from doing the child things that he enjoys like yo-yoing and challenging his roommate in five or six different games in a day.

But that's just one side of this new folk hero who has come down from the mountains to break the world indoor record and run the second fastest mile ever recorded.

He likes classical music, is a voracious reader (he read 12 novels on Christmas vacation) and held a season ticket to the local theater group. He also likes to fish and drink beer with his buddies and keep company with the coeds.

Though he is a bundle of contradictions, this young superstar remains as uncomplicated as a map of his hometown of Columbus in the hill country of southwestern North Carolina. As he describes it, it's "one street and two stoplights."

Though success came at him as a blur over the winter and into the spring, setting a world indoor record of 3:55 and posting the second fastest mile ever run with a 3:53.2 in the Penn Relays, Waldrop seems determined not to become a victim of his glory.

You approach him convinced he's going to hang his straw-thatched head, scuff the ground with the toe of his racing shoe and say "Aw, shucks." Instead, he fixes you with his blue eyes and speaks directly. His comments are crisp, to the point, basically modest but always with a flicker of confidence.

He grew up at the foot of Chocolate Drop Mountain and trained for his high school races on a path around the baseball and football fields at Polk Central, which is bounded on three sides by a chicken farm, a cow pasture and a corn field. Most of his races were run on paths around other baseball fields. ("Ours wasn't measured," he said.)

He has retained his down-home warmth. He reminds you of John Boy. Heywood Hale Broun of CBS, in town last week to interview him, said Tony "looks like he should be milking a cow."

But this is no ordinary country boy. He is extremely bright. He was an Eagle Scout back in Columbus. He came to the university on a Morehead Scholarship, a prized merit grant awarded primarily for academic achievement. He has flirted with Phi Beta Kappa at Carolina.

In sum, he's something special.

In this day when so many athletes are playing their way toward fat professional contracts, Waldrop steadfastly maintains he will not run for money.

"I don't think I could ever enjoy running with money as a motivation," he said. "I run for fun. When I quit enjoying it, that's the day I quit running."

But there is no doubt that a huge check will be dangled under the nose of this wiry young mountain man who wanted most of all to be an 880 runner and started running the mile only at the insistence of his high school coach. He says he doesn't think he has the capability of a 3:50 mile (Jim Ryun's world record is 3:51.1) but expert coaches like Villanova's Jumbo Elliott say he'll run past 3:50 like it's not there. And that will rocket him to even greater international fame.

Too, there is a young Tanzanian named Filbert Bayi whose career is paralleling Waldrop's. They may soon be competing head-to-head for recognition as the best in the world. Such a rivalry would bring even more attention and probably lower times.

Waldrop will run in the California Relays in a couple of weeks, then in the NCAA and AAU Championships. He is going to join a California track club and run with it for a year, after which he plans to drop track and return to Carolina to get a degree in law or perhaps in physical education and become a coach.

"Four years at Carolina sure have gone by fast," he said. "I've done a lot more that I ever dreamed I'd do."

March 25, 1978

Memories of Hardrock

Remember Hardrock Simpson? The old thong of leather had almost slipped out of mind until a clipping bubbled up from the melange in my desk drawer. It told how a group of white-collar workers over 30 years of age had lost almost eight pounds apiece in a jogging-walking program.

"By the 12th week," it said, "they were covering three miles in an hour or more."

Child's play. Good for the health, of course, and highly recommended by all of us guys who stay in shape climbing in and out of a golf cart. A toddling step beside the feats of the great Hardrock, however.

Paul Simpson was and, as far as I know, still is a postman in Burlington. He walked or ran a 12-mile mail route every day until he was 59. Then they gave him a motor scooter.

I've never gotten over Hardrock agreeing to ride a motor scooter to deliver his mail. I don't care if he was 59. I like to think he fought it with everything he had. I like to think maybe he challenged it to a race.

He would run anything – man, beast, machine, a clock or simply the years. He won most of the time.

He's out to pasture now. Until he was 58, he would run a mile for every year on his birthday but he had to give that up on his doctor's advice and cut down to seven miles a day. Plus his mail route, of course.

Simpson, who acquired his nickname of "Hardrock" by playing every minute of every game for two years as a football guard at Burlington High, estimated he ran 160,000 miles from the time he was 15 until he quit.

In 1928 and again in 1929, he ran in the cross-country Bunion Derby, covering 3,863 miles from New York to California.

He once finished fifth in the famed Boston Marathon, narrowly missing a chance to compete in the Olympics. The top three finishers qualified.

For $25 in lower classification, $200 in the higher minors, Hardrock would run around the field for the length of a baseball game.

He would even work doubleheaders. He figured he covered an average of about 18 miles during a single game, 25 during a twin-bill. He was struck by a baseball only once, that a foul tip.

He would also run as a promotional gimmick for grocery stores, funeral parlors and assorted other enterprises.

Simpson feared nothing that moved. He once challenged a submarine to a race from Norfolk to Jacksonville but the U.S. Navy felt that was a bit out of the line of duty and nixed the contest.

"I would have won," Hardrock said.

Some of his greatest and darkest moments came in races with animals.

He once outran a horse from Burlington to Kinston and back but, shame of shames, he was beaten two years in a row in a run from Benson to Newton Grove and back by a mule named Maude.

In 1927, the steel-legged runner took on a horse in a distance race. Hardrock ran the horse into the ground after 144 miles.

"The horse got so stiff in the hips," he said, "they had to get a block and tackle and load him in a truck to get him home."

He mistreated another horse even worse in 1958. He lost to the nag in a 157-mile race from Salt Lake City to Roosevelt, Utah, but Hardrock lived to run again. The horse didn't. The animal expired at the conclusion of the duel.

Simpson said he ate lots of fruit, vegetables, meat, honey and raw oatmeal.

Raw oatmeal?

So that's how he beat the horses.

April 25, 1980

Rascals

People who have run 26 miles, 385 yards and lost probably don't think the Rosie Ruiz Incident is funny.

After that distance, they probably don't think anything is funny but especially the possibility that this woman ran only a portion of the Boston Marathon Monday, came in first among women entrants and was crowned with the laurel wreath as champion of her sex.

Not having run farther than two miles at a time in the past several months myself, I'm amused.

I don't condone cheating. If she cheated, she should confess, not only to cleanse her soul but to give due honor to the real champion.

But I enjoy rascals, so long as they don't do anybody serious harm.

I've gotten a kick out of Barry Bremen, who goes around posing as a star athlete. He's a life insurance salesman in Bloomington, Minn., but he's gained national fame and had fun doing it by warming up for major league baseball's all-star game in a Yankee uniform, warming up for the NBA All-Star game wearing a genuine warm-up suit and playing nine holes during a practice round with a couple of pros at the U.S. Open last year.

I smile at the revelation that a Dr. Richard W. You of Honolulu became known in Hawaii as "Mr. Olympics" while posing for 24 years as a member of the U.S. Olympic committee.

I chuckle at a man named Terry Jackson, who went from city to city posing as Bobby Joe Mason, a member of the Harlem Globetrotters, and staging clinics.

The gentle sting has its humorous side.

And frankly, I think running was getting a little too big for its britches, anyway. It needed a little dose of humility.

I don't think we'll ever know whether Rosie Ruiz, a trim, 26-year-old native of Havana who works in a New York City office, actually ran the full distance or snuck in somewhere along the line and loped home ahead.

Unless, of course, she decides to 'fess up and sell movie rights.

If Ruiz is cheating, she's not going at it in a very professional manner.

If she were pulling a bank heist, she'd show up without a gun and forget what she wanted to say in the note to the teller.

She'd take a bus for her getaway, forget to take off her mask and wouldn't have the correct change.

People who perpetrate a sting usually plan it carefully. If this was a sting, Ruiz could've written the plan on the head of a pin and had space left for the entry list.

Ruiz didn't even bother to learn to speak running. She didn't know the meaning of such basic terminology as "splits" and "intervals."

And she didn't sweat enough to suit the experts.

Compared to the other entrants, who finished lathered up like

Secretariat after the Belmont Stakes, she arrived at the finish line looking like she had just stepped out of a deodorant commercial. She didn't have any "salt streaks," they said, explaining that marathon runners become streaked with the salt of their own sweat.

The men's winner, Bill Rodgers, who says he's won four Boston Marathons, commented that Ruiz didn't look like someone who had just run a marathon and he said there was no way she could've improved her time of 2:56.29 in the New York Marathon last October to 2:31.56 in Boston in such a short training period.

What Rodgers apparently didn't know was that Ruiz may have taken the subway in the New York Marathon and you know how undependable public transportation is.

In the New York marathon, Ruiz was credited with finishing in 23rd place and her time qualified her to run in the Boston Marathon.

But Susan Morrow, a freelance photographer in New York, says Ruiz didn't run the New York Marathon. Morrow said Ruiz rode the subway with her to the finish line. Wearing her running outfit.

That seems fair. It's more difficult for a woman to ride a New York subway and survive than to run a marathon.

Films indicate Ruiz didn't even finish the New York marathon and a study of 28,000 photographs of that race don't contain her Latin features. Given this, Fred Lebow, director of the race, labeled Ruiz "a phony."

Geez, what a grouch! Maybe she didn't know she was supposed to finish. And if she didn't finish, how come that gave her 23rd place?

Two Harvard students claim they saw Ruiz jump into the Boston Marathon about half a mile from the finish. Could be. Maybe that's where she got off the subway.

When it comes to running, I'm a middle-of-the-roader. I run some but not seriously. I am an advocate. It's good for the body and mind and competitive running must be rewarding. And yet I break up laughing at some of the deep meaning ascribed by some gurus to putting one foot in front of the other.

Most of America is probably laughing today about Rosie Ruiz and the Boston Marathon. I think sometimes that may be a better exercise than running.

September 18, 1988

Not Just Any Sprinter

Who was that walking into the interview room at the press center at the Seoul Olympics? Jackie Collins?

You could just catch a glimpse of her and from here she looked a bit like Collins. The paparazzi – that's Italian for boorish clowns with cameras – had her hemmed in, jostling and stumbling big-eyed and frantically with her as she moved toward the podium.

She looked a bit like Jackie Collins but younger. Who, then, could command this kind of attention, drawing more than 500 media people from around the world? Cher, of course! Semi-nude. With a deep tan.

Wrong again. It was Flo Jo. Florence Griffith Joyner. A sprinter.

Not just any sprinter. She's the one who wore those brightly colored body suits with one leg missing at the U.S. Olympic trials, where she also burned the world record for 100 meters – 10.76 seconds – to cinders with a 10.49 that may stand for two decades.

And the one who also, incidentally, will be favored to win a gold medal in the 100 and could be a co-favorite with East Germany's Heike Dreschler to win the 200.

But enough of the nuts and bolts. What we have here is a sex goddess with leg muscles like Herschel Walker's, a woman who sweats a lot but could be doing perfume commercials. Her picture has been on every magazine cover but *Mechanics Illustrated* in the past few months.

Who ever thought we'd be asking a woman who can run as fast as O.J. Simpson could in his prime what her attire will be when she runs in the Olympics?

But we did. They did. Griffith Joyner, who really is a beautiful woman, was wearing a red-and-white warm-up suit for the press conference (gossip columnists have to include that kind of information, see) and had the obligatory sunglasses perched atop her head.

She said she would be required to wear the basic U.S.Olympic team uniform but had brought along several flashier models in which to train. Minds conjured images. (Not mine. Hey, look at me. I'm laughing. OK, maybe I did wonder if she brought the lacy one.)

She has a voice like velvet, which doesn't do any damage to her charm.

Someone asked Griffith Joyner, who is 29, 5-foot-7 and 130 pounds, how she felt about the focus on her appearance since the trials a few months ago. In all fairness to Griffith Joyner, the answer probably shouldn't be revealed because in print it's going to sound like something a Miss America cheerleader-wanting-to-change-the-world might say. And that's just how it sounded.

"I haven't set out to change track or the image of women in the sport," she purred. "What I've done, I've done because it's just me.

"Young girls say they want to be like me. I tell them, don't be like me, be better. I tell them to follow their dreams and stay in school."

Griffith Joyner's performance in Indianapolis – the outfits and the destruction of the world record – jacked up her appearance fee at track meets from $1,500 to 25 grand overnight, and she turns down as many offers as she accepts.

Not bad for a girl who grew up in the ghetto with 10 brothers who "knocked me down in football and beat me up in basketball" because she could outrun them. A young woman who a couple of years ago, after winning a silver medal in the 200 in Los Angeles, was a slightly plump bank secretary.

Now, she trains two or three times a day, "three or four times harder" than she trained a couple of years ago. She is determined to win a gold medal, perhaps two or three (a third in the 400 relay), and confident she can do it.

"I don't feel any pressure," she said. "I won't allow it."

As she rose to leave the press conference, cameramen engulfed her again. They pushed and shoved and knocked one another spinning and fell over chairs.

Fortunately, the writers were a bit more dignified. None asked her if she would be wearing those long fingernails she wore in the '84 Games. And I couldn't get close enough to see.

From Pool to Politics

July 26, 1978

The Last Pool Room

The sign says simply Plaza Pool Room.

And that is what it is, hunkered back there on Thomas Avenue between Central and Commonwealth, a genuine, by God, pool room.

Not a "cue lounge" or "billiards parlor." Not one of those spacious, brightly-lighted, antiseptic places that carefully projects the image of a "family" place. Not one of those lounges that has a few undersized tables set in among the drinking tables and the Foosball games, where guys take their girlfriends.

The Plaza Pool Room is a survivor.

Progress has killed off most of the real pool halls. The Plaza and the Independence Cue Lounge, so named because it once fancied itself a modernistic, family place but has since reverted to an old-fashioned pool room – and ought to be called that – are about the last of their kind in Charlotte.

These are pool rooms like those that used to make you feel so deliciously evil when you played in them as a high school kid. There were still mothers then – and there may still be – who thought a pool room was not a fit place for their young'uns. Men drank beer there and smoked and cursed and gambled and, for all anyone knew, might even talk about you-know-what there.

On reflection, maybe it was that feeling that the police might come through the back door at any time (for what reason, I cannot now imagine) that made the places so fascinating. That and the knowledge that this was a place for men only. And the things that tugged at the senses – the clack of the balls, the mingling odors of smoke and beer and food, the faces that always seemed faintly mysterious.

The Plaza Pool Room is everything my pool rooms were.

It is Monday night. The Yankees and Royals are on the TV that sits above the beer cooler and crackers and Rolaids and cigars and the picture of Steve Garvey. Four or five men sit at the counter drinking beer and smoking and watching the game.

There are four regulation pool tables, a snooker table and a bumper pool table in the Plaza Pool Room. Back in a corner at one of the tables, near the oil heater and the toilet, two men play nine ball. One, obviously in need of a hurtin' song, keeps poking quarters into the jukebox in the other corner at the rear of the room and punching No. 162, and Bonnie Tyler's husky voice fills the room with "It's A Heartache." This makes it difficult for the men at the counter to hear the ballgame.

Harry Panos, the proprietor, takes care of it. He semi-politely tells the man to can the music until the ballgame's over.

There are priorities in a real pool room. Music is not high on this list.

Harry Panos is a nice-looking, solidly-built 38 year-old man who has been in the pool room business "off and on" since 1959. He is a family man but his pool room is not a family place and he doesn't want it to be. A second home, as one of the regulars described it, yes, but for men only. Respectable, by all means, and trouble-free, but a man's place.

"We have some women come in here," said Panos, "but we don't really want them. We like women, of course, but I figure when a fellow comes in here, say like on a Saturday afternoon, he's here to get away from women, shoot some pool, drink some beer and watch the ballgame with some other guys.

"The family places where the women go are good for pool. But I don't encourage women to come in here."

You know the Plaza Pool Room is the genuine article because it has a jar of pickled eggs, a jar of dill pickles and a jar of hot sausages on the counter.

The front of the building is not well lighted. It appears to be closed at night when it isn't.

The walls are a deep brown halfway up, then a dingy color that might once have been an off-white or a yellow. They are decorated with the ancient symbols of pool rooms – beer signs, cartoons clipped from magazines and newspapers, hand-lettered signs that say, "In

God we trust, all others must pay cash" and "No profanity" and "Helen Waite is our credit manager – If you want credit, go to Hell'n Waite."

There is a picture of a very fat nude, a picture of some shapely legs and a clipping of some bare-breasted natives of some foreign country that looks like it came out of *National Geographic*. Remember that?

There's a sign advertising the second annual N.C. Dixie Classic Nine Ball Tournament in Fayetteville. There's a "Hee Haw" pinball machine in a front corner, some peanut dispensing machines on one wall and a mirror. The mirror, you conclude, is for the salesmen and other business types who drop in during working hours and want to check their appearance before they go back on the job.

Another indication that the Plaza Pool Room is the real thing is the occasional visitor passing through town who stops in to see if there's any action. The shooters that we call "hustlers," some of the best in the country, guys with nicknames like Midnight Mike Segal and St. Louis Louie and Larry (The Iceman) Hubbard and Hippie Jimmy Reid, come by the Plaza from time to time.

In the world of pool, that lends class to the place, authenticates it. Unfortunately, says Panos, there are no top-notch players in town nowadays who can shoot the visiting hotshots without "spots," a handicap.

Primarily, though, the Plaza Pool Room is not inhabited by professionals but by men who have been coming there regularly for years to shoot their daily games on the snooker table. ("You can set your watch by them," says one regular. "You can bet on what time they'll walk through that door every day.") And it's a place for a man looking for some guys to talk with and drink beer with, shoot a little pool with and watch the ballgame with.

It's a real pool room, one of a vanishing breed.

June 8, 1986

Contentment

The sun was high but there was still a bit of morning freshness in the air, and so we sat outside Bob Rose's home and talked.

Rose's home is a tired-looking, white 1973 Fleetwood Cadillac with darkened windows and license plates – one from Nevada, one from North Carolina – that read B ROSE. It sits in a concrete shopping center parking lot on the outskirts of Chapel Hill, close to a dogwood tree and a little rose garden, a few yards off a busy highway.

Rose opened a metal folding chair for me, and he sat in the front seat of the car, facing out the door. As we talked, we were joined by Rose's friend, David, who had brought him a plate of food for lunch. David took a seat in the other folding chair and said, "Eat your lunch before it gets cold," but Rose put it aside.

Through the open door you could see a transistor radio, some newspapers and two issues of *Town and Country* magazine. Clothes hanging from a rack and assorted other belongings were visible through the plastic coating of the rear window.

Bob Rose, 66, was captain of the North Carolina basketball team in 1942 and all-Southern Conference in 1941 and 1942. Newspaper accounts depict him as a campus hero of considerable magnitude back then, and one lists him among the best to wear a Tar Heel uniform before the post-World War II era.

He talked of his service in the war as a Marine pilot, of owning an auto dealership in Cherry Point and of running a real estate brokerage office in Las Vegas, where he had about 30 employees, and of selling Florida real estate and such, remarking that he had made a lot of money. He mentions, as an aside, that he used to take his yacht down the Inland Waterway to Sea Island, Ga., and spend several days vacationing at that ritzy resort.

And then, he says, he retired in 1980 and came back to Chapel Hill.

He has been living in his present location for about a year. He worked for a while as a ranger at Finley Golf Course and a few weeks at the cafeteria that serves as the training table for Tar Heel athletes. At the moment, he is unemployed.

His blue eyes were bright as he talked of all his ventures, but when the obvious question was asked – what in heaven's name are you doing living in a car in a shopping center parking lot – his eyes grew sad and a cloud came over his face. He shuffled his sneakered feet and wrung his hands nervously and pulled a cigarette from one of half a dozen packs on the floor of the car. "I do what I have to do," he said, looking me squarely in the eye and making me feel that he was saying, "You must know the answer."

Clearly, he didn't want to talk about it. He told me a few things about his plans to change all this, but said he would appreciate it if I wouldn't put them in the newspaper.

I had come to Chapel Hill to find the story of what had happened to this onetime hero, but he seemed so content, except when he was questioned about it, I was reluctant to dig deeply into it.

What was I going to do, write that the man is a derelict? He isn't.

What we see is a tall, handsome man with neatly trimmed hair the color of snow clouds, clean shaven, dressed in shorts and a golf shirt, deeply tanned from hours sitting in a field behind the shopping center enjoying the sun. He has a lot of the look of the late Bear Bryant about him, and the same gravelly voice.

What we see is a man who could put on a three-piece suit and hold his own in a board room but who, instead, might be dubbed the king of the shopping center parking lot. People flock around him because they enjoy his company, like to listen to his stories and play a few hands of cards with him on a produce box with a rug thrown over it.

He's healthy ("I haven't seen a doctor since I went into service in 1942").

He has friends. He hangs around a barbershop because there is conversation there. "Ten or so of us meet for breakfast every morning," he said. "And in the afternoon, 10 or 15 people drop by to visit. A golf pro, doctors, lawyers, all kinds of people. We talk sports, play all-star sports trivia, go putt on the practice green at Finley, play softball, shoot pool in the student union. I really enjoy people."

I asked where he ate. Some say he subsists on his social security checks, but he denies that. He said he eats at various restaurants around the area and at friends' homes. He said he bathes and shaves at various places and does his laundry at a Laundromat in the shopping center. He said Dean Smith gives him and his girl friend complimentary tickets to basketball games, down on the first or second row, where the heavy contributors sit. He speaks authoritatively about the team.

At one point in the conversation, a pickup truck drove past and the driver honked his horn. Rose waved and said, "That's ol' Charley." A woman walked by pushing two infants in a stroller. Rose waved to them and chuckled.

He told stories of coming out of Smithfield, attending Riverside Military Academy, where his roommate was Tommy Prothro, later a famous football coach; of coaching Butch van Breda Kolff in the service; of playing with all-American George Glamack and against Bones McKinney and John Belk and Banks McFadden.

He knows a great deal about Charlotte and Greensboro and Raleigh and Chapel Hill, and can reel off the names of influential people in those cities, sometimes accompanying them with accounts of personal encounters. He knows a lot about the business of those places, about their growing pains, about their plans.

He tells delightful stories, sitting there in the parking lot in the sunshine, smoking his Cambridge cigarettes. You forget for the moment where you are. You could be sitting beside a pool at a resort hotel talking with a captain of industry, except for the traffic roaring by.

I don't know what brought Bob Rose to this humble domicile, where the heat of the sun sears him and the cold of the night chills him ("I'm tough"), where heroes are not supposed to end up.

But if they want to know, someone else will have to probe deeper. I'm going to leave him alone. He may sleep a troubled sleep, he may have problems with which he can't cope, but I came away feeling here is a man who has found a measure of contentment in an old Cadillac in a shopping center parking lot, that a lot of people can't find in comfortable homes.

He has friends and memories and a dogwood tree and a rose garden and the sun. For him, that seems to be enough.

July 27, 1981

The Pavilion

Benny McGuire, a famous "fat man" whose stomach almost touches the ground when he sits, chants into a microphone in front of Ripley's Believe It Or Not Museum, "....See a genuine shrunken head...the world's weirdest graveyard..."

Across Ocean Boulevard people are buying foot-long hot dogs at Peaches Corner. Foot-longs have been sold there for so many years, it's a landmark.

The odors of the long, thin cafe – food, beer – spill through open doorways into the street to mingle with the other smells – cigarettes, popcorn, cotton candy, perfume, exhaust fumes.

The sound of a recording, Roseanne Cash singing "Seven Year Ache," lurches out the door of The Bowery, a long-famous beer drinking establishment. The sound blends with the others – the throb of automobiles lining the streets bumper-to-bumper, the piercing screams from the roller-coaster, barkers, the bing-bong of pinball machines, an addling cacophony.

Sunburned mamas fuss at sunburned young 'uns tugging at them and whimpering. Boys in cutoff jeans walk the streets in search of girls walking the streets in hopes of finding boys, to the silent sound of Jimmy Buffett singing "Fins to the left, fins to the right..." The sidewalks are packed with people, walking, looking.

It's Saturday night at the Myrtle Beach Pavilion.

If there is a focal point to the 60-mile Grand Strand in summer, this is it, these three or four blocks of loud, glittering carnival. It is to the Strand what Bourbon Street is to New Orleans.

Here you can see, along with the genuine shrunken head and the weird graveyard, such spectacles as "the world's largest selection of knives and jewelry," men making fudge in a store window, "an old English torture chamber with tortures actually used long, long ago," and the Baden Band Organ which has angels made of what appears to be plaster of Paris that are striking bells and drums and whirling in dance to the sound of organ music while people, either smitten by a fit of culture or just plain tired, sit for long periods watching the repetitive moves of the figures.

Other people sit wherever they can find a place and watch people like themselves walk by. Vehicles line Ocean Boulevard, crawling in both directions along the narrow avenue, "dragging" like a film clip from "American Graffiti." There are more Trans-Ams and pickup trucks than anything else.

There are the standard rides – roller coaster, ferris wheel, merry-go-round, Tilt-A-Whirl, bumper cars and a few newer ones – to delight the young and daunt the older sunburned souls.

The mechanical bull craze that has swept the country has made its way to the beach. There's always a crowd around it to watch some macho type in tank top with tobacco in cheek get thrown on his cud.

Shorts, tops and sneakers or clogs are the standard dress for Saturday night at the Pavilion. The only attire that gets a lot of notice is the overdress – women in dresses and high heels carrying purses – or the underdress which could be the guy in black dress slacks and black dress shoes with no shirt, the better to show off his muscular upper body.

Next to food, T-shirts look like the big sales item. Several stores peddle them with iron-ons dealing largely with such themes as sex, rock musicians, motorcycles, marijuana, beer and cowboys.

You can, in the words of the barker, "git your pitcher made with a live lion or tiger." These are baby lions and tigers. You can get the devil scared out of you at haunted houses. You can buy a live hermit crab. You can dance to live music in a hall that stands on one of the spots where the kids who invented the shag and danced first to beach music used to wear out their penny loafers and ballet slippers.

You can see a gathering of people looking into a window where two men are smoothing large cakes of fudge. You wander on down the street wondering why people would stand and watch guys make candy, then you realize you were doing the same thing.

And you watch people spray paint T-shirts and try to shoot basketballs through hoops and ride bumper cars and fall off the bull and you check out the people walking and riding by.

Fascinating place, the Pavilion, on a Saturday night.

July 26, 1976

Poor Man's Deep Sea

A few hundred feet away, the gleaming sand of Garden City Beach was almost too hot for barefoot walking as the July sun came down like a blowtorch. Inland a ways, the ocean breeze died against the pastel-colored cottages and everything baked in the stillness.

But out near the end of Garden City Pier, there was a brisk, steady wind blowing. Ed Washington turned his mahogany face into it, looked out over the gently rolling Atlantic and said, "This is the best air-conditioning in the world. We got air-conditioning at home but all it does is blow house air around. Out here, it's all fresh. That's one of the reasons I come out here so much."

Ed Washington is a pier fisherman. More devoted than most, no doubt, but still one of that ever-changing, indefinable clan, grouped right along with the sunburned tourists in walking shorts who bring their Styrofoam coolers, beer, rods and reels, bait shrimp and visions of mammoth catches out along the wooden planks leading away from shore, give it a few hours and then disappear for another year.

Washington is a regular, though, at what amounts to the poor man's deep sea fishing. He buys a "season pass" for $27 a year. He is 62 years old. He lives at nearby Pawley's Island with his wife. He pours some concrete when there is work available but they don't pour enough concrete in Pawley's Island to keep him busy, he said. "That's why I can fish so much."

You walk out the pier, past an old woman in a bonnet sitting alone, clutching her fishing gear, hunched over watching the water below; past two boys, youngsters, untangling their lines that got crossed; past a man in walking shorts and undershirt, sunburned, wearing a Budweiser hat and explaining to his sunburned wife, who is fat and wearing a bikini, how one catches fish, although his cooler is empty.

You walk past all these and the others and you come upon Ed Washington. He is standing alone, peering out at the water. He has three lines out. The poles lean against the rail, in little notches that have been cut for them. The tip of one of the poles bends and shakes. It is a bite. Ed Washington cuts his eyes toward the bobbing tip but doesn't move. The rod quits moving. He looks back out at the blue water.

A man who has been watching this, leaning against the rail, says, "Don't you have to set the hook when you get a bite? I've always heard you have to give a tug on the line when you got a bite." Others on the pier had been giving mighty jerks at the feel of a nibble.

Ed Washington said, "Heh, heh, folks say they be hookin' a fish but a fish hook hisself. You don't have to be jerkin' on the rod. You might even pull the hook right out of his mouth. If he's gonna be hooked, he'll hook hisself."

Another rod bent. Ed Washington watched it for a moment and decided he had a fish. He began reeling it in, not with the quick, excited movements of the average pier fisherman but easily, slowly. He had a keeping-sized whiting. He removed it from the hook, dropped it into an ice chest that also contained some other fish, his bait shrimp and a package of bologna for his dinner. He was going to be there awhile, he said, because he was waiting for the incoming tide. That's when the big fish come in, he said, on the incoming tide.

Summertime is not the best time to fish. Ed Washington knows that, of course. He has lived at Pawley's Island all his life and fished for most of it and he knows the best fishing is in the late summer and early fall, when the weather cools and the spots are running and you can pull them in as fast as you can drop a hook into the water. But that isn't why he is out there, just to catch fish. He is out there for the same reason a lot of the "regulars" – of whom there are about a dozen, he estimates – are out there. Because it is a good place to be.

"I don't do it just for the fish," said the dark man with that distinctive accent found around the Charleston area. "If I did, I could catch all my wife and I needed in no time a'tall. I just like to be out here, to think and enjoy the breeze and look at the water.

"I catch a lot of fish but I just freeze 'em and sometimes my sons come and get 'em. One lives in Missouri, one in Virginia. I always thought Virginia was a fishin' city but my boy says there ain't no fishin' around where he is."

Ed Washington eyed a cooler filled with water in which a couple dozen small croakers floated, bent, their white bellies up. "Ain't worth keepin'," he said. "Ain't big enough. They gonna spoil, too, if that fella don't get 'em on ice. Fish spoil fast." Ed Washington shook his head. He knew the man was a novice but he didn't feel inclined to say anything to him about the croakers. "Mostly," he said, "I just listen." He prefers the times when there aren't many people out there, he said, but he has learned to be patient with all kinds of folks.

Croaker is one of the standard catches from the piers, said Ed Washington. Others are spot, whiting, bluefish, flounder, drum and pompano. Nothing exciting, like the great sports fish that can be caught far off-shore from the boats.

Ed Washington said he had never been out into the ocean on a fishing boat. "Had some chances," he said, his eyes wandering across the long horizon, "but that's a big piece of water out there."

There is no need for Ed Washington to get on a boat and go out there. He is not fishing just for the fish and he is not likely to find any more contentment out there than he can find on the pier. It's a good place to be.

August 3, 1981

Prince of the Pier

He doesn't look like much. He's thin as a pool cue. He has stringy bleached blond hair that hangs to his shoulders. His upper front teeth are missing, a fact you don't notice at first because of his blond mustache, and you guess he got them knocked out at the same time he was hit beside his nose but he says no, the teeth were pulled. The raw spot beside the nose he thinks came from a policeman's billy club.

He got drunk the other night and was thrown in jail. The next day, he couldn't remember much but he was so sore he said he must have resisted arrest.

His arms have tattoos he drew himself and, if you look closely, you can see the "tracks" of needles he's used shooting drugs.

Some people would probably call him worthless, but a lot of people think he's kind of special.

He hangs around the pier a lot. Lately, it's been just about all day every day because he's been out of work. "I was helping build that big place where you see the crane up the beach there," he said. "The boss, he's real religious and he said he had to let me go because of my record."

He shows up every day, wearing tight-fitting jeans to cover the tattoos on his legs, and a T-shirt. He sets up his mackerel rig on the northeast corner of the pier, then helps other folks cast their lines or bait their hooks or identify a catch or he just converses with them.

Kids love him. All the other regulars share baitfish and time with him. He's a happy man and he helps keep the others happy.

He's the Prince of the Pier at Myrtle Beach.

He seems surprised that you notice he's helpful to others, surprised and pleased. "I'll help anybody," he said. "If people had helped me, I wouldn't be where I am today."

He's 24 now but his eyes, the color of the ocean, are the eyes of an old man. He can no longer see out of his left eye. He was playing darts after using drugs and stuck a dart in his eye.

"I haven't used no drugs since then," he said. "It's been about a month now since I got out of the hospital."

He left his home in a small South Carolina town, where he was raised with four brothers and two sisters, by his father, who was a preacher but quit preaching to work in a cotton mill, and his mother, who died a few years ago.

He wants to go back there and live but he can't, he says. They'd point at him and say, "There's the guy who stuck the dart in his eye while he was drugged up," or, "There's the guy who stole that car."

Oh, yes, about the stolen car. What he did was rent it and drive it to the San Joaquin Valley in California and he never got around to returning it. He was back in his hometown a while back and the man he'd taken the car from spotted him. To stay out of jail, he now pays $25 a week until he's paid the man $1,000.

There was that time, too, when his brother stole a pickup truck and the two of them took off for Florida. They stopped beside a swamp and he painted flowers and hearts and crosses and a devil holding a pitchfork, things like that all over that ol' pickup. "I'm kinda artistic, and I just wanted to paint some pictures on the pickup," he said. "I guess we're just crazy, is all."

They drove the truck to Mexico and on the way back, they were stopped by border guards and the vehicle was searched for drugs. "One of them guards looked at us – my brother had a beard but I wasn't old enough to grow one yet – he looked at us and at that painted pickup and he said, 'I'll bet you we find at least five pounds on this one.' And the other guard said, 'Ten pounds, at least.'

"Well, all they found was all we had. We had two grams of

marijuana hidden in a five-pound sack of grits and derned if that dog of theirs didn't dig right through that bag of grits and find that stuff."

The Prince of the Pier was married once, for two weeks.

He traveled with this one girl a lot, though. They hitchhiked across the country and back a couple of times (he's thumbed across and back four times and driven it once), once living in a tent for three months on the bank of a lake in Tennessee, keeping their beer and perishables cool by sinking them in the water.

There was another girl, too. He and his brother were working for an oil company in Florida. They'd both gotten themselves a motorcycle and they'd bought a car and saved about $1,000. "Best job I ever had," he says, shaking his head. "I shouldn't have ever left it."

But they met this girl who had inherited $4,000 and they took off with her, partying their way across the country, until they had partied away all of their money and hers.

He expects to find work soon, maybe on a shrimp boat. He's done a lot of things – construction, plumbing, digging and cleaning septic tanks, digging ditches, building chimneys, cleaning boats, working as a deckhand. "Name it and I can do it," he said, "and if I can't do it, I'll tell you I can because nobody's gonna hire you if you say you've never done that kind of work before."

His conversation, sitting on the pier with the sun and wind washing over him as he waited for the mackerel to bite, was laced with mentions of his mother and father.

"I've never worried much about anything, except my mom," he said. "My mom never touched a beer, never said a cuss word. Like the song says, the only hell she ever raised was her children.

"We've been a bunch of rowdies, I guess, stealing that car and that truck. And I got another brother that's done time up in Columbia. And a sister we ain't heard from in three years.

"I never got over my mom dying, the way it was. I was out west somewhere and I called home on Mother's Day – this was about four years ago – and she was sick. I started thumbing home and I got stuck in Albuquerque for three days before I got a ride out. It took me seven days to get home and when I got here, my mom had been buried three days."

He sat running a finger over the tattoos on his arm, some of which have been scratched over as a new girl replaced an old one. "Yeah," he said, looking out at the ocean, "I've got some regrets. I wish I'd never done no drugs. And I wish I'd done a better job of raising up and made my daddy proud of me. I imagine he thinks I'm pretty sorry.

"But if I can get me a piece of land here and settle down with a good job, maybe he'll change his idea about me. I hope so. He was a hard man, but I guess he had to be. I talked to him on the phone the other day and he said, 'Son, if I ever whupped you for something you didn't do, I'm sorry.'

"That sure made me want to go home but I can't, not right now."

June 30, 1975

The Curse

The journey began in the cool, fresh early morning darkness of the farm where we had come to visit old friends Ben and Sue Rogers in Pink Hill (pop. 500) in eastern North Carolina tobacco land. Ben loaded his son Craig and my son David into an automobile and pulled his boat. I climbed into a pickup truck with Cecil (Shep) Sheppard, a neighbor, and we hauled Shep's bass boat behind us.

Shep is a jolly man who repairs heavy farm equipment for a living and lives for the days when he can go fishing. His girth attests to a lifetime of good feeding.

As we rambled through the flat countryside along narrow, winding roads into dawn, Shep, a chew of Red Man tucked comfortably into his jaw, spun yarns of fish pulled from the waters of Pungo Creek, our destination.

Pungo Creek opens into the Pamlico River. Part of it is fresh water – the first mile or two from the point where we put our boats in. Then it turns brackish. Shep said he had caught bass, bream, speckled robin, gar, striped bass, sea perch, flounder, trout and assorted other fish in Pungo. I thought perhaps I should warn him about The Curse but decided against it because he was clearly excited about the prospects for the day's fishing and I didn't have the heart to dampen his enthusiasm.

I have lived with The Curse all my life. What it is is an uncanny ability not to catch fish. Not only do I not catch them, the people with whom I am fishing don't catch them either. Occasionally, I have dredged up a few whiting while bottom fishing or a few crappie around old tree stumps, things anybody could do. But never a big fish. Never a bass big enough to keep.

That's what I wanted. To hook a good-sized bass and experience what others had told me about, to see a big one come out of the water twisting and slapping its tail like the pictures on the covers of *Field and Stream*. But despite assurances from Ben and Shep that it would happen in this place on this day, I sat thinking about The Curse as we pushed through Washington – Little Washington, they call it – to the creek.

The point where we launched the boats was no wider than a backyard swimming pool. But in five minutes, we were out of the overhanging trees and bushes, in a great, unspoiled wonderland of wide waterways skirting small islands of marsh grass as high as your head.

As we pushed farther and farther away from civilization, the creek widening as we went, a serenity settled over me. The Curse no longer mattered so much. I knew I could spend this day in this place and leave totally fulfilled if I didn't catch so much as a small bream. On days when that urge to go fishing – a mysterious urge that tugs at every man from time to time – had come over me, this was the kind of place I had envisioned but I had no idea that such a place existed any more.

We moved up several yards from the bank of an island and Shep cut the gasoline engine and cut on a tiny, quiet electric motor which he could operate, along with the steering, with his foot while he fished. Our casts brought up nothing but an occasional thin stalk of dead marsh grass. The Curse was working.

Shep fussed softly. "I can't understand it," he said, spitting tobacco juice into the water. "We ought to have three or four by now. Always do." I felt guilty but said nothing.

Tired of the fruitless casting, reeling, casting, reeling, we snuggled up close to the bank of another island, hooked worms onto lines hung from cane poles and went after smaller stuff. A speckled robin, a beautiful orange and yellow fish, took Shep's bait, raced around with it, then yielded to his strong pull and was dumped into the ice chest. Seconds later, I boated one. "At least we weren't shut out," I said.

We stayed there, plunking worms into the tiny cut in the island, until we had caught about a dozen robins, then went looking for Ben and the boys.

They had three bass and clearly were not impressed with our catch.

Shep and I, fired by the sight of their bass, began plugging again. We tried Graveyard Point, which looked promising but yielded nothing. We eased up Jack's Creek, narrow and windless, where the full blast of the sun could be felt. My suntan, earned on golf courses, was turning red. So was Shep's face, though it was shaded by a cap.

The drought finally broke when Shep boated a bass barely big enough to keep. I breathed a sigh of relief. At least The Curse had not spoiled his day completely.

We went back over waters we had worked before, easing along the banks. Several times, the water behind his lure roiled but nothing struck. It served only to heighten his excitement, though.

We went back and caught a few more robins and by then, it was late afternoon and I still hadn't caught my bass. "I'm not going to catch one," I told Shep. He spat and said, "Yeah, you are. 'Fore we get out of here, you'll have one, I guarantee.

"Here, try this redfin lure. It'll get 'em."

I flipped it under an overhang of grass and felt that certain tug. I had a fish. It struggled deep and then to the surface. "Little'un," said Shep. It looked big to me. We boated it and he said to throw it back, but I said measure it first. It wasn't a keeper. The Curse.

He hooked a couple and put them on ice. I dutifully kept casting, though by now I was weary and convinced it was foolish to continue. I flicked the redfin onto a little point jutting out from the island and suddenly it happened. The line tightened and the reel sang.

The water broke and a bass, fighting my lure, leaped high. It looked like a whale. Shep began to laugh and shout, "Keep the tip of the rod up and keep a tight line on him." I wrestled it to the boat and he netted it. It was a good three pounds if it was an ounce. Shep chuckled. "Heh, heh, heh. told you so. Told you we'd get you one 'fore the day was over."

I stood up and yelped like a man cheering a touchdown pass. The Curse had been broken.

The journey home in darkness was a treasure in itself. I was tired but it was a good tiredness. I lay back on the seat with the night air blowing on my face and smiled as the truck hummed along with Shep telling stories, spitting out the window and occasionally interrupting his tales to say, "Well, sir, you beat me, didn't you? Heh. Heh."

I never did tell him what else I had beaten.

August 8, 1984

Something to Cheer

The Midnight Mission hunches on the corner of Fourth and Los Angeles streets in the aching gut of Skid Row.

The men who shuffle into the mission for free meals are street people to whom life is an empty bottle and home is wherever they lie down at night under a piece of cardboard or a few pages of newspaper or the sky.

For them, the Midnight Mission is a wasted lifetime away from the splendor of LA's Olympic Games, but the fever of the great sports spectacle is so pervasive in this sprawling city it has crept even into this refuge. Men whose days are ordinarily consumed by the quest for a bottle in which they can escape the reality of hopelessness are spending more time at the mission because someone connected with the Games thought to send them a television set last week.

They sit in the rows of seats in front of the TV, clutching paper bags or oily little carry bags or tiny packets which hold everything they own, and watch the Olympics and for awhile they are lifted.

Some wear the Olympic badges the mission gave them and there are bright Olympic posters on the concrete block walls.

They were watching the canoe races Tuesday morning. "They don't get very excited about stuff like that," said Clancy Imislund, a husky, good-natured man, a one-time alcoholic who had his front teeth kicked out in a Phoenix jail but who has had his mouth and his life repaired and is now director of the mission. "But when track and field or swimming or basketball, anything they can identify with, comes on, they're up and cheering.

"We're very pleased with the effect. You've got to remember, their overt reactions are secondary because their life is such an inner-directed thing, so anything that pulls them out of themselves is good, anything that focuses their attention for awhile."

"It's good to hear them cheer, because they really don't have a helluva lot to cheer about," said Lee Hopson, the assistant director. He knows. A few years ago he was coming to this same mission for a handout, just another Skid Row bum.

"A lot of them will be bragging about this next year, telling people, 'I was in Los Angeles during the Olympics.'"

A big, black man who was leaning over the edge of drunkenness weaved up to Hopson and asked moistly, "Is it true we've won 11 gold medals? (The figure was actually in the 40s.) I wish the Russians was here so we could get some of that.

"Americans are not scared of Russians. The Russians are coming, the Russians are coming. Bleep the Russians."

He ambled to the door, thrust out his chest and said, "Be proud," and walked out.

Alfredo Nueva, a short Filipino with silver hair spilling down onto his shoulders from beneath a cowboy hat, sat in one of the rows listening to Frank Gifford and Kathleen Sullivan talk about the Games.

"I've watched most of the Olympics," he said, "but my game is judo. I'm a physical education teacher. I've been a black belt for 24 years. I was the lightweight champion of the United States last year."

He's 62 years old. His mind is obviously filled with fantasies. He says he was in the Bataan march, he earned a wartime commission and made lieutenant colonel, he once threw the world judo champion to the floor in five seconds and he might compete in the next Olympics. His mind is not so gone, though, that he can't experience the same emotions the rest of us feel when The Star-Spangled Banner is played and the U.S. flag is raised at the Olympic awards ceremonies.

"We cry," he said. "Look at me, I cry just thinking about it." And he wiped a tear from his face.

Robert Grove is a tall, lean, well-spoken man with blue eyes that tell you they've seen a lot of fire and rain and sunny days when he could not stand the pain. He carries his belongings in one hand, a toothbrush, a comb, a razor, a pen "for making notes," a bus pass to get him from one mission to another and a couple of pieces of identification.

"It's all I've got," he said. "I'm waiting for some money coming from home. I got mugged about a month ago. I lost my money, my bedroll, my identification and my trumpet."

He used to be a musician, he said, playing night clubs and circuses and rodeos.

"I've lost 13 horns in about seven years," he said. "Some of them were stolen but sometimes I get a little loaded and walk off and forget where I left them.

"Occasionally, I get into sporadic drinking spells. I just blew $100 a couple of weeks ago celebrating my birthday (his 67th). I set the troops up. That's what I call the guys around Skid Row."

Grove said he's proud to see the United States doing so well in the Olympics "but it's nice to see other countries win, too. I always believe in 'may the best man win.'

"Sometimes, though, I get a little emotional when I see an American getting a medal. There have been a few occasions when I've kinda had to steel myself against tears. I've been close to what you might call the breaking-up stage.

"Even a television program can manipulate your feelings. I've felt that a few times."

I'll carry a great many touching images of these Olympic Games home with me but none will be more enduring than that of these men who have been buffeted so awfully hard by the winds of misfortune sitting there, shoulder to shoulder, with their eyes on a TV set watching people play games.

Even a television program can manipulate your feelings.

June 5, 1980

Summer Images

Images shimmering on a hot June day, patches of Charlotte at play:

• A jogger lopes along the streets of a leafy neighborhood in the early morning, wearing radio earphones. His face reflects the pain of the run, then suddenly bursts into a bright smile at something he hears on the radio. Murphy in the Morning, probably.

• Caddies waiting for bags at Quail Hollow Country Club play "Graveyard," their own miniature golf game. The course winds through a small patch of trees. The caddies argue good-naturedly about the quality of their shots that bound crazily along the ground they've worn bare in places.

• Tennis shoes slide, dig, twist in the clay at Olde Providence Racquet Club as a doubles match unfolds. The game ends and the empty court, streaked and pocked, looks like a modern painting.

• A blocky, blond kid of maybe 12 years rides a bicycle up a neighborhood street, notices a couple of girls sitting on a front stoop and pops a wheelie, cutting his eyes to see their reaction.

• A man of perhaps 25, his skin glistening with sweat, shoots alone on a playground basketball court. He puts on some moves – head fakes and cuts and a behind-the-back dribble – and you know there's an announcer in his head describing the action, screaming, "And Dr. J, working his way through traffic, goes behind his back, driving, goes up for a layup..." And he throws up a "brick" off the backboard.

• Old men argue whether Carter will be re-elected while they shoot snooker. Their game is a daily ritual they've been observing at the same hour, same pool room for years. Long ago, they learned it was unnecessary to name the bets or say things like "nice shot." On Sundays, when the pool room is closed, they wait for Mondays.

• Parents, a small cluster, sit in the stands of a high school gym in early evening and watch their youngsters' gymnastics class put on its year-end "show" and at least one of the students reminds them of Nadia.

• A heavy-set, gray-haired man takes a seat behind home plate at Crockett Park, slings one leg over the other, lights a cigar and watches the O's alone. He shows no emotion. He just watches. He could be a scout. More likely, he's a man who loves baseball and has no one left with whom to watch it.

• A service station mechanic takes his lunch bag and a fishing rod to a pond off a neighboring road. He alternately takes a bite of his sandwich and casts into the red-brown water. Nothing hits his lure. It's too hot for the fish to bite. Att he end of the hour, he reels in one last time, picks up the paper from his lunch and heads back, cleansed, ready for an afternoon's work.

• Daylight is just creeping over the trees as a station wagon, loaded with young'uns and groceries and towels and all the other things – but most especially, loaded with anticipation – backs out of a driveway and turns its nose toward the beach.

• A man wearing a gray suit and carrying an umbrella walks alone along a downtown street in the flow of people going to work. Suddenly, he stops, takes his stance facing a mirror in a window and drills an imaginary tee shot down the concrete fairway with his umbrella, holding his pose to study his follow through. He nods almost imperceptibly and continues on down the street.

• Two little boys, barefoot and shirtless, hunt crawdads in a section of creek where overhanging branches give the effect of a cave.

• A couple of three-piece suits are having coffee in a shop in one of the high-rise buildings downtown. They are smiling a lot and nodding agreement with each other. They are talking about how Carolina will do next season. Not next football season. Next basketball season.

• A man with the unmistakable look of a traveling salesman looks over the magazines in a hotel lobby shop. He thumbs through a *Playboy* and puts it back. He picks up a *Sports Illustrated*, pays for it and starts out. He stops, goes back, picks up the *Playboy* and buys it, too.

• The Atlanta Braves flicker on the TV screen. And in front of the TV, a man sleeps.

July 9, 1987

The Faces of Pool

Pool rooms – real ones – should be cool and shadowy and possess a certain coziness.

They should regenerate a hint of the iniquity that our moms warned us could be found there when we were growing up.

They should be populated with men whose countenances are road maps of intrigue to be read in our imaginations by the lights hanging above the tables.

Rob's Roost, on N.C. 115 near the Metrolina Fairgrounds, is a lounge, but the furniture has been moved out this week and pool tables moved in for the Charlotte Nine-Ball Championship. The full flavor of a pool room has been captured.

They could have shot "The Hustler" or "The Color of Money" there.

Indeed, Grady Mathews, one of the contestants, had a bit part in "The Color of Money," a movie starring Tom Cruise and Paul Newman. He lost a match with Newman.

He says the movies were OK but not true to life, "just workman like, stereotypical jobs, what the public wanted."

Mathews, 44 with glasses and thinning hair, is known as "The Professor." He acquired the name for his affinity for crossword puzzles. Plus, he said, "I always like to look at the philosophical, esoteric side of life. I've made a lifelong study of the intricacies of pool, not just what happens but why."

Nicknames abound in the sport. New York Blackie, The Giant Killer, The Rifleman, Spanish Mike and The Pearl are among the shooters here.

The Professor had just knocked off the fabled ex-hustler "Weenie Beanie," whose real name is Bill Staton and who has appeared on the Johnny Carson and Merv Griffin Shows.

As pool has moved deeper into tournament competition, said The Professor, hustling has diminished.

"There are still a few hustlers," he said, "but not as many since pool players have begun to gain public acceptance.

"I used to hustle. I had all kinds of disguises. I pretended to be a mechanic, a hair dresser, various things.

"I would bet you could let me off in any town in my underwear with no money and, without sending for money, I could be 500 miles away the next day with money in my pocket. Hustlers know how to talk to people."

Not that money doesn't change hands. Rob's Roost is open 24 hours a day this week. After the tournament action has ended, players "get together, let their hair down," is the way The Professor put it.

One player opened his garage and auto parts shop in Ayden in eastern North Carolina on Tuesday morning, worked until late afternoon, drove to Charlotte, won his first tournament match, played one-ball from midnight until 1:30 Wednesday afternoon, then won another match. One assumes he was not playing for his health. He said he would get five or six hours of sleep, then start shooting again.

Some of the players in the tournament are local hotshots but of the 28 men players, eight rank among the top 20 in the Professional Billiards Association ratings. The Professor is a three-time one-pocket world champion and has won half a dozen nine-ball tournaments. He said he writes for two trade publications, gives lessons and exhibitions, plays in tournaments, gambles and sells cue sticks and his income is about $50,000 a year.

He carries a $1,000 cue stick. Most pros, he said, use cuesticks worth about $600.

"I'd lend you my car or my wife but I wouldn't let you touch my cue stick," he said.

Four matches are played simultaneously. Spectators sit in bleachers or stand in the shadows. The first man to win 11 games wins the match. The players, most wearing jeans, sneakers and untucked sports shirts, move silently around the tables sizing up shots or sit watching their opponents, showing no emotion. The rich click of the shiny balls can be heard above the soft conversations of spectators. There is a faint odor of beer in the air.

There are no flashy cue-twirling Tom Cruises playing. But you can almost feel the presence of Minnesota Fats and Fast Eddie Felson in the place, eyes darting from ball to ball, cue sticks flicking backward and forward, mind working against mind.

"You get tired," said the man who had been up for a day and a half, "but nerves, that's the thing."

If you don't have nerve, you don't belong here. You're going to lose to some face with long highways and long nights etched in it.

February 22, 1973

Unsinkable John Brophy

For some reason, I never saw John Brophy as a blackhearted villain. Though he has raged against player, fan and gendarme across the Eastern Hockey League for as long as the frosty game has been in the South, he remains more mischievous than malicious.

That may be hard to accept when just two nights ago, Brophy, now wearing the colors of the New Jersey Devils, had to be subdued – more or less – by the police at the coliseum to put a stop to a fight he didn't even start.

But when the storm in him subsided and he agreed to banishment from the game, he skated across the ice wearing an impish smile and flashed a victory sign to the Checkers fans who were booing his behavior – many of them the same fans who used to cheer him when he played for our village. No doubt, he felt better for it all, fulfilled, in a fashion.

Brophy, 40 years old now with combat ribbons from more EHL teams than he can count on one fist, is not easily provoked.

He is basically a cheap shot artist who can accept – indeed, appreciate – a good cheap shot aimed at himself. He has always chosen his adversaries with great care when possible, selecting those he figured he could intimidate or whip and avoiding bigger, more hostile opponents.

Once embroiled in battle, though, he sometimes loses his head. He carries the conflict to the point of insanity, fairly inviting the world to come and taste one of his knuckle sandwiches. Properly enraged, he would stick fight King Kong.

Brophy was one of the original Charlotte Clippers, who were later to change their name to Checkers. Burned out of their arena in Baltimore, they finished out their season in Charlotte and met with such success at the gate they decided to move to the city permanently.

Brophy was 24 years old with the hair of a 60-year-old. He was immediately dubbed the Gray Ghost. As an incendiary, he excited the male population and as a good-looking roughneck, he won the favor of the ladies.

He won it in such abundance, when he was dealt away in 1960, women besieged the Checkers office with calls and letters of protest, demanding that he be reclaimed.

Brophy had questionable judgment, to say the least.

Charlotte was playing Philadelphia in a pre-season exhibition game in a tiny arena in Valley Forge, Pa. The Philly crowd hated Brophy from past encounters and rode him from the moment he put a skate on the ice.

It seemed a good time and place to let discretion be the better part of valor but Brophy, thriving on the hostility, broke his stick over the head of a Philly player, which has always been unacceptable practice in ice hockey and most everything else.

There was no penalty box. Brophy had to serve his time on the first row of the grandstand. He didn't get seated before a fight erupted and a riot was very nearly touched off.

Brophy let that one simmer down without pursuing it to any great lengths but there have been countless other occasions when he wouldn't quit.

During a regular season game in Philadelphia, he carried the fight into the penalty box and to the fans and to the police – six, I believe

– who were trying to subdue him. He was holding his own until a couple of cops located a length of chain in the penalty box, wrapped it around Brophy's neck and brought him to rein long enough to haul him off to jail, still wearing his bloody uniform.

And, as some seem to recall, smiling.

He has also been arrested in Greensboro for fighting fans. They say he wiped out his own teammate in a fight in an elevator, rendering the poor guy unfit to play for several days. They also say he smashed the windows – glass, sash, everything – out of his hotel room in a fit of rage over something.

Laid end to end, his penalty minutes would probably run for a year or two. He has spilled enough blood to lay ice for a hockey game.

He hasn't changed. At the Charlotte Coliseum Tuesday night, he fought one Checker, tried to fight the coach and struggled with several policemen who were trying to handcuff him.

They never did get the cuffs on him. He was thrown out of the game but as far as he was concerned, he had won a victory of sorts. He exited smiling.

May 8, 1984

A Pretty Good Quarterback

Athletic feats generally grow over the years where the famous are concerned.

Charlie "Choo Choo" Justice says, "The older I get, the greater I become."

Burt Reynolds occasionally is referred to as a former all-America football player when in fact he was never an all-star of any kind.

Not so with Jesse Jackson, the former quarterback-linebacker from Greenville, S.C., who would be president. Go in search of Jackson the football player and you find that no legend has grown around his gridiron feats. He is remembered for his leadership and determination but there are no memories of Jesse Jackson outlined against a gray October sky doing wondrous deeds. Which explains why, though he's featured in the media every day, rarely is there a mention of Jackson's football playing days, which were between 1961 and 1963.

Walter Holtzclaw of Charlotte, who was a basketball player at N.C. A&T in Greensboro when Jackson was a football player there and has maintained a friendship with the presidential candidate, provides the bottom line on Jackson's football playing days:

"Jesse wasn't the man, but he was a pretty good quarterback."

The man, according to Dr. Bert Piggott, who coached football at A&T when Jackson played there, was Cornell Gordon, who later was Joe Namath's backup on the New York Jets team that upset the Baltimore Colts in the Super Bowl.

"Jesse did a lot of playing but Cornell was entrenched at quarterback," says Piggott.

There are no statistics to tell us how many passes Jackson completed, how many yards he ran. Drexel Ball, the sports information director at A&T, says either no stats were kept or they were lost in a fire that destroyed many of the school's athletic records. Yearbooks show that Jackson was a member of the teams but don't tell us how many touchdowns he scored.

Jackson first flowered as a football player at Sterling High in Greenville, S.C. The Rev. J.D. Mathis, who coached him then, says, "Jesse was our quarterback for four years. He had a very outstanding career at Sterling. He was our all-time leader in pass completions.

"He was very versatile. He was a good runner, had good size and had a keen knowledge of the game. He could read defenses and check off at the line of scrimmage even then.

"He was bigger than most kids his age. And he was very competitive. He didn't believe in second place. He always played to win.

"You could see his leadership qualities even then. He just stood out in a crowd. People just flocked to him and he was very comfortable with them. That's one reason we played him at quarterback."

Piggott first learned of Jackson by mail from A&T alumni. The letters urged Piggott to take a look at this young quarterback, who stood 6-2 and had a strong arm.

"We sent a battery of coaches to try to recruit him," recalls Piggott. "Spent eighty dollars."

Jackson chose to go to Illinois, though. He remained there one season, apparently realized he wouldn't get to play a lot because even in that more enlightened Midwest area, people were not ready for a black quarterback (that's not gospel, it's what some of his friends suggest), left Illinois and came to all-black A&T.

"He was our second-string quarterback," says Piggott. "For a while, we alternated our first and second teams as starters to develop depth and so he got to start some.

"He could throw but he wasn't as fast on his feet as Cornell. He had the ability to run and was good at it but not like Cornell.

"He could call plays with acumen. He could pick the right plays. I only called the plays in key situations.

"I don't remember him messing up other than a couple of fumbles and interceptions, the normal things that happen to quarterbacks."

It was during these days that Jackson first became involved in the black movement, joining sit-ins and picketing and marches that launched him on a career as a prominent black leader.

Wylie Harris, a physical education teacher at Johnson C. Smith who played for A&T, recalls that several members of the team were "involved in sit-ins and going to jail together in Greensboro."

He also remembers Jackson as being "pretty big, pretty rugged, pretty rough" and one who was persistent, who "was going to stick to something, no matter what."

Piggott says Jackson would speak up for what he thought was right, sometimes to the coaches.

"He could talk, get his message across well," says Piggott. "He had a head on his shoulders. He was also a team man. When one guy would be falling apart, in need of discipline, Jesse would get him back in line. He'd say, 'Come on, this is our team. Let's go.' "

Jackson still expresses his appreciation for his football scholarship when he and the coach get together.

Jackson came from a poor family. The man who married his mother when Jackson was 2 years old and gave the child his name was a janitor.

"Jesse still says that he ate two of every three days he spent at A&T and if it hadn't been for his scholarship, he wouldn't have eaten at all," says Piggott. "He seems to feel A&T helped him when he needed help. He seems to feel the scholarship saved his bacon.

"I knew he had the stuff to be a quarterback. He had to have the stuff to be a leader. But I didn't realize that he had the potential in him that was discovered later."

May 30, 1974

Armed and Dangerous

You remember Spiro Agnew, don't you? The fellow who conked Doug Sanders on the head with one of his wayward golf shots.

His successor, Gerald Ford, wrestling grimly with the Quail Hollow Country Club course in the Kemper Open Pro-Amateur, almost achieved the same notoriety – armed and dangerous – with one swipe of his driver.

It happened on the par-5 10th hole. The vice prexy, gunning for extra distance, hit a screaming hook and then he started screaming, "Fore!" as the ball curved sharply left toward two young ladies making their way toward the green.

The ball ripped through the branches of a small tree and cleared the heads of the spectators by about a foot and wound up in an unplayable lie in a patch of honeysuckle. The girls continued on, oblivious of how close they had come to being famous.

A voice in Ford's gallery said, "You're starting to look like Spiro."

The vice president was teamed with pro Tom Weiskopf, Gov. Jim Holshouser and evangelist Billy Graham for the four-and-a-half hour struggle with God's green earth. God won. Weiskopf, the defending Kemper champion, somehow managed to keep his game together for 17 holes while his partners thrashed around in the trees and sand and tall grass but it finally rubbed off on him at the 18th.

He drove under an azalea bush and made a rather vice presidential seven on the par-4 hole. A man can take just so much.

Despite his political affiliation, there is nothing conservative about the vice president's golf game. He takes a very strong grip, pounds his tee shots lustily, gambles from the rough and putts like a blacksmith, frequently rolling the ball well past the cup.

His score? Well, he would probably like this covered up, but here's how I figured it:

He didn't finish out the 10th hole after driving into an unplayable lie, taking a drop and then hitting across the fairway into the woods. I reckoned the best he could have made had he continued was a nine.

Giving him that nine and conceding some putts he didn't have to hit after Weiskopf or one of the others had taken care of the hole for the team, Ford, a 17-handicapper, shot 50-52–102.

That's not all that bad when you have a Secret Service man in your hip pocket and another hanging off the end of your club and a third examining the ball for bugging devices and photographers kneeling directly in your lie with their cameras clicking and whirring.

The Secret Service men scoured the woods ahead of Ford's foursome, scanned the crowd constantly, trailed at his heels and all the while tried to be inconspicuous. They wore sport shirts that bulged at the hips with weaponry, had plugs in their ears for radio contact and sweated a lot.

On the first tee, the vice president told his companions, "Call me Gerry, not vice president." The foursome posed for a picture and Holshouser said, "Tommy can smile now. He hasn't seen us play yet."

After a shaky start, with two conceded bogeys, Ford ripped a fine drive around the dogleg on the third hole, hit a nifty approach shot 18 feet to the left of the cup and two-putted for his only par of the day.

On the fourth tee, he hooked his drive into deep rough. He turned to Weiskopf in exasperation and said, "Now, what am I doing wrong?" He got a free lesson and it helped on the fifth tee when he slugged out a 225-yarder right in the heart of the fairway. He had another good drive on the sixth hole but then the lesson wore off.

The crowd was sympathetic, congratulating Ford or Graham or Holshouser on good shots that weren't, agonizing with them when they found bunkers or missed putts and occasionally exchanging good-natured conversation with one of them.

The 17th hole was ringed with spectators. It's a par three with water between the tee and the green. As Ford stood over his ball, ready to swing, a voice from across the pond rang out: "Watch out for the Watergate." Ford didn't look but smiled and slammed his tee shot into the gallery behind the green, taking no chances with the water.

Graham hit the green with his tee shot and got a big roar. When he reached the green, he told the gallery, "You sounded like a bunch of Baptists over here." A moist voice piped from the crowd, "You want a beer, Billy?"

He didn't but I did. I popped a top and three Secret Service men went for their guns.

November 7, 1980

The Little Dutch Boy

Athletic reputations have a way of growing with the years. Now that he has been elected President of the United States, "Dutch" Reagan may became at least an honorable mention All-American.

But it's difficult even for a president-elect to cast off the encumbrance of playing without distinction in the interior line at tiny Eureka (Ill.) College.

Besides, his coach is still around to attest to the kind of player Ronald Reagan was for the Red Devils.

"He wasn't an outstanding star," said Ralph McKinzie, 87, who coached Reagan from 1928 to 1931 and who still pitches in at Eureka as an assistant. "He was a rather skinny type of individual.

"He was a very conscientious, dedicated, hard worker and pretty much of a leader. He never gave me any trouble.

"I never dreamed he'd be a politician," McKinzie recalled by telephone. "I always thought he'd be a broadcaster. After practice, he'd grab a broom or something with a handle and act like he was broadcasting a game. He made up the names, all of it. He was very good at it."

Reagan was so good at it that it led to a job at WHO, a 50,000-watt station in Des Moines, for five years before he went into movies.

"Dutch" Reagan (his father gave him the nickname because he supposedly looked like a little Dutch boy with his hair hanging over his forehead) walked into the station and asked for a job. WHO was planning to start broadcasting Iowa football games and needed someone to do the play-by-play.

They gave Reagan a tryout on the spot. They put him behind a microphone and told him to go ahead and broadcast an imaginary game. He gave them several minutes of the kind of thing he'd been doing to entertain his teammates and fraternity brothers, and the job was his.

He began doing Cubs and Iowa Hawkeye games as well as other events such as dance remotes, track meets, Golden Gloves boxing and fairgrounds auto racing.

His big sponsors were Wheaties and Kentucky Club pipe tobacco.

"He made a game seem real," recalls Myrtle Williams Moon of

Des Moines, who was program director at WHO at the time. "He could make you see a game. He had a great flair, a great imagination."

Myrtle Moon developed a lasting relationship with Reagan. When her husband was fatally ill seven years ago, Reagan telephoned her and asked, "Would it help if I came?"

Today, Myrtle Moon says, "When he was elected president, I felt a little sad. Isn't that funny? It's such a big thing.

"But I know he knows what he's doing. And he won't have to do it alone. He has the ability to turn things over to others. He was that way when he was at WHO. He hated detail."

Listeners remember that Reagan was burdened with losing Iowa teams except for one year, but he kept his broadcasts lively. Iowa did bless him with one player of unusual quality, a running back named Ozzie Simpson, nicknamed the "Ebony Eel."

When Simpson got the ball, Reagan's favorite expression was "It's a hippity-hop to the left" or "It's a hippity-hop to the right" and then, "There goes the 'Ebony Eel.'"

He also favored "Holy cow" during football broadcasts and "Socko" during baseball games.

H.R. Gross, for 26 years a Congressman from Iowa and now retired in Arlington, Va., was news director at WHO while Reagan was there. Gross points out that Reagan worked under very difficult circumstances during baseball season.

Reagan broadcast the Cubs games from a studio, re-creating the action from sketchy accounts sent by Morse code. The information he got might say simply, 'S,' and Reagan would go into detail about the pitch and the swing and the strike.

"Oh, he could improvise," said Gross. "Sometimes the wires would go down and he would have to ad lib, describing events that may or may not be going on, until the wires could be rerouted."

On one occasion when the wire reports stopped with a man at the plate, Reagan had the presence of mind to have the batter foul off 17 pitches, meanwhile having the pitcher take a "slow, a very slow" windup.

Jim Zabel, sports director at WHO for the past 35 years, remembers listening to "Dutch" Reagan. "He was a heckuva sportscaster. To this day, he's one of the best I've ever heard. He was in the mold of Bill Stern and Ted Husing or, among today's broadcasters, Keith Jackson.

"He has a great memory. He can still recall details of games he broadcast.

"A few years ago, I asked him what would've happened if that telegram (summoning him to Hollywood) hadn't come. He said 'I would've remained a broadcaster.' Of course, he would've moved up to a network."

Reagan usually wore his "E" letterman's sweater and a hat while broadcasting football games.

William Burghardt, who would coach N.C. Central from 1937-1942, played center beside guard Reagan at Eureka.

Now retired in Lanham, Md., Burghardt says, "I don't want to say that 'Dutch' was the greatest guard the world has ever known, but he was one of the most dependable men I ever played beside. And he was durable. We didn't have platoon football then. He and I usually played 58 to 60 minutes. The only time we ever came out was when we were hurt."

Burghardt's most vivid memory of his old teammate is one that runs contrary to the picture painted of the candidate Reagan during the campaign.

"I was one of three blacks on the football team," said Burghardt. "The Midwest was pretty tough for a black at that time. There was no such thing as a legal sign of segregation, but you could go one place without a problem and go to the next block and get insulted."

The Eureka team stopped in LaSalle, Ill., to spend the night in a hotel en route to a game at Elmhurst College near Chicago. When the desk clerk refused to give the blacks rooms, Reagan stepped in.

Burghardt recalls, "'Dutch' said, 'I have the solution. Give me taxi fare and I'll take them home with me tonight. (His home in Dixon was only about a dozen miles away.) We'll get a few hours of sleep, eat breakfast and catch a cab back here in the morning.'

"And that's what we did. That was unusual for Illinois at the time, but I don't think Reagan even remembered it until I brought it up not long ago."

It was Reagan's broadcasting that led him into the movies. He annually went to the Cubs' training camp at Catalina Island off the California coast to study mannerisms, appearances, batting stances, etc., for use on his re-creations.

In 1937, Reagan dropped into a nightclub to hear one of his old girlfriends sing. She arranged for him to take a screen test. Later that year, the telegram came, calling him to Hollywood for his first film.

Myrtle Williams Moon remembers him running down the stairs shouting "Myrtle! Myrtle!" and waving the telegram.

She also recalls his first film, *Love Is On The Air*, in which "Dutch" played the role of a radio announcer.

"It was a crummy movie," she said.

These Are Personal

August 20, 1978

A Few Words To My Son

This one is personal. If it seems at times that I'm dropping names, I'm not. Some of the most impressive people I've met are not even mentioned here and some of them aren't even famous. This is just something I wanted to say.

The first of my young flew the nest today. He's going away to complete his college education with the intention of becoming a sports writer.

I've never encouraged him in this direction, though I have helped where I could. I've tried for years to nudge him toward medicine or dentistry or sales, point out that the people in those lines are the ones you see most often at the bank and the golf course, but he said he would rather write sports than work for a living.

All of this has put me to thinking. I've been writing sports for the *Charlotte News* for 29 years. I figure I've written 7,250,000 words, give or take a million, and not counting the thousands of pages I've thrown away when the words wouldn't come out right. At times, putting one word after another is like lifting an anvil, but I have never thought of it as work and I still don't like to see the paper come out without something in it that I've written.

So, how can I tell him he's making a mistake? How can I tell him he should be an orthodontist or a stockbroker or a banker? I can tell him he'll never be a millionaire but he can quote someone who once said that a sports writer doesn't need to be a millionaire, he lives like one and treads where even millionaires cannot.

I can tell him about the routine office work but it wouldn't matter. He has sat too many nights and listened to me tell about interviews with greats like Mickey Mantle, Ted Williams, Joe DiMaggio, Joe Namath, Woody Hayes, Ara Parseghian, Bill Russell, Wilt Chamberlain, Julius Erving, Jerry West, Arnold Palmer, Jack Nicklaus, Ben Hogan, Patty Berg, Chris Evert, Evonne Goologong, Ken Rosewall, John Newcombe, Bobby Unser, Richard Petty...

About the colorful characters like Billy Joe Patton, Ilie Nastase, Argentina Rocca, Clayton Heafner, Titanic Thompson, Lefty Driesell, Al McGuire, Jim Piersall, Casey Stengel, Curtis Turner...

About the manager of the Davidson basketball team who was pressed into service as a reserve during scrimmages because the ranks were so thin and who finally got into a game one night and scored a basket and then, when the game was over, went back to picking up the towels and jocks. About the scared kid fresh off a boat from Cuba who hung around Griffith Park and lived with the groundskeeper until the late Phil Howser, who saw something special in him, found a team for him to play with, a kid named Tony Oliva...

About the realization that I had seen something done that had never been done before when I saw a Russian woman break a world track record. About the chills I felt watching Ben Hogan limp up the 18th fairway at Augusta. About seeing a no-hitter. About watching Jack Nicklaus beat Johnny Miller and Tom Weiskopf in the greatest Masters of them all. About seeing Arnold Palmer with a tear in his eye when he missed the cut and perhaps – though he wouldn't say it – realized for the first time that he was no longer the great player he had been. About seeing Joe Namath's knees for the first time, with the surgical scars around them, and wanting to turn away. About seeing Archie Griffin run for more than 200 yards in his first big game...

I've told him about all the places – Hawaii, Scotland, Ireland, London, San Francisco, New York, little Canadian towns where the hockey teams trained, Notre Dame on a football weekend, Pinehurst in the spring...

About the warm and lovable people I've gotten to know, too many to mention here, but people like the Buckey twins, George Karl, Cedric Maxwell, Leo Hart, Gordie Tottle, Moe Savard, Minnie Mendoza, Phil Howser, Dick Tiddy, Peggy Kirk Bell, Pete Tufts, Richard Howard, Dennis Satyshur, Waban Thomas, Wahoo McDaniel, the Crocketts, John Morrell, Bobby Jones, Monte Towe...

There's a lot more I've told him about. Of course, there are writers in the big cities who travel far more, see many more stars, catch a lot more of the big events. But then, they don't get to live in Charlotte.

I've been thinking about all these things because my first-born is going off to become a sports writer. I've talked to him about all those other professions but the truth is, I wouldn't trade with any of them. So, son, I hope you make it.

July 6, 1970

In the Good Old Summertime

It's summertime.

It sizzles in the city's streets but there are cool places to sit and contemplate the season, and the memories rush in:

• The tent we made of hopsack that burned down when we tried to have a wiener roast inside it.

• Discovery of a stable in my endless wanderings, where somebody left perfectly good pitching horseshoes lying around.

• Our baseball games, played for hours, with no shirts, no shoes, only an occasional glove, a repaired bat and a ball wrapped in black tape.

• The summer I delivered groceries on a bicycle for $1 a day, $1.50 on Saturday, and learned the valuable lessons from the older, wiser delivery boys. They were blacks who taught me how to sneak a pint of ice cream into the basket for my own consumption and better yet, how to shoot dice, which made me feel deliciously evil.

• The sleepless nights before the beach trips, spent walking with my friend Ray or sitting on his front porch, sneaking a smoke and talking about girls and baseball and occasionally stealing over next door to swipe grapes from the neighbor's vine.

• Standing barefoot in the rushing water after a storm.

• Real lemonade, with slices of lemon and chunks of ice.

• The warm, deep dust of a country road beneath bare feet.

• Riding our bikes down narrow lanes, through the woods, to the creek gurgling under the trees, tossing in a simple line and hook and my heart pounding as I brought to the surface a fish as big as my hand.

• The day we sneaked the .22 out of Ray's house, shot a sitting rabbit, then told tall tales of hitting it on the run.

• Playing baseball in the quiet street with the girls, gallantly lobbing the pitches in to the pretty one, fogging it in to her sister. The sweet smell of soap and the freshness of their dresses when we went back that night to play Monopoly.

• The dawns that found us at the country club, wading the pond, squishing mud between our toes and finding precious golf balls, which we used to play some of the back holes with a five-iron and a putter until the members came along and scared us off.

• Skinny dipping on the Sunday school trip to the mountains.

• My precious BB gun, a Red Ryder model, bought with money I had saved for months, and rubber guns, made from a piece of wood, a clothes pin and a slice of inner tube, great for shooting flies.

• The plum thicket, where you could find shiny, yellow plums and build a hideout.

• The money we made from soft drink bottles we returned, including some chipped and cracked ones culled from the rejects behind the bottling company.

• The awe of the river.

• The week at my uncle's house. He was a preacher and his church was having a revival meeting. The visiting evangelist could eat more fried chicken, biscuits and gravy than any man I'd ever seen. We'd be sitting around on the front porch drowsing on a hot, lazy afternoon, when the evangelist would suddenly shout, "Amen, brother!" and startle hell out of us. And when he pounded the Bible that night, leaped across the front row of seats and warned us all we were going to the devil with liquor, cigarettes, women and lipstick – none of which I used at the time – I could feel the hot breath of Hades on my neck, though the most sinful things I had done at the time were to swipe a handful of peanuts at the store, "smoke" Indian cigars, bust open a watermelon in a field and eat it, and sneak a look at the corset ads in the Sears catalog.

July 12, 1973

Down to the Sea

Nowadays when we go to the beach, we take a house at Garden City with air conditioning and thick carpeting and a color TV. Or maybe a room in a luxurious motel with the ocean lapping just outside the window to lull us to sleep in our comfortable oversized beds. That's the way it is when you're grown up and can afford to treat yourself to an occasional vacation.

I guess it beats what we used to do when we were teenagers but I'll swear, when I sit down and think about it, it seems the way we did it then was better. We could live at the beach for a week for the money we spend on a dinner up at Calabash now.

Ray and I always went together. He was a good influence on me. He started me smoking and cussing and chasing women, although I wasn't very good at any of them at the time and never did master but a couple of them.

We thumbed to the beach. We would start on Monroe Road across the street from the Oakhurst School and the thought that we might not make it that day never entered our minds.

It would usually take about five or six rides for us to make the beach. Once we were picked up by a big, redheaded man in a Ford coupe who said he was a stock car driver. He drove with one hand and drank from a pint of whiskey with the other.

He stopped beside a cotton patch and let us out. He was turning into a dirt road to visit his girl and he said if we were still out there when he came back, he'd take us on down the road. As soon as he was out of sight, though, we ran back up the highway, and planned to hide if he showed up again.

We tried to time our trips so that we would be at the beach at the same time Bill was there with his family. We could sleep on his porch and his mother was a wonderful woman who insisted we take most of our meals with them. We didn't protest very strongly because we figured we were doing Bill a favor by taking him with us when we went chasing women.

I don't think the women ever realized we were chasing them.We never caught any of them.

We would "drag" the boardwalk and go down to Spivey's to look the crowd over but there was usually somebody getting hit with a beer can or a fist down there and we didn't stay there long. We hung around the other dance pavilions and listened to songs like "Sixty Minute Man" and "Sleeping In A Hollow Log."

Mostly, we played bingo. Money that should have gone for such necessities as "world famous" foot long hot dogs was squandered at the bingo parlor.

There was a guy no more than our age hired to stand in front of the bingo parlor and invite people in. He had worked up a clever delivery and he could really "snow" the girls.

I was so smitten by this, my fondest dream was to become a bingo barker and spend the summer at the beach, tossing out cute lines at the passing people, winking at the pretty girls and being recognized by the "popular" crowd at the dance pavilions.

We tried sleeping on the beach a couple of times but the sand blew all over us and it got cold as the night wore on. Sleeping in a car wasn't much better. It was hot and the mosquitoes swarmed and there were usually three or four other guys sleeping in the car, too, so you couldn't lie down.

It was pretty terrible, I guess, but at the time, it seemed worth it, just to be at the beach.

We never rode much except the bumper cars. Mostly, we gambled. You could shoot corks out of pop guns at packages of cigarettes which had silver dollars attached to them by rubberbands. If you knocked the package off the shelf, you got the money.

Ray and I kept at it until we had figured out how the guy operating the place had set the guns, which wouldn't shoot straight. We were well on our way to cleaning him out when he leaned over the counter, kind of raised his lips up over his teeth like a snarling dog and told us to get the hell out of there.

We tried to think of some way to bring legal action against him but we forgot about it a few minutes later when we heard "Wine Spody-Ody" blasting out of a hot dog joint.

The most money either of us ever had at a time was $30. Once we made it a week on $7 each. And when Sunday afternoon came and it was time to go home, we wouldn't have a dime between us.

But we would hit the highway – our shirtsleeves rolled high to show off our tans, our peroxided hair golden in the sun – and miraculously thumb our way home. Still chaste.

August 29, 1979

Yogi, Danny and Beth

I'd love to listen to a conversation between my wife, Beth, and Danny Ozark, manager of the Philadelphia Phillies.

The other day, Beth watched a woman jog down our street and remarked, "Look at that beautiful stride. She's as graceful as a gazebo."

Ozark wouldn't even have blinked.

He's the guy who, trying to allude to Alphonse and Gaston, once said of his decision as to who would play third base in an important game, "I don't want to get into a Galphonse-Aston act."

Beth, bless her, wouldn't even have blinked.

These lapses are accepted with a shrug by our friends, once they learn she's apt to clobber the language from time to time. But it takes some getting used to. Like the time she mentioned a peliquin.

One of our guests leaned over to his wife and whispered, "What the hell's a peliquin?"

His wife, who knew Beth better than he, said, "It's part pelican and part penquin, of course."

"Oh," he said.

Beth, after she had sung a couple of ad lib lines to a song and made them rhyme, exclaimed, "Hey, I'm a regular Oscar and Hammerstein."

She also complained that if television didn't show so many replays, the games wouldn't last so long.

She's not dumb. She married me, didn't she?

If Danny Ozark were dumb, would he be a major league manager?

But Danny says, "Half this game is 90 per cent mental." He says, when asked about his team's morale, "It's not a question of morality."

He says, "I have a good repertory with my players." He says, "Even Napoleon had his Watergate."

He says, "Mike Andrews' limits are limitless."

All of this comes to mind because a book entitled *The Book of Sports Quotes* by Bert Sugar has fallen on my desk and I find it difficult to keep my nose out of it.

As you might expect, I'm especially fond of the malapropisms. I thought of Beth when I read that manager Wes Westrum said, after losing a close game, "Gentlemen, you've seen a cliff dweller."

Some of them are light, some serious, all fun to read. Like Garry Maddox, describing his first grand-slam home run. "As I remember it, the bases were loaded."

Yogi Berra is perhaps the most quoted man in the book. He's another who could have a beautiful conversation with Beth.

Quoth Yogi:

• "If the people don't want to come out to the park, nobody's gonna stop 'em."

• "A nickel ain't worth a dime anymore."

• After hometown fans in St. Louis threw a day for him in 1947, "I want to thank you for making this day necessary."

• "You're never out of it 'til you're out of it."

• "How can I hit and think at the same time?"

• Upon hearing from his wife Carmine that she had just seen *Doctor Zhivago*: "Oh, what's the matter with you now?" Beth would love Yogi Berra.

Or Manager Johnny Logan, who said, "I heard his footprints coming down the hall."

Some others I like: Ring Lardner: " 'Shut up,' he explained." Lee Trevino on tour golf: "My wife tells me she doesn't care what I do when I'm away, as long as I'm not enjoying it."

Wit Oscar Levant on the marital breakup of Joe DiMaggio and Marilyn Monroe: "It proves that no man can be a success in two national pastimes."

Writer Morris Sigel on the performance of Craig Morton, a born-again Christian, in the '78 Super Bowl: "He might have found Jesus, but he's having a terrible time finding (Haven) Moses."

And here's another Beth would listen to and wonder why it was even quoted:

Sam Bowen, a Boston Red Sox draftee in 1974: "Right now, I feel I've got my feet on the ground as far as my head is concerned."

Uh, I'll be right home, Dear. Did you remember to call the man today about the floor-to-floor carpet you wanted?

October 29, 1989

The Frost Is on the Turkey

Just a few weeks ago, we presented in this space some malapropisms and assorted other humorous remarks by such figures as Danny Ozark, ex-manager of the Philadelphia Phillies; Yogi Berra, former star and now a coach with the New York Yankees, and Beth Green, who is going to be formerly Mrs. Ronald Green if I don't quit writing about her.

Today, we return with more words to lose your mind by, these by Jerry Coleman, the recently-appointed manager of the San Diego Padres; Emery Wister, retired entertainment and business writer for the Charlotte News, and Beth:

After taking the poodle for an early morning stroll Monday, Beth came in and announced, "It's cold as blue blazes out there."

You may recall that it was she who said, "If they didn't show so many instant replays, the games wouldn't last so long."

To that, she has added, "If everybody drove small cars, there wouldn't be so much traffic."

Wister is proud of the fact that he was "the last person to interview Clark Gable alive."

He made reference to "the hangman's ax."

In a fit of eloquence, he said, "The frost is on the turkey."

He also commented that "the worm is on the other foot." And one that, to this day, we haven't figured out, something about "up the walls of the blue Pacific."

Coleman is the latest Master of the Malapropism, replacing Ozark, who said such things as, "Even Napoleon had his Watergate," and "His limitations are limitless."

Coleman's best have come during his seven years as broadcaster of the Padres' games before consuming the managerial reins. (I know.)

Some Colemanisms:

"On the mound is Randy Jones, the lefthander with the Karl Marx hairdo." (Presumably he meant one of the Marx brothers – other than Karl.)

"We're all sad to see Glenn Beckert leave. Before he goes, though, I hope he stops by so we can kiss him goodbye. He's that kind of guy."

"There's a fly ball deep to centerfield. Winfield is going back, back ... he hits his head against the wall. It's rolling toward second base."

"Rich Folkers is throwing up in the bullpen."

"He slides into second with a standup double."

"Grubb goes back, back, he's under the warning track, and he makes the play."

"The big ballpark can do it all."

"Young Frank Pastore may have just pitched the biggest victory of 1979, maybe the biggest victory of the year."

"If Pete Rose's streak was still intact, with that single to the left, the fans would be throwing babies out of the upper deck."

"Hrabosky looks fierce in that Fu Manchu haircut."

"Bob Davis is wearing his hair differently this year, short and with curls like Randy wears. I think you call it a Frisbee."

"Next up for the Cardinals is Barry Carry Gary Templeton."

"George Hendrick simply lost that sun-blown popup."

"Those amateur umpires are really flexing their fangs tonight."

I think all this is catching.

I heard a record at a friend's house the other evening and remarked, "Hey, that's Glenn Miller before he died."

I know this – I'm gonna have to start listening carefully to everything I write.

January 4, 1980

A Bad Code

I figure God invented the common cold to punish people who have ticked Him off pretty good but not enough to qualify for full wrath.

I've been trying to figure what I did to make Him drop the deluxe, long-lasting model on me.

I don't recall having done any uncommon sinning lately.

Whatever the reason, though, this one could run longer than The Sound of Music. It started before Christmas, lasted through the Gator Bowl in Jacksonville – where it seemed to be diminishing – and then, like a hurricane going back to sea, picked up strength again at the Peach Bowl in Atlanta.

I bought medicine that is supposed to decongest you and relieve the aches and pains. I still sounded like Rosanne Rosannadanna.

I tried to set up an interview with Famous Amos Lawrence, North Carolina's will-o-the-wisp running back, the day before the Gator Bowl game.

I approached Amos in the lobby of the team's hotel. He kind of backed off, then politely excused himself and did some great broken field running through the lobby.

"Whut's wrog with hib?" I asked my friend, another writer.

"I can't imagine," said my friend. "It might help, though, if you'd wipe your nose."

I bought a box of Kleenex and some aspirin.

"Maybe you ought to eat some chicken soup," said my friend. "My mom used to say chicken soup would cure colds."

That evening, I ordered chicken soup.

The waiter said, "We don't have chicken soup."

"Whod kide do you hab?"

"Turtle. You ought to try some turtle soup for that bump. My mom always said turtle soup was good for pimples and, boy, you've got Super-Zit there in the middle of your face."

"Whod bump?" I said. "Thad's by does. It's red because it has Kleedex rash."

"Nose? Looks like a pimple to me," said the waiter.

At the airport after the game, I tried to get some chicken soup. All they had was cream of asparagus. I bought some cough drops.

Atlanta was warm, then cold and damp. So was my room. You could sand your fingertips and turn the thermostat with the touch of a safecracker and you still couldn't get warm, just hot or cold.

I phoned room service for some chicken soup. Sorry, the voice on the other end said, cream of mushroom. "Must be something wrong with the connection," said the voice. "You sound weird, sir."

I tried to say, "Same to you, fella," but I had a coughing fit.

I approached Clemson coach Danny Ford in the lobby and told him I'd like to do an interview.

"What's happened to your eyes?" asked Ford, retreating a little. "They look like Jim Stuckey's been standing in the sockets with his cleats on."

"I godda code," I blubbered.

"Well, look uh, I'll see you at the game, okay?"

I went looking for some chicken soup but couldn't find any. I bought some nasal spray and eyedrops and a bag of taco chips.

It was raining and snowing when I left Atlanta. It was raining and snowing when I got to Charlotte.

My wife Beth met me at the airport.

"You look awful," she said. "New Year's hangover, huh? You'll never learn."

"Code," I said.

"What?"

"Code. I still hab my code."

"Still? You're impossible," she said. "Silly, why didn't you get yourself some chicken soup?"

April 17, 1980

The Paper Hanger

I know why Hitler was so mean.

He was a paper hanger, that's why.

Before he became dictator, he hung paper for a living. It was probably while he was slapping another sheet up on somebody's parlor wall that he thought up blitzkriegs and that other destructive stuff.

I recently spent two evenings wallpapering my son David's bathroom. Ordinarily it wouldn't be a two-night job, but the first night, I hung the new wallpaper on top of the old wallpaper.

It fell off a couple of days later.

So I waded through the new paper on the floor, pulled off the old and started rehanging the new. Beth was sanding a piece of furniture in an adjoining room.

"Why do I have to wallpaper?" I asked her. "I'll bet Arnold Palmer doesn't have to wallpaper."

"How much money does Arnold Palmer make?" Beth asked.

"Oh, a million or two a year," I said.

"And how much do you make?"

When I didn't answer, she said, "That's why you hang wallpaper and Arnie doesn't."

I wondered aloud why David couldn't hang the paper and Beth said it was because he was working on a school project.

"Well," I said, "I ought to be working on my novel."

"The world has waited this long," Beth said dryly. "It can wait awhile longer."

"But I've got this torrid sex scene in mind that I want to write."

Beth looked up from her sanding and said, "Wouldn't it be easier to write about something you know?"

She got up and walked over to where I was slapping paste onto a piece of wallpaper.

"Why are you holding the brush so funny?" she said.

"Funny? You call this funny? Harry Vardon didn't think it was funny. This is the Vardon overlapping grip, employed by most of the world's finest golfers.

"So that this evening won't be a total waste of time, I'm working on my Vardon grip. I want my hands to be more familiar with each other the next time I play golf."

"Well," said Beth, giggling, "be sure one of them doesn't get the other in trouble."

Then she checked out my handiwork.

"Seve Ballesteros hits his tee shots straighter than you hang wallpaper," she observed. "Don't you think you could smooth the paper better with a three iron? You know you've never been worth a darn with your pitching wedge."

"I'm trying to develop a better relationship with my pitching wedge," I said.

"Whatever turns you on."

As a strip of paper turned loose from the wall and curled over my head, I growled, "Someday, when I sell my novel, I'm gonna hire somebody to do all this and all I'm gonna do is play golf and have fun."

Then I heard something I couldn't believe – some heavy words coming from the next room. Now, the heaviest thing Beth has said in two years is, "I'll double your two diamonds." But here she was, quoting:

"If all the year were playing holidays,
"To sport would be as tedious as work."

And like an exclamation point, she added, "Shakespeare."

"Where'd you ever learn any Shakespeare?" I said.

"I just looked it up in the Dictionary of Quotations," she said. "See, it's right here under 'work.' "

Believe me, I know why Hitler was so mean.

December 18, 1980

The Tree Hunt

We were talking about how the sport has gone out of looking for a Christmas tree. The longer we sat in front of the fire and drank wine, the more convinced we became that, as a sport, it is doomed.

Commercial interests have ruined it, we agreed. It has become possible to buy a Christmas tree that was grown for one purpose in life, to stand in someone's window for a week or two and look pretty.

These trees are trimmed into shape as they grow so that they will look like a Christmas tree.

That's a little like raising deer on a hunting preserve for people to shoot. Both are conveniences that take the sport out of the hunt, we lamented as we poured another dollop and studied the flaming logs.

The best Christmas tree hunt we ever had was the one in Huntersville. A relative on Beth's side of the family owned a big spread of land there with lots of trees on it. We loaded up the kids, who were mere tads at the time, and her parents and drove up to Huntersville on a Saturday morning.

It was a perfect day for stalking the elusive tree. It was bitter cold and the sky was dark with the threat of snow. We spent a couple or three hours wandering in the fields and woods and exploring a ramshackle and abandoned barn where we found some perfectly good – if rusted – pitching horseshoes.

We found some good Christmas trees – cedars, of course – but we couldn't just cut one down and haul it to the trunk of the car.

We had to look for The Perfect Tree.

The kids found something wrong with every one we discovered. Or we did.

It began to rain and freeze and we had to make a choice and head home.

We said it was the prettiest tree we'd ever had.

We always said that, though.

Once we went to a golf course that had just opened and hunted around the rough there for a tree. The pro said it was okay. We flushed a covey of quail and found a cut Titleist but Christmas trees were scarce.

That's how it ought to be, though. What kind of sport is it if there's no challenge?

We finally settled for one that looked too short and scrawny but once we had decorated it, we agreed it was the prettiest we'd ever had.

I don't recall ever having gone alone to hunt The Tree until this year.

I don't think I will again.

That's pressure.

It seemed to be a good idea at first. I had this day-off and everybody else was busy. I thought I'd just run up to a lot and get a tree and save the others the trouble.

I tried the supermarket first because I'd heard about tree prices this year and I heard the prices were lower at the stores. I guess they were picked over by the time I got there. The supermarket was asking $20 for a tree that was shaped like Ralph Sampson, only shorter.

I tried one of the lots. I found a tree I liked. A woman running the place said it would be $45.

I said I didn't want to buy the land, just the tree.

She didn't laugh. She didn't even smile. I wished I hadn't said it.

I tried another lot. And another. And another. I was hot in pursuit of The Perfect Christmas Tree. All it required, I figured, was patience and a trained eye like my own.

Every tree was flawed. I couldn't take one because it was too thin, another because it was too fat, one because it had a vacant space where a limb should've been.

I could hear David: "That tree's really slack."

I could hear Edie: "Why didn't you buy one that's shaped like a Christmas tree?"

I got tree fever. The lot attendant, a woman who looked like someone's mother, recognized the symptoms and said, "Take your time, honey. It takes everybody at least half an hour to pick out a tree."

I said, "Just give me a tree, any tree, and tell me how much I owe you. I can't handle any more of this pressure."

She picked one out and I paid her and loaded it into the trunk of the car.

We decorated it that night and everyone said it was the prettiest tree we've ever had.

"Nothing to picking out a tree now," I said. "Used to be a real challenge but the sport's gone out of it."

July 6, 1981

July Fourth in Pink Hill

It is late afternoon on Independence Day in Pink Hill.

I am sitting at a picnic table beneath a live oak tree that looks to be at least 200 years old, a tree that might have been a sapling the day the Declaration of Independence was signed.

The tree stands beside the home of friends we've come to visit, Ben and Sue Rogers. The house is more than 100 years old. Thoroughly modern inside, it has a tin roof. Last night, I lay in bed and listened to rain falling on that tin roof, a magical, musical sound I hadn't heard since I was a child, a sound I had thought with regret that I might never hear again.

A few feet away, Bear, a big, lovable old dog, lies sleeping in the grass.

All around, there are great fields of corn and tobacco and, across the road, black cows graze.

There is a breeze blowing and except for the birds, it is quiet.

They celebrate July the Fourth in a special way in Pink Hill, a tiny dot on the map in eastern North Carolina about 15 miles from Kinston. It's a genuine celebration – warm, unpretentious, a Rockwell painting of grassroots Americana.

It's a perfect way to commemorate the winning of freedom, with music and games and the laughter of men and women who are still close to the soil. And yet it's an unnecessary statement. In this place, beneath this old tree that could tell you how it was those two centuries ago, the sense of freedom, of all that we love about our land, washes over you like the breeze.

I've spent most of my life in cities. I've dined in fine restaurants, been to elegant clubs, seen things of enormous magnitude. But I would count the Pink Hill Liberty Festival among my favorites. Two blocks of Broadway Street are closed to traffic.

The day begins with a flag-raising ceremony and a pancake breakfast on the lawn of the bank. There's a softball tournament, a foot race, a horseshoe tournament. There's an arts exhibit, a crafts exhibit, a booth where you can get your face painted with all sorts of designs.

There's an "authentic costume" contest and a "country look" contest. The Methodist church has games for children.

All up and down Broadway, booths offer hot dogs and barbecue and pastries and ceramics and Christian books and fresh vegetables – fat red tomatoes, glistening purple eggplant.

The best is a booth where you can get a plate of fried or barbecued chicken, collards or green beans, potato salad, cornbread and cake – a truly fine meal – for $2.50. The aroma of the chicken frying is maddening.

You get yourself a plate, find a place on the tailgate of a pickup truck, sit down and eat while you listen to the country music that echoes over the street. "Mamas, don't let your babies grow up to be cowboys..."

One of the featured events is the tobacco-spitting contest. Trophies are awarded to the three contestants who can launch a load of juice the farthest.

Everybody knew who would win this year. Clyde Dunham. He wins every year. An auto repairman, Dunham, a big man with a quick smile, says he doesn't practice, he just spits out the door of his auto shop when he's working, which has helped him develop his technique.

A Kinston radio station did a live broadcast of the contest.

For the second consecutive year, Lorne Howard finished second. His time will come. He's only 14 years old.

Tonight, there'll be a street dance and at midnight, there'll be fireworks in Kenneth Maxwell's pasture.

The Pink Hill Liberty Festival helps keep alive old values and freshens our senses for the land about us.

Still, they don't really have to do it.

They could just sit out under this old tree and look around at the fields and listen to the birds and feel the breeze and love this land.

There's a decoupage hanging in the home of Ben and Sue Rogers. It says:

"Go placidly amid the noise and haste, and remember what peace there may be in silence."

March 17, 1982

Plato, the Thief

A newspaper story about a basset hound who hangs out at Queens College in Charlotte, scrounging food from students, sent memories of Plato gallumphing across my mind.

Not *the* Plato.

This is Plato our late basset hound, a scoundrel through and through but as lovable a soul, man or beast, as I've ever encountered.

As a pup, he had such a look of total absence on his warped features that we decided to name him Plato for the same sort of reasons that people name toy poodles Killer.

Plato was your typical basset hound, with some minor alterations. His feet were extra large and the hair on his tail as wavy.

He had so many wrinkles and folds, he looked like a pile of rumpled laundry. Bassets appear to have been put together by a committee, anyway, with ears too big, bowed legs too short, body too long, jaws too slack and big eyes that would have you believe that all the sins of mankind throughout history have been visited upon the breed.

Most bassets, I suppose, are lazy. Not Plato. He rarely got in a hurry but he stayed fairly active.

Unfortunately, most of his activity was on the shady side. He wouldn't hurt you for anything. Oh, he might lick you to death. But he had the soul of a second story man.

He was a thief and an escape artist who had run afoul of the law – meaning, of course, the dogcatcher – more than once.

Plato stole a lot of shoes.

People would leave their sneakers or work shoes outside, on a back porch or in a utility room, perhaps, and Plato would find them and fetch them home to us. Neighbors would come calling and ask if our four-legged Willie Sutton had snitched a particular type of shoe and we'd say, "Just look through the shoes here on the back porch and see if any of them belong to you."

Plato also brought home such items as toys, underwear and a tube of caulking. His biggest heist was a stuffed monkey about twice his size that he must have had a devil of a time getting home.

Emboldened by his successful crimes, Plato went for the big score. He tried to steal a lawnmower.

You are thinking about this time that I'm lying but I'm not. I saw him in a neighbor's driveway tugging on a mower. He moved it a few feet but finally gave up.

A neighbor phoned one morning and said, "Look out the window, in the street."

We looked out and there lay Plato in the middle of the street on a newspaper, as if he were reading it. Maybe he was. He certainly was paying no attention to the traffic.

It was this kind of arrogant behavior that got him into trouble with the law.

The leash law was passed during the height of Plato's adventures. (I've sometimes wondered if he was the reason.) That meant no more wandering the neighborhood in search of booty. It meant no more afternoon swims in the creek, an unfailing ritual with Plato. It meant no more romantic interludes with his lady friend.

Rather than fence in the yard, I decided to put Plato on a rope attached to a clothesline. That would allow him to run but would keep him in the yard. I hated to do that. It broke my heart. Have you ever had a basset hound look at you with those sad eyes while you were tying him up?

It didn't work. He broke the rope and ran off and stole some copper tubing. Before I could get him back into irons, the dogcatcher had collared him and hauled him to the pound. We bailed him out, and this time, I used a chain rather than a rope. As I attached it around his neck, I decided I was going to give him to someone who lived outside the city, where he could have his freedom again. I wasn't going to keep him imprisoned even if he was an incorrigible.

He didn't stay in chains long. He unsnapped the clasp from his collar and took off. Now, you say, he's gone too far. He's lying for sure this time.

Let me put it this way. Nobody in my family unsnapped that clasp and yet Plato escaped so many times, with clasp unsnapped, the dogcatcher just took to knocking on our door and saying, "Mr. Green, I caught Plato again. Here he is and here's your citation."

I didn't get around to finding Plato a new home soon enough. As I've indicated, he regarded automobiles with obvious scorn, taking his time crossing the street and looking at screeching cars as if to say, "Hey, don'tcha see I'm walking here?"

Ambling down the street one day, he was hit by a car.

We think he died happy. From the direction he was traveling, we figured he was coming home from either a matinee with his lady friend or from casing that lawnmower again.

July 8, 1982

The Klutz

I think I've known you long enough now to make a full confession.

I'm a klutz.

It may shock you to learn that I'm not the devilishly suave, sophisticated person I'm sure you think I am. There are a couple of reasons I've decided to come out of the closet at this time.

My wife, Beth, just bought me a beautiful white linen jacket. I know that soon I'll wear that jacket to a nice affair and, along about the hors d'oeuvres, I'll drop vegetable dip right down the lapel and spend the rest of the evening holding my hand over my chest like a man singing the National Anthem.

That thought occurred to me at the golf course the other day when I set my golf bag on the back of a cart, climbed in, drove off and heard my clubs clattering to the cart path.

Klutz.

I've tried to hide this for years and, in fact, attempted to deny it in my own mind, but the realization has become undeniable. I'm not certain exactly when I knew.

It might have been on a trip to the beach. We were invited for cocktails at one of those ultra-rich, high-rise condominiums. We were sitting on the patio about 14 floors up, looking out at the ocean, holding those little plates of finger food and I was saying, "Yes, when I played the Old Course in Scotland..."

I dipped a shrimp into the sauce and as I lifted the shrimp to my mouth, the sauce splattered onto my white slacks. I tried to wipe it off with a paper napkin with a nice print on it. The ink rubbed off, mixing with the sauce.

Beth did one of those "Oh, Ron!" numbers on me.

From there, we went downstairs to dance. Have you ever seen a guy dance with one hand held over his, uh, lap? That was me.

Or maybe it was the next night. We went out to a seafood place. I had on a new golf shirt Beth had bought me. I spread some butter onto a hush puppy, raised it to my mouth and felt the butter pour onto my shirt.

Beth didn't see that. Nobody did but Franny, my ex-friend, and I. I signaled Franny to keep her big mouth buttoned, but she said in one of those sing-song voices, "Ron, why don't you just dip your hush puppy on your shirt?"

I spent more on dry cleaning that week than I spent on food.

Most of my shirts start out being solid colors and end up being polka-dotted. I can be sipping wine with friends, regaling them with wonderful stories of the places I've been and the things I've done and look down and find that I'm suddenly wearing something that looks as if it were tie-dyed.

I stick fountain pens in my pocket with the cap off and a couple of hours later notice what looks like an oil spill spreading across myself.

The lawn mower won't start for me. It starts for Beth. We don't have many flowers in our yard. I've mowed them down.

I hate to do carpentry work around the house because I hate black thumbnails.

I pack for a trip, grab my suitcase and pour the contents onto the floor. I forget to fasten it.

Klutz.

I'm zero for life at adding my expense accounts accurately. Pat, the lady to whom I turn them in, has to stifle a laugh every time I show up at her desk.

More than once, I've walked into a parking lot and tried to get into someone else's car. That's embarrassing, especially when the owner of the car is watching.

I was playing golf in the mountains last year. I stepped over a trap rake and caught the head of the rake with my cleats. It snapped up, and the handle slapped me in the back, sending me stumbling across the green.

My playing partners asked what was wrong. I told them a bee was flying around my head, but I think they suspected something because I was speaking in a gasp.

I've felt worse pain. Like the time the dentist pulled a tooth before the novocaine took effect. Or the time I walked into a glass door.

Klutz.

I know embarrassment. There was the day last year a companion and I were hurrying to catch one of those trains that transport you from one terminal to another at the Atlanta airport. The doors were closing, but I yelled to my friend that we could make it. He stopped. I made it, but half of my coat didn't. I had to tug my coat out of the door while the other passengers stood watching me and, no doubt, wondering why I hadn't waited two minutes for the next train. "Late for my plane," I said. "There's not another flight out to Bombay for days."

I was going to jog one day this year when I was covering the NCAA Final Four in Lexington, Ky. I had brought all my gear. I got dressed and started to put on my running shoes. I had brought two shoes for my right foot, none for my left.

I won't tell you about getting stuck in the tree last autumn when I was trying to shake down the last of the apples. There is only so much indignity a man can take.

Did you ever go to the men's room and, while you were washing your hands, splash water on the front of your slacks? People could get the wrong idea. I spend a lot of time in men's rooms, trying to get those blow dryers turned in the right direction.

Things like that keep you humble.

Life's rough when you're a klutz.

August 23, 1984

The Game of Gardening

If I had known gardening was a competitive sport, I don't think I would've gotten into it.

My psyche is already bruised by my fading golf game, which once was fairly decent but has suffered from neglect and, some say, the years.

My jogging is also an embarrassment to me. I jog one, two, sometimes three miles but when I get around one of those leathery people who wear Adidas shoes to dinner at the club and the subject of running comes up, I always feel like a wimp.

Adidas Shoes to Wimp: "You run? Oh, you jog one to two miles. Yes, I run a little. I try to do five to 10 miles a day. No, not every month, every day."

I'm all for running or jogging, whatever those leathery people want me to call it. I do it because I think it's good for my physical and mental health and because it feels so good when I stop and it enhances the taste of beer.

But I have let it become a competitive thing in my mind. I pass a guy on the street – going the other way, of course; I never pass anyone when I'm jogging except mothers out strolling their babies – and I say, "Geez, he's really cookin' and I'll bet he's already done 15 miles." So I pick up the pace until he's passed.

That's what I hated about disco dancing. It was competitive, everyone trying to outdance everyone else. It is enough of a challenge to keep from falling down when I'm dancing.

Then I got into gardening. Vegetables. I thought I'd just put out a few tomato plants and see what happened.

I didn't realize I would be getting into a kind of agricultural Olympics.

I mention this now because my garden is doing its annual el foldo. It has no endurance. It exits faster than an Atlanta Braves pitcher in Dodger Stadium. Here it is only the middle of August and I'm looking at a barren wasteland within a week. And my neighbors' gardens still look like a picture out of a fertilizer catalog.

(Between you and me, I'm kinda glad my cucumbers are dying. I have funny-looking cucumbers. They're fat, shaped like watermelons. On the other hand, my radishes never got fat. They looked like thermometers.

(I don't really mind. Maybe the cucumbers wouldn't have been misshapen if I hadn't walked on their vines so much. It's just that you don't want fat cucumbers in competitive gardening.)

If you have a garden, you know how the game is played. It's one-upsmanship of the highest order. Or lowest. Rivalry is fierce. Michigan-Ohio State Fierce. North Carolina-N.C. State. Just more subtle. Always subtle.

You say to someone, "You ought to see my tomato plants. They're going crazy. We picked a dozen tomatoes yesterday. Want some?"

And he says, "No, thank you. I just took several bushels to the people at my office and I'm shipping a trailer-truckload to an orphanage."

And I'm wimped out again.

I thought I was tilling the soil early this year. My neighbors had sneaked and tilled theirs two weeks earlier, while I was away at a golf tournament.

I tried a different fertilizer. Not good enough. You should try my kind, said my neighbor. It had more phosphorous or something in it. My manure's better than your manure, that's the name of the game.

Another thing. How come my neighbor John's garden always looks as neat and orderly as a company of Marines in a parade and mine looks like something along the Amazon. A month after I plant the garden, you need a machete to get through the weeds.

John's tomato plants look like they're wearing three-piece suits, standing straight up, every limb in place, each holding perfectly shaped tomatoes. My plants look like Tommy Lasorda in a baseball uniform. I couldn't keep them tied up if I used handcuffs and leg irons.

My neighbors' gardens are still green. Mine looks like a motorcycle gang has camped in it for two weeks. It's so brown, I'm afraid it's going to catch fire.

At any rate, it's all dying – except for the okra. I can grow some okra, boy. Even the neighbors say that.

I wish someone would say I'm a good putter but in this competitive world, you take what you can get. If it's okra, it's okra.

April 29, 1986

Ace and the Kids

"You've had a nice day, haven't you?" said Beth, the wife of the man they call "Ace," because "Dad" and "Mr. Green" are inappropriate in a game of home run derby or two-on-two basketball.

Your sons – Ron and David – are not comfortable saying, "Nice air ball, Dad."

"Nice air ball, Ace," that's OK. Sweet arrows to the heart of the spindly-legged jump shooter with shards of silver hair glinting in the springtime sun after he has leaped inches off the patio and lofted a wayward shot toward the rusting hoop.

Your daughter's fiance, Johnny, feels uncomfortable saying, "You made good contact, Mr. Green," when the plastic bat whips around and the Whiffle ball darts downward and gallops across the back yard.

It's not a compliment. Contact hitters are guys who can't hit one downtown, or in this case, over the split rail fence into the neighbor's back yard. Contact hitters don't win home run derbies. They bounce the ball back to the pitcher, or, when they tag one, into the plum tree spreading its purple arms in right field.

But, "You made good contact, Ace," that's OK.

It makes us all equals, erases the years that separate the lean young man from Philadelphia and the weathered relic from Charlotte.

Yes, it was a nice day, one Roger Kahn, the author who knows and can articulate the sporting relationship between fathers and sons, would describe as "full of innocence and sunlight."

The kids were all at home, what used to be their home and, in the hearts of their mother and father and in-laws-to-be, will always be their home. It was a weekend for lying in the sun, washing the cars, listening to beach music coming from the jam box sitting on the patio, cooking burgers and hot dogs on the grill and reaching deep into the ice-filled cooler for another beer.

And for games.

Competition – soft as the snowball flower blooming at the corner of the house, but competition, nonetheless – welled up early, as it must when guys sit around arguing the merits of Mike Schmidt and Curtis Strange and the Sixers and the Celtics and the sun is shining and there are balls and bats and basketballs lying around in full view.

David won the home run derby in extra innings, catching a hanging curve ball and putting it over the honeysuckle crawling along the neighbor's fence.

Johnny and Ron and the Ace lost.

In the late afternoon, someone bounced a basketball and the game was on. The Ace and David lost. As best he could figure, the Ace was one for 10 from the concrete. Funny, he can hit those jumpers when nobody's around to guard him.

It was the sunshine, probably. It's hard to find the bucket when the sun's in your eyes.

Darkness settled softly, and moments after the burgers and dogs were cooked, a thunderstorm drove them indoors. Johnny and Edie won the Trivial Pursuit game, holding off a late rally by David and Diana, answering a "brown" question, which everybody hates and usually can't answer.

The storm passed in time for a few games of Putt-Putt. The Ace couldn't get the hang of the wet greens. Ron took an early lead, built on it and weathered a late rush of birdies off David's blade to score a victory.

As midnight crept by, the kids watched a late movie and Ace lay in bed reading Herbert Warren Wind's collection of golfing essays, *Following Through*, tales of Bobby Jones and Ben Hogan and Byron Nelson and Arnold Palmer and Jack Nicklaus. But his thoughts kept going back to the day of innocence and sunshine, to the Whiffle balls that darted in on his fists, to the reverse layups that hit the backboard and bounded over the basket into young waiting hands, to the Trivial Pursuit questions about Rabat and Shakespeare and to the putts that clanked off the sideboards.

Everybody had won but the Ace.

He put the book down and lay there for a while, thinking. It had, indeed, been a nice day.

And a day of defeat.

The Ace got out of bed, went to the den and said, "Tomorrow, golf. Real golf. Be there."

And he went back to bed. Smiling.

August 9, 1983

35 Years in Sports

On the front page of the *Charlotte News* on Aug. 2, 1948, there's a story about Israel threatening to resume war and another story that says Duke Power has been granted a rate increase. On the sports pages, there's a note in a column that says a writer named Hank Beaudouin has left the *News* for Baltimore and is being replaced by Ron Green.

Some things never change.

On the anniversary last week of my official employment by the News (I had worked part-time for a couple of years before that as a boy wonder), some folks in my house suggested that I write about my 35 years of observing and recording the bounce of the ball.

I'll not fall into that trap. I'm not going to haul out the scrapbooks of my mind and burden you with clippings of yesterday.

First thing you know, I'd be sorting through the faces, looking for the one I enjoyed the most. Sooner or later, I'd come across Billy Joe Patton and stop there. He was the one.

Sheriff Andy Taylor in golf spikes is what he was. He had a backswing faster than an airplane propeller and he hit Titleists into places where the sun could never shine. But after milking the situation for all of its drama, filling the time with folksy chatter, he would hit shots that magically flew up through the limbs and, after a moment, you would hear the cheers as his ball lit on the green.

He was a bold, free-spirited, colorful, exciting amateur from Morganton, a lumber salesman by trade, who gambled away the Masters when he had Ben Hogan and Sam Snead beaten in their prime, who nearly won the Open and who cut a wide swath through amateur golf, just a-smilin' and a-talkin' all the way.

Sometimes now I think perhaps we made him up.

No, I won't take up your time with the yellowed pages. I'd probably lapse into a drab soliloquy about the figures I came across in those years who had a mythic quality about them, who seemed bigger than life. Joe DiMaggio. Bear Bryant. Billie Jean King. Bobby Jones. Ted Williams. Ben Hogan. Gordie Howe. Argentina Rocca. Choo Choo Justice. Bill Bradley. Bjorn Borg. Johnny Unitas. Jerry West. Secretariat. Perhaps there were others but they don't come immediately to mind.

Ah, Secretariat. Now, the mention of that name would start me reminiscing about lovely moments, patches of time painted on my heart and you wouldn't want to hear all that.

I'd just get a faraway look in my eye and start talking about that fresh, clean autumn morning in Kentucky before a football game when I visited Secretariat at the farm where he had been retired and the old gentleman who cared for him brought the great horse out of its stable for me to see and told me how Secretariat loved to roll in the grass and would nip you if you weren't careful.

And about April mornings in Pinehurst walking with Richard Tufts to watch the North & South and a misty day at Pebble Beach when Tom Watson chipped in to beat Jack Nicklaus. And a steamy night in Las Vegas when we foolishly dreamed that Muhammad Ali would come back and beat Larry Holmes.

Old Madison Square Garden and Reynolds Coliseum when Everett Case was directing a pounding symphony of red – that image would come flooding back. Limerick, Ireland, when we sat boozily laughing at our own naughty limericks. The ghosts of 500 years who made us quake as they watched us tee off at St. Andrews.

The enormity of Super Bowls and the glory of October afternoons at Texas and Oklahoma and Ohio State and Notre Dame and the most beautiful place to see football played, Kenan Stadium.

The Masters, 29 of them now, with spring in full flower and Arnie – my man Arnie – in the chase. Greensboro Coliseum the night N.C. State beat the arrogant and unbeatable UCLA, the single most thrilling moment of my 35 years on the beat. That stunning instant when Carolina finally won it all for Dean Smith. Those games that State strung together to win the NCAA basketball title last season, which taken together made up the best story I've seen unfold in sports.

The bustle of airports. Press rooms. The columns that worked. Late night in the lounges when the stories flowed as freely as the amber. Hot nights at the baseball park. Cold nights when ice hockey was alive at the coliseum. The first lap at the speedway that took my breath away. Breakfast in Monterey. Lunch in Sausalito. Dinner at Scandia and Mama Leone's. Fishing with my sons at Grandfather Mountain. Tobacco spitting contests on the Fourth of July in Pink Hill. Golf at The Dunes.

Well, there's more but I said wouldn't carry on like this.

But if I did, I'd have to mention the colorful characters who have made it more fun, like Ali, Joe Namath, Lou Holtz, Hot Rod Hundley, Lee Trevino, Doug Sanders, Clayton Heafner, Ellis Clary, Curtis Turner, Sandy Grady, Doug Moe, John Brophy, Bones McKinney, Billy Martin, Reggie Jackson, Jim Valvano, Lefty Driesell and so many others. And the boxers, I couldn't forget them. I loved the fight crowd here – Snooks Howard, Waban Thomas, Joe Lassiter, Honest Jawn Allen and the rest.

And I'd have to mention the sweet souls. So many of them. Phil Howser. Walter Davis. Alec Guion. Sutt Alexander. Gordie Tottle. Moe Savard. Minnie Mendoza. Kenny Dennard. Jeff Mullins. George Karl. Dick Tiddy. Richard Petty. Gene Verble. Jim McNulty. Slug Claiborne. John Crane. Gene Thompson. Don Smith. Walter Reynolds. Johnny Palmer. Dick Snyder. Dave Moser. Bill Foster. Cat Whitfield. I shouldn't have started this. I can't name them all.

If I ever decided to do a column about all this, I'd choose Jack Nicklaus as the athlete I most admire of all those whose paths have crossed mine.

As I said, though, I've decided not to write about these things. Like Neil Diamond says in the song, yesterday's gone.

December 16, 1990

Why I Love Sports

Sixty-five reasons why you gotta love sports:

Chicago and Green Bay at Soldier Field on a snowy day.

Tailgate parties.

"My Old Kentucky Home" minutes before the Kentucky Derby.

Wimbledon.

The Yankees and Red Sox at Fenway Park.

Pinehurst.

The Olympic 100-meter dash.

Coaches' cliches.

"Gentlemen, start your engines!"

The minor leagues, where dreams take root in the dust.

Easy Goer and Sunday Silence, hoof to hoof down the stretch.

Trout fishing.

"It's fourth and one at midfield and...they're going for it!"

The short seventh at Pebble Beach.

Magic Johnson vs. Larry Bird.

The Stanford band.

Al Davis.

The Cowboys vs. the Redskins.

The look in the eyes of the athletes when they've won at the Olympics and their national anthem is being played, their flag being raised.

Duke vs. North Carolina in hoops.

Harry Caray singing "Take Me Out To The Ballgame."

Hotdogs.

Joe Namath.

The Super Bowl.

Legion baseball, a relic of the past.

Boston Garden.

Arnold Palmer.

High school football, around which lovely memories grow.

Ted Williams' last at-bat, a homer.

The old Jimmy Connors-Bjorn Borg matches.

Greg Norman five shots back starting the final round.

The Duke crazies at Cameron Indoor Stadium.

Babe Ruth.

New Year's Day bowl parties.

Arguments.

Augusta National in April.

Tommy Lasorda, when he was still fat and had barbecue sauce on his chin.

Football games at Clemson, Tuscaloosa, Ala., State College, Pa., Baton Rouge, La.

Secretariat.

"Outlined against a blue-gray October sky..."

Richard Petty.

"Peanuts, getcha hot roasted peanuts!"

Dodgers vs. Giants.

Nicknames – The Splendid Splinter, Monsters of the Midway, Fightin' Christians.

Michael.

Kentucky, Indiana, UCLA, North Carolina, the four synonyms for college basketball.

Play-by-play announcers, love ‘em or hate ‘em.

The Final Four.

Bradshaw, Swann, Stallworth, Harris, Blount, Lambert, Webster, et al.

“The Boys Of Summer.”

One second remaining, one point down, two free throws.

The World Series.

Chris Evert.

“Why don’t you come over and watch the game with us?”

The British Open.

Fight songs.

Joe Louis.

Yankee Stadium.

An October Saturday morning at Notre Dame.

Don Shula.

Clemson-South Carolina, Oklahoma-Nebraska, Ohio State-Michigan, Alabama-Auburn, Notre Dame-Southern Cal, football with feeling.

The 19th hole.

“Today I consider myself the luckiest man on the face of the earth.”

Split-fingered fastball, nickel defense, give-an-go, dead solid perfect, dinger, personal best, flat out – the language.

Sports pages, with a cup of coffee.